HITLER'S
PRISONERS

Brassey's
MEMORIES OF WAR
Series

Outstanding memoirs that illustrate the personal realities of war as experienced by combatants and civilians alike, in recent conflicts as well as those of the distant past. Other titles in the series:

HITLER'S PRISONERS

Seven Cell Mates
Tell Their Stories

ERICH O. FRIEDRICH

AND

RENATE G. VANEGAS

BRASSEY'S, INC.
WASHINGTON, D.C.

First Memories of War edition published in 2003

Copyright © 1995 Brassey's

First paperback edition 1999

Library of Congress Cataloging-in-Publication Data

Friedrich, Erich O.
    Hitler's prisoners: seven cell mates tell their stories / Erich O. Friedrich and
    Renate G. Vanegas.
      p. cm. — (Memories of war)
    ISBN 1-57488-600-2 (alk. paper)
    1. Friedrich, Erich O. 2. World War, 1939–1945—Personal narratives, German.
    3. World War, 1939-1945—Prisoners and prisons, German. 4. Prisoners of
    war—Germany—Biography. I. Vanegas, Renate G. II. Title. III. Series.

D811.A2F745 2003
362.2'1'092243—dc21
[B]   2003041806

Brassey's
22883 Quicksilver Drive
Dulles, Virginia 20166

10 9 8 7 6 5 4 3 2 1

To my wife, Hilde, who lived through the cataclysm of World War II and who safeguarded my notes from 1945 and brought them to the United States

and

To my grandchildren, Sonia, Alex, and Cito—may they never experience the horrors and agonies of war and the repressions of a totalitarian government.

ACKNOWLEDGMENTS

My father and I are most grateful to those friends and family members who have encouraged us to complete this work. Without their support and generosity this manuscript would not have made it to publication.

We want to acknowledge a few friends in particular. One was James E. Wise, Jr., who felt strongly that the contents of this book should be shared with the modern generation and who encouraged us and gave us valuable advice.

We appreciate Carl Peter Hanson, who was kind enough to assist us with his editorial skills and suggestions to improve the manuscript. We thank Carl for his valuable time and his devotion to a project which had lain dormant for many years. Friends like Carl and Jim help make the world a better place.

We also want to thank Jenilu Richie and many other friends too numerous to mention who encouraged us.

In addition, we would like to thank my husband, Germán Vanegas, for his guidance, support, and time spent on extensive research to bring this work to its completion.

CONTENTS

PREFACE

Many books have been written about World War II, from the Nazis' and Hitler's rise to power, the pain and death on the battlefields, and the immense suffering of the Jews to the ultimate victory of the Allies.

Beyond these many books is another story—a story never adequately told until now. This book is the story of the other people in Hitler's Germany—not the Jews or the Nazis, not the persecuted or the persecutors, but those who were caught in between.

This book is based on my father's secretly kept notes about his wartime experiences on the Russian front and subsequently in a Nazi mental hospital in Berlin. When, as a thirteen-year-old girl, I first read my father's notes, I was both fascinated and horrified, although I did not yet understand the true meaning of this critical period in Germany's history.

Years later my father explained to me his reason for writing these notes: a solemn promise made by him and his fellow inmates that whoever survived would tell the unvarnished truth.

After his release from the asylum, my father served a sentence in the Brückenkopf Wehrmacht prison in Torgau, where he became an aide to a staff sergeant. While performing his more mundane daily tasks, he thought about his cell mates at Buch, the Berlin asylum. These men, their stories, and the kinship they shared had left an indelible impression on him. He became so obsessed with these thoughts that he decided to set them down on paper, but his fear of getting caught and the scarceness of writing paper made this an impossibility.

When my father was released from prison in July 1944, he was hospitalized in Bad Tölz for an operation on his left hand, which had been mangled by shrapnel on the Russian front. It was during the three-month recuperation period that he finally had an opportunity to record his thoughts. Because conventional writing paper was extremely scarce, my father did most of his writing in pencil on discarded wrapping paper, which he cut up into letter-size pieces.

In the early summer of 1945, my father's grandfather gave him a portable Continental typewriter. Because his left hand was disabled, he taught himself to type one-handed and laboriously transcribed his written notes. Now, fifty years later, he still uses the same typewriter.

His notes were typed single-spaced, at times on both sides of any available paper, including discarded voting handbills. After fifty-eight pages he felt his recollections were complete, and he tore up his handwritten notes. Although he was at home, my father felt apprehensive during the tumultuous transition of a war-torn Germany to peace and hid his typed notes behind the linens in our dining room china closet.

In the years that followed my father struggled to survive and to help rebuild his devastated country. Considering himself very fortunate, he devoted his energy and efforts to his new work as an investigator for the Coburg police department, a position assigned to him by the U.S. Armed Forces. With his excellent memory and passion for detail, he solved every criminal case that made its way across his desk, in spite of the extremely difficult postwar conditions.

A lengthy court case against the city of Coburg, and ultimately against the state of Bavaria, occupied most of his free time. He felt angry at being labeled a subverter of the Wehrmacht, rather than being recognized as a political victim of the Nazi regime. He had served his country on the Russian front, had received the Iron Cross second class for valor and the wound badge, and had had to endure an unjustifiable prison term for subversion. It took almost five years before his record was rectified; in the spring of 1952 he was declared a political victim and received compensation for the unjust suffering and imprisonment he had endured.

As the years passed I encouraged my parents to come and live with me and my family in Virginia. In the mid-1970s my parents sold most of their belongings and their home of thirty-six years and immigrated to the United States. During the moving process, my mother salvaged my father's notes and brought them along.

Once retired and with more free time, my father was encouraged by family members and friends to construct a more detailed manuscript and consider publication. With this encouragement and still feeling bound by his old oath, my father wrote a 360-page account based on his notes and remarkable memory. It is the story of seven young men who, as they shared a prison cell for a brief moment in history, reminisced openly and poignantly about their lives, and who by the end of their ordeal shared a kinship that is seldom found in any group. Most of the seven were soldiers imprisoned for crimes against the Nazi regime, but among them were also a Jehovah's Witness and other opponents of the war who were waiting to hear if they were to be sentenced to death. Their hopes, wishes, and expectations for a better future could unfortunately not be realized.

The narrators are not historians, scholars, or men of political greatness; they are average Germans whose lives were overwhelmed by the extraordinary tragedy of this era. A student, a vintner, a farmer, a hairdresser, a furrier, a worker, and a clerk describe their experiences of the economic and social conditions in Germany from World War I to 1943.

Although this book does not pretend to be a full history of Nazi Germany, my father made a great effort to capture the texture, tedium, emotions, and suffering of these times as he lived them. Some names of people and places have been changed to protect privacy. However, his representation of the cell mates' stories is as they told them.

While translating the manuscript, I conferred with my father on a daily basis. I had many difficulties in translating an unedited version of a manuscript and also felt that the format was not appropriate for publication. Once the translation was completed, we agreed to use the techniques and structure of a novel to tell the story. There were many questions that arose in my mind, such as how my father could remember in detail all the stories told to him by his cell mates. When I asked him, his explanation was simple: his experiences had been so painful and traumatic for him, who had never before been incarcerated with a group of people or shared their most intimate thoughts and feelings, that he will always remember the smallest details of those four weeks at Buch.

Renate G. Vanegas
June 1994

CHAPTER 1

THE PRISONER

On the morning of December 9, 1942, the monotonous rumbling of the wheels of the express train blended with the throbbing in my forehead. I was headed for Berlin with only a guard for company. I was not handcuffed, but my guard kept his eye on me constantly, as if he were afraid I might try to escape. Otherwise, his manner showed that this was a routine assignment for him; he didn't utter a sound as he sat watching me.

I rested against the cushioned seat and stared out the train window but was oblivious to the passing scenery. My thoughts wandered from the pain of the wound in my hand to the events of twenty-four hours before, when I had been arrested. Although it was now a full day since my arrest, it seemed as if only a few minutes had passed, so clearly could I remember all that had happened.

I had been one of many wounded soldiers bedded down in a huge dance hall that had been converted into an infirmary inside a small town in northern Bavaria. After two days at the hospital my hand, which had been torn apart by a piece of Russian shrapnel and had undergone extensive surgery, was finally beginning to respond to treatment. I was lying in my bed, reading a newspaper, when the large hall door was thrown open and a captain and two soldiers appeared, followed closely by the chief of surgery.

The officer and the soldiers were armed and wore steel helmets. The patients turned their heads as if on drill to face the approaching group, who, to my dismay, halted at my bed. With expressionless faces, they clicked their heels and stood at attention while the officer shouted, "Are you Private Erich Friedrich?"

Blood rushed to my face. I answered, "Yes, sir, I am."

"Get up!" barked the captain. "You are talking to an officer!" I jumped to my feet and stood at attention as he continued, "In the name of the German people, I hereby put you under arrest. You have violated the will of the German people by maliciously subverting and demoralizing the entire military establishment by maintaining—after refusing to make the German salute—that you have had it up to here with the system, and by contradicting Reichmarschall Hermann Göring by stating that you didn't get shit to eat for days while serving on the eastern front. You are hereby ordered to stand trial in Berlin before a general court-martial."

The officer bent his head slightly, and his small, piercing eyes looked directly into mine before he continued, "Do you have anything to say?"

"I protest this arrest," I said. "You can't throw me into prison in my codition; I was just operated on two days ago and have an open wound."

The officer's response was swift and to the point: "You'll be taken to another infirmary in Berlin before we continue with you." The group spun around and marched out of the hall, leaving a stunned audience behind.

At first I wasn't afraid. In fact I almost burst out laughing when another patient came over to tie my shoelaces for me; he was trembling so he could barely perform that simple task. After I gathered up my clothing and personal belongings, I was led out of the room by an orderly. As I passed one of the fellows I had played chess with earlier in the day, he remarked, "Well, Erich, this is the gratitude of the Fatherland."

"Be careful what you say, or the same thing will happen to you," I retorted.

I was taken to a military barrack outside the city of Coburg, where I spent the night on a hard wooden bench in an unheated room. It was so cold that I trembled uncontrollably. I removed an old army coat dangling from a nail on the door and covered myself, but the smell of mildew made me sick to my stomach. From my wounded left hand a searing pain shot through my arm, shoulder, and neck; it became worse the next morning, when I was taken to the train station and placed on the train, where I had been ever since.

When the train passed through the city of Jena, my attention was diverted from my memories of the day before. As a young man I had spent many happy days there, and I thought about my wife and my little daughter, how my little girl would be standing in front of the decorated Christmas tree with a glow of anticipation on her face. But Christmas, the celebration of the birth of Christ, was only a dream for me now—it no longer existed. It struck me that my family would probably not even be told what had happened to me.

I raised my head from the seat cushion and nervously massaged my arm, hoping the nagging pain would abate. Apparently the sergeant was human after all, for he noticed my suffering and asked, "Didn't they give you anything for the pain?"

"No," I answered. Since he at least was talking now, I decided to find out what he knew of my situation. "Do you know where I'm being taken?" I asked.

"It's someplace in Lehrterstrasse in Berlin; that's all I'm allowed to tell you," he said.

"Do you think anyone will notify my family?"

He shrugged. "I really don't know."

"Perhaps in Berlin I can drop my wife a few lines on a postcard," I suggested cautiously.

"I don't think that's permitted," the guard replied, "but possibly I can do that for you. We'll see when we get to Berlin."

This was not much of an assurance, but it sparked a little flame of hope in me.

We continued talking as twilight fell and the dim lights came on in our compartment. Even though I felt miserable, it was good to have someone to talk with. The sergeant asked me about my injury.

"In Russia," I explained. We talked about the war, about combat. The guard confessed that he had never been on the front.

It was dark as the train approached Berlin. "Ah, Berlin at night!" I thought. Bright lights, the gay and happy life of fabulous nightclubs and fancy cabarets, a metropolitan city with everything to offer. I wondered how it would be now, in the third year of the war.

Berlin was blacked out; it seemed as if the entire city had gone to sleep. When we got off the train, we were relieved to find that the streetcars were running, but we had difficulty finding the one we wanted. When we finally found the right streetcar, the conductor said, "Wounded soldiers don't have to pay."

It was only a short ride to Lehrterstrasse. The wind bit into our faces as we walked two long blocks from the streetcar stop to an immense, dark, foreboding building, even more depressing than the rest of the city. The sergeant took my arm and led me through an iron gate to another door, where he pulled the doorbell cord.

A cloud of warmth billowed into the winter night as a young, clerkish-looking soldier opened the door. The sergeant handed him my document file, which the man studied carefully while we entered the large, almost bare room. The room was illuminated by only two lights suspended from a high ceiling, and crossing it to the single desk seemed to take forever. From behind the desk a private materialized, still sullen from sleep, to see what was happening. Straightening his uniform jacket while coming around the desk, he took the papers from the clerk, leafed through them, and laid them on the desk. He signed one of the sheets and returned it to the sergeant, who abruptly departed, leaving me standing awaiting my fate. The question now confronted me of where I was and what was going to happen to me. Scared and confused, I felt abandoned.

Time dragged on, and fifteen or twenty minutes later, I found myself standing inside a dark cell. By fumbling around, I was able to find a bunk. I lay down fully clothed.

It must have been around midnight when the door opened, a ceiling light came on, and another man was pushed in. In the sudden light, I had just enough time to see how filthy the room was before the door closed again and the light went off. The newcomer crawled onto the upper bunk without saying a word. Apparently he had body lice or fleas, because he scratched himself constantly. This really annoyed me; I had managed to avoid these pests in Russia by sleeping outdoors rather than inside infested huts or sheds. Here, I realized, there would be no escape.

The following morning, two guards came before dawn and took me to a solitary confinement cell, where I stayed without food or water for two days. On the third day an attendant brought me a slice of bread with some margarine smeared on it. On the twelfth of December, I was transferred, along with several other inmates, to Tegel, another prison in Berlin.

At Tegel, for the first time since my arrest, I was allowed to get medical help. The doctor was a mousy-looking character who wore big horn-rimmed glasses and seemed very unfriendly. He gestured at me to sit down and asked why I was there. When I told him, he gave a short, humorless laugh and said, "Well, that'll teach you a lesson. You should have kept your big mouth shut. Anyway," he added, "the head of the infirmary surgical department has declared you medically fit to be imprisoned."

He unwrapped the gauze bandages. The stench of the open wound was horrendous, and yellowish pus oozed out all over what was left of my hand. Pointing to the washbasin, he told his assistant to soak the "mess" and bandage it up again. I asked for something to ease the pain, but the doctor replied that painkillers were needed on the front for the fighting men, not for prisoners of my kind. He was clearly untouched by my suffering.

I almost went insane as I endured more than a week of excruciating pain before seeing the doctor again. He had me rebandaged but refused to have me admitted to a hospital. I was becoming frantic; I didn't know where to turn for help. As I was leaving the doctor's office to return to my cell, the doctor's adjutant, a corporal, asked me if I was from Thuringia. When I said that I was, he said, "I'm also a Thuringian, and I'll make sure you go to a decent hospital."

I didn't take the adjutant's promise too seriously because I doubted a corporal could do what the doctor, a brigadier general in the medical corps, had refused to do. To my utter surprise, the following morning an attendant opened my cell door and told me to collect all my belongings and come outside. I quickly grabbed my few items and rushed out of the cell. "You wait here," said the attendant. "Another inmate will join you, and then you'll be transported to the Buch prison infirmary."

Shortly thereafter, the door across the hall opened, and the shrunken shape of a man, his eyes empty and expressionless, limped out, only to collapse on a stretcher that an orderly had brought for him. The poor man was whimpering with pain. A few other inmates joined us, and, together with two guards, we were on our way. During our short ride in the van, one of the soldiers told us that Buch was only for mental cases or prisoners whose fate had already been decided. Now I was chilled with fear, and my high hopes began to disintegrate.

As we approached Buch, I studied the layout. It consisted of several large buildings surrounded by massive red-brick walls three to four meters high. Driving through the gate, we entered an empty, dusty courtyard. In its center was a single brick structure with iron-barred windows, which were painted a dirty white, staring down at us sightlessly. On the left-hand side of the compound was another building that looked as desolate as a charnel house; ravens were perched on and flapping around its roof. Otherwise, there was an almost eerie stillness in the yard and even in the air. A storm brewing in the west made the birds restless, and, cawing raucously, the entire flock rose up and flew away as our truck entered the compound.

The silence was broken when we entered the central building. The roaring voices of the guards assaulted my ears and vibrated through the corridors, guttural words echoing off hard walls and floors. It was as if each wanted to outscream the others.

A private who was standing by the registration desk saw the sergeant and shot out his arm in a salute.

"Tell the sergeant major I have some more from Tegel," said the sergeant as he returned the salute and handed him our files. The registration procedure that followed was brutally simple: I had to remove my uniform and all my clothing and was frisked from top to bottom, outside and in. The seriously injured soldier brought in with me was still lying on his stretcher, moaning in pain. One of the passing guards kicked the stretcher viciously. His boot thudded into the man's ribs while he remarked that they were going to "teach him to forget about moaning and groaning." I stifled an urge to punch the guard. A bitter taste flooded my mouth and seeped into my throat. I swallowed hard. I wanted to reach down to aid the broken body, but I remained motionless. I never saw the wounded man again.

Once I had completed my "registration," I drew a long, deep breath. I was led down a windowless corridor, whose dreary gray walls had a suffocating effect on me. An uneasy feeling, a premonition of what lay ahead, overcame me when the sergeant's boots stopped in front of a cell with the number seven painted on its wooden door. I had arrived.

CHAPTER 2

THE CELL MATES

There were seven others in cell 7, sitting on benches and lying on the beds, when I was shoved in.

The door slammed shut behind me. I staggered, struggling to stay upright. When I had composed myself, I said, "I'm Erich Friedrich. Who's in charge here?"

An understandably mistrustful silence followed. Finally a youngish fellow in civilian clothes piped up, "I'm Willi Weber."

I nodded at the round, friendly face that had at least acknowledged my presence.

Another man, his legs dangling from a bench close to the window, pointed wordlessly to a figure lying on the bed near the door. The uniformed man on the bed glanced at me out of the corners of his eyes, barely moving his head, and said in a hoarse voice, "What do you want?"

I shrugged. "My freedom."

He smiled humorlessly. "Call me Herms," he grated. "That's my last name, and that's all I want to be called." He was an angular-looking man in his twenties with a pronounced beak nose and crooked teeth. "If I let people call me by my first name, they'll lose respect. After all, I am the spokesman." Herms's eyes narrowed as he focused on my bandaged arm. "What kind of injury do you have?"

"It's only my hand. Otherwise I'm all right," I replied and moved farther into the cell. The wooden floor creaked beneath my feet with each step I took. Somehow I felt happy to be with a group of people, and the cell wasn't too bad; it even had two windows, although they had been painted over from the outside with white oil paint. A bit of light penetrated through the paint and gave the place a less sinister appearance, and there was a visible clear spot in the glass where, as I discovered later, one could look out into the courtyard.

The cell was crowded with three bunk beds and two single cots with a small night table next to each. A narrow wooden wardrobe stood in one corner, and a square table and several chairs occupied the other. Since the beds were covered with what must at one time have been white linens, I began to think this was an infirmary after all. A comfortable glow of heat escaped from a radiator covered with a sheet of perforated metal.

As I continued my initial inspection, the door was unlocked and opened. A skinny, silent guard brought me a few of the items that had been taken from me during the frisking. Aside from my mess gear and spoon, I also received a small comb, a toothbrush, and a chunk of lye soap.

A prisoner dressed in a heavy gray cotton shirt and loose-fitting slacks who introduced himself as Franzl came up to me and offered to share his night table with me. He was a small man, his voice was gentle and calm, and his accent identified him as an Austrian. I guessed him to be in his late thirties. His caring, trusting, and almost fatherly disposition made me like him instantly.

As I stored my few possessions on the night table, a hand touched my right shoulder. As I turned, another inmate introduced himself as Alex. Franzl, speaking in a low voice, pointed to a man with reddish hair who was still sitting at the table. "And this is Richard; he never has much to say." Richard nodded his head slightly and resumed staring at his hands, which were also covered with fine reddish hair. Franzl then explained the house rules to me: "Reveille is at six A.M. Everyone has to get out of bed unless he is too sick to move. A guard comes in at seven and takes us to the washrooms, where we stand in line to use the toilet, wash, and shave. The shaving gear has to be returned afterward. Whoever wants to see a doctor has to request permission from one of the guards the night before. Our laundry is collected every Thursday and brought back to us on Saturday. By the way, you're not allowed to lie in bed during the day, but they can't enforce the rule too strictly because by the time the guards manage to unlock the door, you have time to get up if you're quick about it.

"Breakfast is at nine and lunch at one, dinner is at six, and bedtime is ten P.M. Outside the cell you are not permitted to speak to other inmates. If you do, you run the risk of being punished severely." That explained why only the screaming voices of the guards and the rhythmic marching steps of their boots could be heard. "At seven at night we get another chance to use the toilet; otherwise we're not allowed. When Phillip is on duty—he's one of the more humane guards—exceptions are made. He allows us to go to the toilet and even smuggles in some painkillers once in a while," Franzl finished.

I felt more comfortable now. Shortly before lunchtime one of the men who had occupied the bench got up slowly and, supported by a cane, limped back and forth, repeating a Latin phrase: *"Morituri te salutamus."* He was tall and lean in his worn-out army uniform, which hung loosely from his body. This haggard-looking man couldn't have been more than twenty-one years old. Even though he was pale and tired, he had a handsome, aristocratic face with large, intense blue eyes, a classic, well-formed nose, and tightly curled, brownish hair.

I noticed that he studied me in passing but otherwise kept looking toward the window. Turning back, he came to a halt in front of me, and with eyes flashing, demanded, "I am Fritz Römer. What have you done? Why are you here?"

I started to answer, but he brusquely cut in, "I know you're another innocent one. In the four weeks that I've been here I haven't met one person who thought he was guilty. Perhaps all the jails are filled with innocent lambs who wouldn't hurt a soul."

For a moment I didn't know how to react or what to say. I wasn't certain whether the man's penetrating stare projected hatred or pain. All eyes were fixed on us.

"Yes," I said, "I too feel that I am innocent of any wrongdoing, but I think I'll wait before telling you my story. But tell me, Fritz, why do the doomed salute you? You certainly don't look like a murderer or a dying man."

"Don't pay any attention to Fritz," said Franzl. "He's beginning to see ghosts now."

"You don't know these hangmen like I do," retorted Fritz. "A Gestapo agent stressed the words 'collaboration with the enemy' during yesterday's interrogation. Now, I'm smart enough to know what that means."

"Does one get interrogated right here on the premises?" I asked.

"Yes," Fritz assured me. "I am interrogated almost daily. Each day they add a new charge to my case. Watch out, Erich; you don't look to be a hard-core crook who has done time before. When the Gestapo agents arrested me, they told me I was being charged with high treason and collaboration with the enemy, among other things. Well, we can talk about this some other time," he concluded. "It's almost lunchtime now."

"High treason is a serious charge," I said. "But since you're wounded and you have served your country, maybe the court will take that into consideration. Very likely you'll get three or four years in prison. I don't think it's going to be more than that." I knew better, but I thought it would calm Fritz down. How wrong I was.

He almost jumped on me as he shouted, "You're all alike! No one dares to tell the truth anymore! You don't think I know what's coming? Everybody lies. But I know for a fact I won't be around much longer. My fate has been decided."

Herms, the only one who hadn't been paying much attention to the exchange, slowly unfolded himself from his bed. Franzl reached under one of the beds and brought up two shiny metal bowls. He inspected them carefully and then placed them on the table.

It wasn't long before we heard footsteps and the rattling of keys. The door was unlocked and opened by a sergeant. Herms, the speaker of the group, stood at attention and reported, "The room is occupied by seven men and one new arrival."

Scurrying timidly behind the sergeant was an inmate in a striped prison uniform who carried a large metal kettle and a pitcher. The sergeant said, "The new man doesn't get any food today" and left. The nervous inmate dumped some potatoes into one bowl and poured a red sauce into the other. He then hurried out, and the door slammed shut. All this happened so quickly I could hardly follow the procedure.

Herms didn't slow down as he counted out twenty-nine rather small potatoes. "Gerhard will get five today, but the smallest ones," he said, referring to one of the inmates with whom I had not yet spoken. Herms did not include me when he divided the food.

Gerhard, a quiet, dignified-looking man, sat on one end of the bench playing with his fingers, acting as if all this did not concern him. He reminded me of a schoolteacher with his buttoned-up white shirt and long-sleeved sweater. Meanwhile, the rest peeled their four potatoes each and proceeded to eat. Reluctantly, Gerhard joined them.

Franzl, the Austrian, asked me if I was hungry, offering me two of his peeled potatoes. I thanked him, saying that I had eaten some bread earlier in the day and that I could wait until tomorrow. I had learned in Tegel that food was not provided on the day of arrival. Nevertheless, Franzl insisted and put the two potatoes on the table. "Erich, there's some salt in the night table drawer; just help yourself."

Potatoes and salt taste excellent, especially when you're hungry. During the depression it had been a standard meal at our house.

Unlike the others, Franzl didn't start eating right away. He bowed his head, folded his hands in prayer, and with closed eyes muttered a few words. When he was finished, he looked up with a serene expression on his face and began eating.

I didn't think this strange, because I knew that most Austrians were strict Catholics and that daily prayer was part of their religious practice. Noticing that I was looking at him, Franzl explained that he was a

Jehovah's Witness and was serving time because of his faith. He had already been sentenced to death and was now awaiting the court's decision about how and when he would die.

Since four of the men were still sitting around the table, I moved over and sat on the bench next to Franzl. The heat from the radiator came through the holes in the metal sheet and warmed our backs. Franzl soon got up from the bench and sat down on the floor, assuming a meditative position. I was intrigued. All I knew about the Jehovah's Witnesses was that they were being persecuted by the Nazis for refusing to participate in the war. Since I was not very religious myself, I'd always felt the Witnesses were deluded. Nevertheless, it was difficult for me to believe that anybody would want to persecute a kind man like Franzl because of his beliefs.

I asked Franzl if his imprisonment could have been prevented. Without moving his head, he said, "I've come to terms with my fate. Soon I'll be with my beloved brother, who died a couple of years ago because of his convictions and his faith. The Lord gives me the strength and the courage to remain truthful to myself and to endure all sufferings, as our savior, Jesus, did." His words radiated contentment and satisfaction.

Suddenly he changed the subject. "If you're going to stay here for a while, try not to eat too much salt or smoke the filter ends of cigarettes. Leave the others alone, unless they actually ask you for help. I've been a prisoner for more than two and a half years and have managed to survive. You can, too.

"Being kept in custody has strengthened my faith to the utmost," he continued, changing the subject again. "For me there is only one redemption—not that you should think I'm waiting for Germany to lose the war—no, that's not the case; my redemption will come the day I have to give my life. I'll know that I've acted correctly and, most important, that I've not taken anybody else's life. I can say of myself that I've tried to make the best of my abilities and live a life free of sin." He fell silent.

Gerhard stood leaning against a bunk bed, staring at me. Finally he asked, "How's your wound? Perhaps I can have a look at it. I worked as a first aider." Since I still felt pain and pressure in my arm, I agreed. As he carefully removed the bandages, the other inmates came over one by one to take a look. Gerhard remarked that the wound had a bad odor and needed to be washed and cleaned.

"You should tell the attendant tonight that you need to see a doctor tomorrow," he said, concerned. "You should also get this arm massaged, or the couple of fingers you have left will become stiff and useless." But when Gerhard took hold of my arm and began massaging it, Herms warned, "Get away from him, you idiot! Take your dirty hands off him." Gerhard let go of my arm immediately and reverted to the shy, withdrawn person I'd first thought him to be. He moped back to the bunk bed and practically crawled behind it.

Herms continued, "Don't you see, he's touched in his head! He was brought here so his mental state could be examined before they chop his head off."

Gerhard did indeed have a frightened, strange look in his eyes. Herms obviously had no compassion for him. "After Christmas, Gerhard will have his day in court," he continued. "Then his distorted brain will be twisted in the right direction. He's just here eating his way through and playing sick. I tell you, I have my doubts about that guy; nobody's going to tell me anyone's called for a hearing these days just because he's sick in the head. I bet he's one of those smart-asses who was caught spying for the Poles and then pretended to be insane. There are a lot of those characters around. Well, the psychiatrist will find out the truth, but that asshole can't fool me."

Gerhard was still squatting behind the bunk bed, looking like a punished child. I felt some sympathy for him. He was not a bad-looking man—short, a bit stocky, with very close-trimmed hair. Gerhard gave the impression that he had had a good upbringing and an excellent education. I guessed him to be around thirty-five years old.

Herms began anew with his accusations: "The guard, Phillip, has read Gerhard's files, and he keeps me informed about what's going on around here." Looking at me, he continued, "I say this just in case you think that you can fool us by claiming you're innocent." Herms was beginning to get on my nerves.

"This is ridiculous," I said. "You don't know anything about me, so you can't possibly make a judgment. I just hope *you're* not sitting in here because you're innocent." I didn't want to antagonize the man, since I knew he was the cell leader, but I had to get it off my chest.

"Thank God, I'm not a traitor," Herms began. "In my eyes that's the worst crime a German can commit, especially when his country is in danger. If I were a judge, I wouldn't fool around with trash like that; he'd be hanged on the spot and without trial." Watch out, I thought to myself, this man's a Nazi.

The room fell silent as everyone became occupied with his own thoughts. There was no escaping it now, I was really in prison. My mind traveled south to the little town in Bavaria where my family lived. I wondered again whether my wife had somehow found out I was in prison. The sergeant had more or less promised me he would write her a postcard. Had he kept his promise? What would her reaction be? I knew she'd be frightened. How often had she told me not to be so outspoken, even among our friends?

Whenever I had listened to the British radio broadcasts, she would drape a blanket over me and the radio to dampen the sound. Then she would go outside and walk around the house to make sure no one could hear, since it was against the law, and even punishable by death, to listen to and spread foreign news. Everyone in Germany was aware of this, yet many careless souls had lost their lives by ignoring those ludicrous laws.

I thought of my war buddies from the Russian front. A few of us who were very close had agreed that whoever survived the war would tell what had really happened and thus balance the distorted propaganda stories.

A rattling of keys interrupted my thoughts. The door opened, and the top sergeant, together with a corporal I hadn't seen before, appeared in the doorway. Herms stood at attention and reported dutifully, "Private First Class Herms, here awaiting trial for second-degree manslaughter. Our cell is presently occupied by seven inmates and one newcomer."

"Who's the newcomer?" the sergeant asked. I thought at first that the question was directed to Herms and therefore did not answer. The sergeant, who looked like a worn-out playboy, snapped, "Don't you have a mouth of your own to talk with? You're not in some kind of sanatorium here; this is a prison, in case you hadn't noticed. Next time stand at attention when in front of an officer, and report properly. Is that understood?"

I had no choice but to reply "Yes, sir." Turning now toward Herms, he barked, "And you, Herms, kindly bring some discipline into this group. That's your job as leader." The corporal who accompanied the sergeant gave me a furious look and hissed between his teeth, "You idiot!"

The door had hardly closed before Herms came over and stood in front of me with his arm raised as if he were about to hit me. "I tell you, we don't need this kind of attention," he said. "That's bad news for all of us. Why on earth couldn't you report to him?"

"I thought he meant you," I replied.

"Next time there will be more action and less thinking, is that clear? Now go read the instructions about reporting to an officer." Herms pointed to a piece of paper hanging from a couple of thumbtacks on the door. I quickly walked to the door and read the typed sheet:

Room Regulations and Instructions for Prisoners

1. When an officer enters, all prisoners will rise and stand at attention. Those who are bedridden or unable to rise must place both arms alongside their legs with their hands extended.

2. The senior prisoner must report on himself, his status, how many persons are present, how many are absent, and for what reason. New arrivals must report themselves.

3. When a prisoner is addressed by a superior, he must stand at attention immediately and report his military rank, his name, and the reason for his imprisonment in said order. Convicted prisoners must report their sentence status and the number of years involved.

4. Whoever is caught possessing drugs will be court-martialed.

5. Speaking outside the cell is prohibited and will be punished severely.

6. Eating utensils and beds are to be kept immaculate.

Several other instructions and prohibitions followed. The sheet finished with the notice that violations of the rules and regulations would be punished with solitary confinement and that repeated offenses would be considered mutiny and subject to court-martial. My life was now governed by these paragraphs.

Willi had been standing by the window, peering through the tiny hole in the paint. Suddenly he turned around and came toward me. Looking at me accusingly, he said, "Thanks to you, we won't get any second helpings today."

"When you're here for a while, it'll become very important to you too," Herms added.

"All right," I answered angrily. "I didn't know the procedure, and it won't happen again. I'm sorry I've caused problems."

"I'm sorry, I'm sorry," mimicked Willi. "That doesn't help matters, and it won't feed us."

Gerhard came out from behind the bunk bed and sat down on the bench. I joined him. "You're so good," he whispered softly, looking at my hand sympathetically and gently touching one of my fingers, which protruded out of the bandage. "You definitely have to go and see the doctor tomorrow. The doctor is really nice," he continued. "All people are nice, except Herms and his sergeant; I get so scared of them." He looked up at Herms with a frightened expression on his face. Herms took no notice of Gerhard.

"God, if only I had a cigarette," began Fritz. Sitting at the table, he rolled up a small piece of newspaper he had found somewhere and stuck it between his lips. He closed his eyes and bent his head slightly backward with a sensual expression on his face. He opened his eyes and asked me, "Do you have anything to smoke? Look in your pockets; maybe you'll find a cigarette."

I emptied my uniform pockets onto the table, and, behold, there was a bit of tobacco mixed in with the dirt. Like untamed lions, Fritz, Herms, and Willi rushed over to help collect the shreds. Amazingly, we were able to get enough tobacco together to roll two cigarettes. Now all their faces lit up with heartwarming smiles—and they were smiling at me! For a moment discontent had flown out the window, and I was a hero. Only Willi remained silent; I guessed he was still angry about losing his second helping of food. Herms laid one cigarette aside and said, "We'll enjoy this even more after supper."

When I realized how much happiness the two cigarettes had brought them, I told them that I'd relinquish my right to a drag. "Tell me," I said to Herms, "aren't prisoners pending trial permitted to smoke?"

"My dear fellow," answered Herms, "they don't need prisons in the war. Our comrades out there are rotting in the dirt, and whoever sits in prison in wartime really has to be an enemy of his country. That's why there are so many restrictions now. Once you're here for a while and you haven't caused any problems, they'll issue you a smoking permit. But getting cigarettes is another story. I'm allowed to smoke and so are Alex and Fritz, but although these two bigmouths claim to be rich, so far neither one of them has come up with as much as one lousy cigarette. We can't buy them here, either."

"If anybody has a big mouth," Fritz exploded, "it's you! You behave as if you were Adolf Hitler in person. The way you mouth off as if you'd been on the front, it sickens me. The truth is, you've never even been shot at. You told us yourself what you did as an army food-supply driver in Norway: you stabbed a man to death while you were drunk. The only reason you were acquitted was because the victim was a Norwegian.

"So," Fritz went on, "now our brave Herms is in trouble again, awaiting trial because he ran over a woman, a mother of two children, while he was drunk. The difference this time is that the woman was a German, not an inferior foreigner. The closest he ever came to the front was watching a newsreel." Fritz's face had turned crimson, and as he drew a breath to continue he was interrupted by an even more outraged Herms. His movements were slowed by the cast on his left arm, which had been fractured in the accident when he had run over and killed the woman.

"Come here so I can punch you in your big mouth, you goddamn traitor," Herms shouted, clenching one fist. "That's what you are! I'll show you tomorrow who I am! I'll make sure you're locked up in solitary. That's where you belong—you contaminate all of us with your slander!"

Fritz shouted even more loudly, "I know you and your kind don't like to be told the truth! And if anyone does tell the truth, you want to eliminate that person right away! All you Nazis are the same, the powerful ones and the small fry like you. Let me remind you of the statement Göring made the other day—'My name will be Meyer if an enemy aircraft is ever seen over Berlin.' Do you remember the air-raid sirens that came on last night? Cardboard bombs, perhaps? No, those were real bombs that were dropped, the kind that kill and destroy. But I can hear Göring tomorrow, saying 'Bombs give us strength.' Bullshit, that's what I say.

"Well, Herms," he continued. "I haven't been as lucky as you were in Norway; I've never stabbed anyone to death. My consolation is that there are still a few Germans left who can't be hypnotized or indoctrinated by Nazi swine and big-mouthed fools like you. I just hope Franzl's prediction that the Lord's revenge will come soon is right. When our eyes are opened, *then* we will learn who the true freedom fighters were and who the cowards were who ruined our country."

"Do you guys hear what this criminal is saying?" Herms snapped. "Tomorrow or even tonight, I'll make sure his big trap is shut forever. It's an outrage, the way he talks."

Concerned that Herms was serious, I jumped into the argument. "Fritz, you get carried away sometimes. You're still very young and have a tendency to look at things with different eyes." Turning to Herms, I said, "We have to educate him a bit more. Let's try to talk to him and get him convinced before we betray one another. If he continues, you can still make your report."

Fritz gave a hysterical laugh. "The day the Russians march into Berlin, you can think about me, because I don't think I'll be around to witness it." He picked up his cane and walked over toward the window, resuming his mumbling of "*Morituri te salutamus.*"

Herms had calmed down, and he sat back down on his bed. He fumbled around with the bedsheets and the blanket as if they were not smooth enough to lie on. Since I had no idea how the other men felt about all this, I turned to Alex and asked him what he thought about Fritz's outburst.

Alex stroked his forehead with his hand. "Victory is ours; the army retreats are no more than tactical maneuvers." So much for Alex. Franzl had already told us how he felt about Hitler and the Nazis, but about Gerhard I could not form a solid opinion; perhaps he really was emotionally ill or even a spy, as Herms claimed. Willi, the youngest of the group, was interested only in food and drink—politics didn't seem to interest him one way or another. Richard, the eighth man, had not said a word, remaining completely aloof from us and our conversation since my arrival.

Once more the corridor outside came alive with activity. The light in our cell was turned on, and the same inmate who had brought us our lunch dashed in. The sergeant who unlocked the door went on to the next cell immediately, so Herms didn't have to make his report. Our waiter placed seven slices of bread on the table. Fritz hobbled over and asked him for a match. The man reached into his pocket and gave Fritz exactly one match, which he immediately placed under his mattress. The first waiter dashed back out, and in came another food server, who smeared some margarine into a bowl and poured some black liquid into a coffeepot.

Herms came over to the table and felt the bread slices, counting them as if he expected more.

Herms divided the bread and margarine. Turning toward me, he explained that I wasn't included but that I could have some coffee to drink. "There's an extra cup on the windowsill; go get it, and you can have some of this brew." By now I was so hungry, I didn't refuse the half slice of bread Franzl offered me. I told him I would reciprocate someday. He just smiled. "No need for that, Erich."

We devoured the food as fast as it had been brought in. Then Franzl explained what would happen next. "It's almost time to relieve nature, to be counted, and to ask permission to see the doctor in the morning—that is, whoever has to. After that, all the doors will be locked and no one is permitted in or out until morning. If you have to go during the night, use the pot in the corner." He pointed to a covered enamel pot.

Once again the doors were unlocked, and we all went out to stand in line for the toilets. There were only two toilets for the approximately one hundred and fifty prisoners, who all had to use them in less than an hour. A few minutes after we returned to our cell, the door opened and the private named Phillip came in with a medical supply box hanging around his skinny neck. He was a slim man with close-cropped hair and small but friendly eyes. He looked like a door-to-door salesman. Phillip pulled the door shut behind him and greeted us warmly.

"Who is in pain?" he asked.

"I am," I answered immediately.

"You're new, aren't you? I can't give you anything until you've seen the doctor," Phillip said. He brought forth a pencil from behind his left ear and noted my name on a piece of paper.

This pleased Gerhard. "That's good, Erich, you get to see the doctor tomorrow."

Meanwhile, Phillip walked over to Herms's bed, felt his pulse, and, whispering, handed him a piece of paper. Alex joined the secret discussion, and Herms hid the piece of paper under his blanket. As Phillip turned away from Herms, Willi asked whether we were going to get something for Christmas.

"Yes. A rope around your neck. Happy flea-biting." He smiled as he left the cell.

"If it weren't for Phillip, we probably would've croaked by now," said Alex.

"The light will be turned off in about an hour," Franzl explained. "Then we go to sleep and hang around another day."

How exciting, I thought. Fritz was sitting on his bed with Gerhard beside him, trying to help him remove his pants. Apparently Fritz had difficulty doing this himself. Curious as to what actually was wrong with his leg, I moved closer. Gerhard started to unwrap the paper bandages, but Fritz stopped him, saying it hurt too much. Fritz looked up at me and answered the question in my eyes: "I was shot in the knee; the bullet went through and completely shattered my kneecap."

Gerhard then walked to my bed and got it ready for me to slip into. As I lay down he drew the gray blanket over me, nodded his head without speaking, and turned away to his own bed. I knew then that the nights would be the worst, filled with the indignity and hopelessness of incarceration. There would be no escape from depressing thoughts. But on this night I had exhausted myself both physically and mentally and fell into a deep sleep.

CHAPTER 3

Day Two

Before dawn broke I was awakened by Alex's restless movements in the bunk above me. With another night of unrelenting pain behind me, I remembered it would be Christmas Eve in just two days. I found myself thinking of my buddies on the cold Russian front and how they were fighting for their lives. By comparison, I felt almost lucky to be in prison; at least I had a roof over my head and a bed to sleep in.

Suddenly the light came on. Everyone quickly jumped out of his bed to dress, make the beds, and prepare the cell for inspection. Before ten minutes had elapsed, the door was opened by a sergeant, who, after listening to Herms's report, ordered us to go and stand outside with our toothbrushes, combs, and soap.

Before breakfast we were ordered to walk around the courtyard in a circle for fifteen minutes. We were not allowed to speak. Armed guards surrounded us; some stood on the three- to four-meter-high brick walls that surrounded the entire complex. The guards watched us closely so that no one would attempt to escape.

It was bitterly cold, and although the fresh air felt good, I was happy when we were allowed to go back inside. Everyone stood close to the radiator to warm up.

Twenty minutes later, the door was thrown open and a sergeant came for Herms. Herms's arrogance melted away with the color in his face. Only a few minutes passed before they returned. The sergeant sat down on the chair and kept a close watch while Herms collected his belongings. Herms had a satisfied grin on his face as he said, "I got four weeks of intensified detention, which I already served while being imprisoned on remand."

"That's enough talking now," interrupted the sergeant. "You're not permitted to converse with the other prisoners anymore."

"Yes, sir," answered a happy Herms. He walked over to the night table to gather some of his other utensils. I noticed that he whispered something to Alex but couldn't hear what they were saying.

The sergeant didn't take notice; instead he looked around the room authoritatively and asked who had been there the longest. Franzl quickly pointed to Fritz. Ignoring Fritz, the sergeant got up and walked over to Alex instead. "You're in charge, starting today," he told him. Alex was stunned. Because he didn't acknowledge the order immediately, the sergeant raised his voice: "Are you deaf, Keminski?"

"No, sir," said Alex. "Thank you, sir."

Herms left without saying good-bye. Fritz was the first to break the silence.

"Thank God that punk is out of here. Now you guys have seen Nazi justice at work. Criminals and murderers go free, while others who simply uttered a wrong word get executed. Now, you tell me that that's justice. I just hope the next guy who gets put in here won't be the same kind as Herms. One can't be careful enough around these characters. That son of a bitch has taken two lives, and who knows what else he's done that he hasn't told."

Alex, obviously occupied with other thoughts, interrupted Fritz's conversation. "Listen, everyone, since I've been appointed your leader, I guess I should at least learn how to give a decent report." He sighed. "If only I knew why they chose me. Not only was I never trained as a soldier, I have no experience of barracks life. Well, let's see," he continued. "First, one has to learn how to salute and stand at attention." He stood up and comically started to salute. We all had to laugh.

"There really isn't much to learn; surely you paid some attention when Herms presented his reports," I said.

"Good," Alex continued, still standing. "I shall start my report with 'Private Keminski here,' or perhaps 'draftee Keminski here, awaiting trial because of subversion of the military. Cell is occupied by seven inmates, all present.'"

He rattled off all this while standing at attention. "What do you think? Will I pass?" he asked.

"Your report looked and sounded professional," I answered. Alex's face lit up with a smile as he sat down, apparently satisfied with himself.

"So you were drafted and thrown into prison immediately afterward?" I continued. "How did you manage to subvert the military in such a short time?" I couldn't help but ask this question.

"If I start telling you my story," Alex said, "it'll be an entire novel. Instead we'd better get busy dividing up the room service. Whose turn is it to clean up today?"

Franzl was the first to raise his hand. "Good," continued Alex, clapping his hands a couple of times. "Let's clean this dump." Grabbing a broom from a corner, Franzl began to sweep the floor, swaying as if he were dancing to the rhythm of a Viennese waltz. Everyone seemed to be in a good mood today, except perhaps Richard, who wore a sinister expression on his face.

Alex faced me and said, "Listen, Erich, you can take Herms's bed if you like. I'll stay in this one for the time being."

That was fine with me, since Herms's bed was a single one and I didn't have to worry about vermin dropping on me in the middle of the night. I still had a phobia about crawling insects, even though Franzl had assured me we were the only vermin in the cell.

Alex's first chance to give his report came when a sergeant entered the cell. Alex did well, and we were all pleased for him. The order was to go and shave. We marched down the narrow hallway to the washrooms and stood in line, awaiting our turn. There were only two medium-sized washbasins in the room, and three men had to share one basin at a time. We knew we had to work fast.

When we returned to our cell, breakfast was brought: the usual ersatz coffee brew and stale bread. This time I received two slices of bread. One I immediately offered to Franzl, who had given me a slice the day before, but he flatly refused to take it. "Yesterday is gone, my friend," he said.

Before we had finished our meal, the door was thrown open and Phillip's voice ordered me to report to the doctor. Franzl practically pushed me out the door, saying, "You have to go, Erich, go!"

The doctor, an older man with receding gray hair, made a good impression on me. He was wearing a crisp white coat over his uniform, which made it impossible for me to tell his military rank. He certainly was a great improvement over the doctor in Tegel.

Phillip helped the doctor remove my bandages. The nameless physician looked at the wound and ordered, "Bathe and dress this." Phillip took me to an adjacent room, where a man in prison garb was folding towels. "Bathe this," Phillip repeated and left the room.

The man took hold of my arm and shook his head. "This certainly doesn't look good; if it isn't handled correctly, you could lose your hand." He removed a small bottle from the shelf, poured some yellow liquid into a dishpan, and added lukewarm water. He placed my hand gently into the pan and asked me how I had been injured. I told him briefly about my experience in Russia and how I had been hit by a grenade.

"I too was wounded," the man said. "I have ten bullet wounds, and two slugs penetrated my left lung. But that didn't stop the military court from sentencing me to six years in prison. At first I was going to be sentenced to death, but because I was also a World War I veteran and the recipient of several high honors and medals, the judges gave me a six-year sentence instead. So far I've served two years. I'm being treated as if I were mentally unbalanced."

"Why such a stiff sentence?" I couldn't help asking. "Did you try to assassinate someone?"

"I'm not allowed to talk about it with anyone," he responded. "I'm not even permitted to write to anybody. So far I've kept my promise. My family probably thinks I died in action somewhere. This bothers me the most, having to keep my loved ones in the dark. At times I truly believe I'm going insane," he sighed. "It's all so ludicrous."

"What was your military rank? How shall I address you?" I asked.

He sighed. "Even about something so insignificant as that, I am not permitted to speak. You're the first person I've said anything at all to since I've been here. I need not ask you not to speak to anyone else about our conversation."

"Of course not. I won't talk."

"I can help you," he continued, removing another small bottle from the sparsely stocked shelf. This one contained a viscous black liquid that he slowly poured over my wound. "This should really help the healing process. Try to exercise your fingers a bit, so they don't become stiff and useless." He wrapped my hand with a paper bandage and I left the room. It felt good having found someone whom I liked and who could help me medically.

Phillip took me back to our cell. Only Alex was there; all the others, with the exception of Fritz, had gone to see the psychiatrists, who came once a week. Fritz had also gone to see the medical doctor. Suddenly Alex became very communicative.

"I do hope we get along better now that Herms is gone," he said. "You have no idea what we went through with that no-good bastard. I just hope he doesn't denounce any of us."

Looking at me somewhat inquisitively, Alex continued, "I guess you were able to tell in the short time you've been with us what a fanatic admirer of Hitler Herms is. He has a big mouth but no true conception of what war is really like. All he did was chauffeur upper-echelon Party members around. I met him before he came to Berlin. My brother-in-law was the proprietor of a Turkish bar on the Kurfürstendamm, and all the military brass used to hang around there. One night, Herms was ordered by one of the officers present to take my sister and me home." Alex blinked. "That must have been fate in the truest sense, for it turned to my advantage. Shortly before he left, I promised him a nice fur coat, provided he visits my sister and gets Phillip to smuggle a food package in for us at Christmas. I hope everything will go smoothly; one never knows who to trust these days. You, Erich, you seem to be okay."

He continued, "Now about Willi, I'm not so sure. He never has much to say one way or the other and only talks about food. You're lucky you were put in here. Other cells are not so congenial."

Alex asked me if I knew Berlin well. I said no. We continued talking for a while longer, and I learned that Alex was the owner of a well-established fur business with partnerships in several other European countries.

Our conversation was interrupted when the door opened and Franzl was pushed into the room by a private. He came over to the table, sat down, and, shaking his head, said, "I've really had enough of this. Why can't they leave me alone? I don't know why they're still bothering me. The psychiatrist told me not to be so stupid as to give my life for something or someone that only exists in people's imagination. He meant God, of course. He added that many of my sort have already been executed and that one more head doesn't matter much. When I was ready to give him an answer, he just told me to get the hell out."

"What kind of doctors are these?" I asked him.

"All I know is that the one examining me is a brigadier general," Franzl answered. No sooner had he finished speaking than the door opened again and Willi entered and joined our conversation. He laughed aloud as he told us the doctor had asked him if he ever saw imaginary people, heard strange voices in his head, or suffered from headaches.

"Just to say something, I played along and told him that occasionally, especially during the night, I see figures armed with knives and other weapons approaching me. Also, during the day when I close my eyes, tigers, lions, and snakes sneak up on me to attack; but then I turn out to be magnetic and have the ability to push them away. Other times I hear a loud tone followed by a high-pitched sound, which grows louder and louder until there is a crash inside my head, and afterward these horrible throbbing headaches start. Usually the pain lasts about an hour and then subsides. Often, I see a dog barking at me but I can't hear the bark. The doctor took notes and mumbled that someday this dog would bite me or the snake would suffocate me. I must have sounded pretty convincing, because he said he would keep a close watch on me."

Now Gerhard returned, walking slightly bent over to his left, holding his hand on his bottom.

"What's the matter with you, Gerhard?" Alex asked.

"These guys are crazy," Gerhard moaned, still holding his hand firmly against his rear. "They injected me with a needle this long." Gerhard spread his fingers wide apart. Gingerly he sat down on the bench.

"I really believe Gerhard is being used as a guinea pig," said Alex. "Just the other day he came back with his head shaved and dark blue markings all over it. You can still see the lines, though his hair is growing back. He lets these guys do whatever they want. In a few minutes he forgets the pain and smiles again. This is very strange. You wait and see. The only thing he seems to be afraid of is the armed guards. They really frighten him. Because of this, in the morning they let him walk inside the compound with the officers. Usually, there are no armed guards there."

Meanwhile Richard had returned, looking angry but not saying a word. Apparently Alex read my mind and said, "Leave him be; he's angry at the entire world and hates everyone. He's been through quite a bit and probably hates himself most of all for his own stupidity. Eventually he'll tell you his story."

There was a rap on the door. It was Fritz with his walking cane. He held it up high in the air and removed a cigarette from its handle. While doing so he smacked his lips as if he were kissing someone. "This very valuable item cost me two slices of bread," he bragged.

"But bread is more important than cigarettes," I told him.

"Listen, you," said Fritz, "for the few days I have left to live, I want to enjoy my vices." He reached behind the metal sheet covering the radiator and removed a match, remarking that it was the last one left. He walked over to the door and removed one of the thumbtacks that were holding up the rules and regulations. With it he carefully divided the match into four pieces. I watched with fascination as he performed the task: first he put the match onto the table and stuck the thumbtack in below its head, slowly dividing it in two. Then he repeated the process and came up with four separate matches. Finally, he walked over to his bed and removed a small piece of sandpaper from under one of the bedposts. Rubbing the fragile match against the paper, he sparked a flame and lit his cigarette. He bent his head slightly backward and took a long, hard drag, inhaling deeply. Then he passed the cigarette to me. "Here, Erich, you didn't have a drag yesterday."

At first I declined, but I quickly changed my mind and took a couple of drags with sheer enjoyment. It did taste good. Fritz smiled. "This will be our dessert tonight," he said, putting out the cigarette and hiding what was left behind the radiator's metal sheet.

Sitting down on his bed and carefully removing his pants, he asked, "You wanted to see my wound? Come on over and I'll show you." He began to remove the bandages carefully. Gerhard joined us and helped him, saying he was better qualified to do so. I noticed how seriously Gerhard took his job. Once unwrapped, it certainly was an ugly sight. There was a big hole where the kneecap once had been.

"Isn't there anything they can do about it?" I asked.

"Nothing," Fritz replied quickly. "Remember, I'm on death row; why waste medical skills or medicine on me? As long as the knee holds together until my execution, that's all those bloodhounds care about."

He began to whimper: "If only I didn't have to die. I'm not afraid to look death in the eye. No, that's not the case—I'd just like to stay alive to see those dogs hanged. I know the execution only lasts twenty-six seconds, to be exact. That's it. You're sent to Plötzensee, placed in a cell, and when the time comes for execution they strap you to a board, take you outside, and chop off your head. Then it's good-bye, world. Franzl," Fritz continued, "just imagine, your beautiful head will roll into a basket filled with sawdust."

Franzl replied patiently, "Fritz, stop talking like that. It doesn't really matter how one dies. The Lord's revenge is eternal, and he will not leave anyone out. Whether these killers will be hanged or punished some other way is irrelevant and is not up to us anyhow."

"I really don't care about my own fate that much anymore," Fritz said bitterly, "but I am concerned about my poor fiancée, my poor Gitta; she's six months pregnant and was accused of and indicted for the same crimes as I." His voice trembled, and tears filled his eyes as his face lost its color. "If I only knew where she was! But I couldn't be much help to her anyway."

Alex interrupted laconically, "She's probably in Moabit."

Fritz's head fell into his hands and in dismay he began to cry uncontrollably. We looked at one another, but no one could find words to comfort him. Gerhard got up slowly, walked over to Fritz, stroked his head tenderly, and whispered, "Please, Fritz, don't cry, please."

Franzl moved to his favorite position on the floor and stared aimlessly into the air. I wondered what he was thinking about; perhaps somewhere he also had a sweetheart whom he missed.

Meanwhile, Willi was busily removing six slices of bread from his night table. "Where did you get all those from?" I asked him.

"I've saved them for Christmas to make sure I won't be hungry," he said. He put the bread back and walked over to the window to look out through the tiny peephole in the paint. I stepped over to join him at the window and asked what there was to see. Without answering me, he stepped aside and let me take a look. Peering through the hole, I saw ice crystals swirling in the wind and a few ravens fluttering around, looking for food, flying from the bare trees to the red-brick wall and back. I could make out another building very similar to ours but somewhat larger in size.

It's almost Christmas, I thought, and there's no snow yet; maybe it's too cold. My eyes began to hurt from the strain of peering through the tiny hole.

Fritz, who was still sitting on his bed, noticed me standing at the window and asked, "Do you see any cars?"

"No," I replied, "everything's quiet."

"Well, look again!" he snapped. "That building across the courtyard is the 'Ascension Place' for our glorious German Reich."

"What do you mean by 'Ascension Place'?" I asked.

"It's supposed to be an old-age home," Fritz explained. "Perhaps because of the Christmas holidays the authorities didn't dare bring anyone today, but just wait until afterward. Then you'll see some action! These poor old people arrive with their little bundles under their arms, thinking that they've arrived at a place where they can enjoy their last days comfortably. Well, it's a place of rest all right. Old folks walk in alive through the front door and leave the place through the back door—dead—by the carload. We've been watching them for a long time now. Those pigs! But what's the life of useless old persons to them? Our society was raised to honor and respect its elders, but apparently not elders who have to be supported. The poor souls are being injected with something that puts them to sleep eternally."

The lunchtime commotion began, interrupting our conversation. Lunch was a bluish-looking barley soup, but since hunger is the best seasoning, we all ate and even enjoyed a second helping, after which we were all in a good mood.

Even Fritz had cheered up; he had stopped weeping and began to hum a melodramatic song. Willi accompanied him with his deeper voice. It was against the rules and regulations to sing, so they were very quiet about it.

Gerhard was occupied with rotating his fingers back and forth. Suddenly he stopped, stood up, and reached into his pocket to remove a comb. He came over to me and asked if he could comb my hair. "Do I look so disheveled?" I asked, smiling, but I allowed him to stand behind me. He combed my hair carefully and seemed to enjoy the task.

Alex was busy cleaning his thick-rimmed glasses. He removed a file folder from a briefcase that he kept under his bed. He was the only one of us who had any files about his case.

Fritz told me he had devised an escape plan. His idea was to scrape with a spoon through the one-brick-thick wall and then let himself down on a rope of sheets tied together. That's where his plan faltered, since there was no way for him to cross over the high outside wall.

"Forget it, Fritz," I said. "With your leg you won't even get that far. Anyway, you're still considered a soldier, and desertion would be added to

your record. You don't need that. It would also reflect on all of us. It's probably considered the worst offense next to treason."

"Do you really think so?" asked Willi. "That's why I'm here."

Meanwhile, Fritz had lit his hoarded cigarette and passed it around the
room. Everyone took a drag except Franzl, who apparently hated smoking.
The afternoon passed slowly, but shortly before dinner there was an air
raid. We could hear the guards out in the hall setting up their positions.
The prisoners had to remain in their cells no matter what happened.

The lights went out. The wind was howling outside, and in the distance
we could hear the crashing of bombs. This went on for three or four hours
as we waited in the pitch dark. Our dinner of two slices of stale bread and
tea was served shortly before midnight. As soon as we had eaten, we fell
asleep.

CHAPTER 4

CHRISTMAS EVE

On Christmas Eve the few guards on duty were in a bad mood because they had to work and would rather have been at home with their families. We regarded the chance of communication from the outside world as a dream.

So we seven decided to make this very special evening and the day that followed as festive as possible. But how? We knew we would be left alone after the evening meal, since the doctors were off until after the holidays.

Phillip appeared in the doorway around one P.M. He looked especially good today, his uniform neatly pressed and a satisfied look on his face. "Who's in pain?" he asked.

"The hell with pain," Fritz joked. "What we need is a couple of cigarettes and something good to chew on."

"Who do you think you are to talk to me like that?" retorted Phillip. "But since it's almost Christmas, I won't report you, and here's something for you." He reached under his medicine box and brought out a small parcel, which he handed over to Alex. "Merry Christmas from your sister." Phillip added, "Please, fellows, not a word of this to anyone. I'm a married man with five kids to support. You know what they'll do to me if any of this gets out. You all have a merry Christmas." With these words he left the room.

Alex held the package in his hands as if he were weighing its contents. He placed it under his bed.

"Come on, Alex," begged Fritz. "Let's have a look."

"No, not until tonight," Alex answered. "We'll open it at the proper time."

The afternoon passed slowly, and our anticipation of opening a parcel not even meant for us made the time pass even more slowly.

At last our cell was locked for the night. Alex immediately removed the small package and placed it on the table. He folded his hands on top of it and, slowly and deliberately, said, "This, my dear friends, is for all of us." He read the card that was taped on top: "To my dearest brother, this is the only happiness I can bring you on this saddest of all Christmas holidays. God bless you and keep you well. Your loving sister, Elfriede."

Alex's voice quavered as he read the last few words. He removed his glasses and wiped his eyes. All of us were moved. Thinking of my family at home aroused a choking pain in my chest.

Alex finally opened the box and showed us the contents: cigarettes, matches, chocolates, candies, and two small jars of marmalade.

Fritz was the first to find some words. "Well, at least there are still some decent human beings left. I must say that Phillip's heart is in the right place." Turning to Franzl, he almost commanded, "Include Phillip in your next prayer."

Everyone in the room felt an inner contentment now. Alex smiled. "I'm so glad all this went off well. I told my sister to give Herms a fur coat and Phillip a fur jacket if they got these things to us by Christmas. I'm relieved because I know now that Herms can't hurt us anymore. Franzl can give us a nice Christmas sermon, and we'll sing a couple of carols before we divide the goodies."

Dusk began to settle in slowly, and a comfortable silence surrounded us. Alex and Fritz came over and sat down next to me on my bed. The others made themselves comfortable on the bench. Franzl, who usually sat on the floor, took a seat on the edge of the bench. Even Fritz, who was usually uptight, was calm as he asked Franzl to begin the sermon. Franzl hesitated, then looked searchingly at each of us as if he weren't certain that we were serious. Noting our solemn expressions, he stood up, folded his hands in prayer, and began in a soft, yet dramatic voice.

"My dear brothers, although none of you shares the light of my faith and in theory we are strangers to one another, I do want to convey to you a few words in the name of Jehovah, who loves us all. I shall cite the words from Holy Scripture that our Lord Jesus spoke on the mountainside. I have chosen these verses because they fit our lives so well. We are peace-loving people and true enemies of war."

It was obvious that he had memorized the verses well, because he spoke them fluently and without a pause:

"Blessed are the poor in spirit, for theirs is the kingdom of heaven.
"Blessed are they who mourn, for they shall be comforted.
"Blessed are the meek, for they shall inherit the earth.

"Blessed are they who hunger and thirst after righteousness, for
   they shall be filled.

"Blessed are the merciful, for they shall obtain mercy.

"Blessed are the pure in heart, for they shall see God.

"Blessed are the peacemakers, for they shall be called the children
   of God.

"Blessed are they who are persecuted for righteousness' sake, for
   theirs is the kingdom of heaven.

"Blessed are ye, when men shall revile you, and persecute you, and
   shall say all manner of evil against you falsely, for my sake.

"We must honor the truth," Franzl continued, "even though it may cost us
our lives. Christmas is the feast of love and peace, peace on earth, and
goodwill to men—this is what is preached from the pulpits. But why do so
many preachers speak of peace on earth and yet not stand up openly and
speak out against war? They even go so far as to bless weapons. How often
do men and their leaders speak of peace, and yet the end result is always
war?" He paused for a moment before continuing.

"Why does man still kill? It's not in man's nature to take another man's
life; probably most of us don't even like to hurt a fly, yet the killing goes
on. The reason is unbelief; most people don't even believe in themselves
anymore. They let themselves be led by their leaders, who, quite often, are
apostles of the Devil himself. Of course, Satan never admits that he's the
Devil; he uses many tricky devices and forms to appear among us. He
influences man with cleverness and even goes so far as to play God himself. One would think that history had taught us wisdom. But has it really?" he asked rhetorically.

"Quite often it's the fear of losing his own life that makes a murderer out
of a man. However, no one seems to think about the consequences or the
kingdom of Heaven. When a country starts a war, it is usually done, so it is
said, because of a threat to its existence. But one has to be very careful in
evaluating this assertion, because quite often the Devil draws tempting
pictures on the wall and stirs up hatred. In reality, war is for many a prof-
itable business and goes hand in hand with murder and robbery. In most
countries murder is considered the most vicious of all crimes. Yet mankind
has lived through it all, and when comes understanding? Perhaps never.
We all know that the Devil will never be killed; he's a survivor.

"As Jehovah's Witnesses we are acutely aware that Judgment Day is
coming very soon and that then there will be heaven on earth. Our Lord
sees and hears everything, and everyone will be judged by Him. Behold,
everyone will have to pay his debts on the day of reckoning. Jehovah will

arrive in glory, and it will be wonderful when the words 'Love thy neighbor as thyself' become reality," Franzl said with emotion.

Franzl looked each one of us in the face. "The crimes that you all have committed are petitions for God, even though you might not realize it now. He means well for you, and I only hope you'll learn to realize it. It will help you suffer your fate.

"I am not a preacher," he continued. "My request to keep a Bible was rejected, so I can't read you anything from the truest of all books, the Holy Scripture. Everything that man needs to know is written in this book. We Jehovah's Witnesses tell the truth, and unfortunately this is our doom."

For a few moments we were all silent, each thinking his private thoughts. Fritz, who apparently was the only one among us who wasn't impressed with Franzl's sermon, stood up, limped over to the table, and said, "Jingle bells, jingle bells, it's time to give Christmas presents."

Suddenly, Richard, who was sitting at the table, looked up and started to sing softly: "Silent night, holy night . . ." We joined him but got only as far as the second verse before our voices broke down.

Alex drew a long breath and rescued the situation. He took out a box of cigarettes and handed three to each of us. In no time the room was filled with smoke. "Just imagine what would happen if one of the sergeants walked in on us now and saw us puffing away," said Willi, a wide grin on his face.

After we finished smoking, Alex distributed the rest of the presents. We lay on our beds, daydreaming about home.

It was Alex who came up with the idea. Perhaps it was because we were all feeling the contentment of Christmas. Perhaps it was because Herms was gone and we could feel more relaxed. Certainly we had drawn close to one another during the evening with the guards away and the unexpected joy of Alex's present from his sister.

"What we must do," Alex explained, "is for each of us to explain his case, not only how he was arrested, but also how his life drew him to the point where this could happen."

Fritz joined in, "We must tell it one hundred percent as it was or as we see it. When each one is finished, we can judge the case for ourselves and reach a verdict." Even the quiet Richard seemed pleased for a change.

Alex suggested that we draw straws to determine who should go first. "Before we begin, we must swear by whatever is holy to us that the information will be kept a secret within this room, even if it means being tortured." We all did agree and then decided we would draw straws in the morning. With thoughts of my family swirling through my head, I fell asleep.

Morning came, and it was unusually bright in the room. Willi roused us. He was looking out the tiny hole in the window. "It snowed last night! The entire area looks as if it were covered with powdered sugar! Come and see for yourselves!"

Feeling relaxed, we prepared to draw straws for who would be the first to tell his story. Alex dug six straws out of his mattress and, as we all watched, carefully broke them off to the same length. Then Alex broke one of the bits of straw in half and threw half away. Turning his back to us, Alex lined up the straws in his hand so that we couldn't tell which was the short straw. Finally, we each drew a straw: Willi drew the short one. He sat on the bench, nervously rocking back and forth while chewing his lower lip. "All right," he said, clearing his throat. "I hope you guys will tell the truth and I'm not the only one just because I have to go first."

Willi looked around at us one more time to assure himself that we weren't joking and that he should begin to tell us about his life. Stiffly and hesitantly, he began.

CHAPTER 5

WILLI WEBER: THE DESERTER

I was born on March 3, 1923, so I'll be twenty years old in a few months—if I live that long. To tell you the truth, I don't really care if I die; it's just that there are so many things I haven't seen or done, and I'm curious about the future.

[Willi pulled his hands through his wavy blond hair and repositioned himself on the bench.]

Let me tell you a little bit about my family. My mother was seventeen when I was born; my father was thirty-one. I used to gaze at their wedding picture, which hung over my grandfather's sofa. I thought they were a nice-looking couple, but unfortunately, as fast as they had gotten married, they were divorced. From what I heard, it was my mother's fault—people said she ran around with other men. Whether that's the truth or not I really don't know, since I was only a couple years old when all this happened. After their divorce my father remarried and moved with his new wife to Silesia, where he had three more sons. The last I heard of him was that he had died in combat somewhere in Poland.

My mother and I lived with her parents for a while, but one day she decided to take off with a married man. That's the last I ever heard of her. I was raised by my grandparents. Soon after I started kindergarten, my grandmother died suddenly; my grandfather took her death very hard. He became a remorseful, grouchy old man, and his mood wasn't helped by his rheumatism and arthritis, which made it difficult for him to walk.

He used to send me to the corner store and would time me to the minute. I wasn't permitted to have any friends, nor would he tolerate any kind of noise. It wasn't much of a life.

We lived in the back of a tenement—a low-rent housing project—from where we could hardly see the sky. My grandfather would sit all day long in a rocking chair staring out the window, yelling at the children playing in the courtyard below. How I used to envy those kids, especially their freedom. I had a corner of the room where I was allowed to play and sleep. Most of my time I spent daydreaming about having a real friend, someone to share my thoughts with or to laugh and cry with. That's why I envied the kids down in the courtyard so much—they were very poor, but they always had so much fun.

When I started school—that was 1929, so I must have been six years old—my grandfather watched me even more closely. I had to be home right after classes, and if I were even a minute late, for whatever reason, he'd hit me with his cane. Obviously, he was very concerned that something would happen to me, because he didn't have any insurance for me. Occasionally he would insult me. He'd say, "You good-for-nothing whore bastard; why am I burdened with supporting you? Not even your father gives a damn about you, he's never sent you a penny. And your mother is a goddamn whore who isn't worth a cent. I just wonder why she turned out like that; your grandmother and I always lived a good and moral life."

My grandfather had been employed as a bookkeeper and received a small pension. Whenever the first of the month came around and he had to pay the bills, he would take his bad moods out on me. That's usually when he started in on me with his insults. I got so used to it that eventually I didn't even hear it anymore.

Thinking back now, I realize I lived like a hermit. I saw my first live cow when I was fourteen years old. The only good thing that came out of living with my grandfather was that he taught me to work with numbers. I was always the best student in my class, especially in mathematics. Since I had an aptitude for figures, he wanted me to become a bookkeeper. When I graduated from grade school in 1937, my grandfather wrote a lot of letters to help me find a position. We got one answer, inviting me to an interview at a lawyer's office. My grandfather had never heard of the lawyer and surmised that he must be a shyster. Nevertheless, he said, it was better than no apprenticeship at all, and at least I would get room and board and he would have peace and quiet for a while. With those words I was sent on my way.

My new employer was an attorney named Dr. Wischnevski, and his business was on the third floor of an old office building near the Alexanderplatz. During the interview he asked me if I knew how to read and write and whether I was good at math. I handed him my report card, and he seemed pleased. He told me I could start working the next day, explaining that the first couple of months were probation to see if I worked hard enough; then I would start receiving a small salary in addition to room and board.

In the office, I was assigned one of the three desks in a dingy-looking room. The light was on all day, since the only window opened onto a light shaft. Besides the lawyer there was an elderly man by the name of Herr Scheda. He lived in the attic of the lawyer's house. He was a kind and quiet person who taught me everything I needed to know, from filing to typing and other basic office functions. After three months I still had not received a salary.

One day Mr. Scheda accidentally spilled ink onto one of the files. Dr. Wischnevski became so outraged that he talked about it for days. When the first of the month came around, Dr. Wischnevski told the old man he was not financially able to keep him in his employ any longer. He told Scheda that he'd been a faithful employee for more than twenty years, but unfortunately these were hard times and one employee was all he could afford. The poor old man sat down at his desk and cried. The following morning, the attorney's sister found him dead in the attic room. He had hanged himself.

Mr. Scheda's death had no effect on Dr. Wischnevski whatsoever. Since my workload had doubled, I was forced to work longer hours and the lawyer asked me to move in with them. My grandfather agreed to this, provided the lawyer would take it upon himself to be responsible for my training and education.

So in 1938, at the age of fifteen, I moved into the same attic room where Mr. Scheda had lived and died. It was a small room with a slanted ceiling and a tiny window. A narrow bed, a chair, a table, and a closet were its only furnishings. Although it was far from comfortable, it did feel good to have a room of my own.

But I found that in moving from my grandfather's home I had only exchanged one bully for another: the lawyer's sister. She was a masculine-looking woman with a downy dark mustache and small, evil dark eyes that seemed to follow me everywhere. I think her favorite pastime was bossing me around like a drill sergeant.

A normal day for me would start at eight A.M. and end at nine P.M. Saturday I had to work only six hours in the morning, but in the afternoon I had to help with the cleaning. Sunday was my day off.

Most of our work consisted of divorce cases, and I got used to hearing ghastly stories. At times I thought about my mother and her lifestyle. If married life was really like this, I thought, then I would never marry.

Besides the room and board, I was given one and a half marks a month in pocket money, which wasn't much but better than no income at all. The meals at the lawyer's house were much tastier than at my grandfather's, and usually after the Sunday noon meal I would ride a streetcar to the outskirts of Berlin. There, on one of the many meadows surrounding the Mügelsee, I would find a nice spot where I felt comfortable. I taught myself to swim, I exercised and played ball, but mostly I just sat around looking out onto the lake, daydreaming about a future that would be wonderful.

How I envied the other fellows of my age who were strolling by with their arms around their girlfriends, giggling and laughing. For some reason girls had no interest in me. This bothered me, and I often wondered if I really was different from my peers. Was I a weird-looking person, or was it the shabby clothes I wore? I decided that it was because I looked poor.

One afternoon I was sitting, chewing on a blade of grass, when a boat pulled up. A gentleman in his early thirties stepped out; he had a dark complexion and a heavy mustache. When he spoke, I noticed his strong foreign accent. "Well, young man, are you all alone here?" he asked me. He invited me for a ride in his boat. Naturally, he didn't have to ask twice.

He was skilled with the sails and handled the boat beautifully as we sailed back and forth across the lake. This, I thought, was the greatest experience I'd ever had. The man spoke very little, but he did mention that he was a Czech working in Berlin. Girls who passed us in their boats flirted with him but ignored me.

You know, I used to stand for hours in front of a mirror wondering what was wrong with me. Since I was already tall and had wavy blond hair, I certainly was not what one would call ugly. I knew I was shy but not unapproachable. Nonetheless, I never had any meaningful relationships with other young people.

Anyway, after we had sailed around the lake for several hours, the man suggested he put me ashore at the same place where he had picked me up. I said it really didn't matter to me as long as it wasn't too late, since I had to take the streetcar back. We then sailed into a narrow inlet, where he dropped me off at a boathouse. We agreed to meet again the next Sunday at my favorite spot. He told me his name was Ralf Bode and I introduced myself.

Ralf and I met again on the following Sunday and set sail right away. There was a strong wind blowing, and at times I thought the boat would capsize. Ralf laughed at me, remarking that I wasn't much of a sailor. "By the way," he would say to make me feel better, "neither am I."

As we got to know each other better he told me about himself, that he had been born and raised in Prague. He gave me his parents' address and said that someday I should go and visit them. At one point Ralf asked me if I was a member of the Hitler Youth. When I said I wasn't, he wondered aloud why they hadn't recruited me yet. I told him that so far no one had approached me. I knew very little about the organization or the politics behind it. Ralf was surprised since he had heard that most youngsters had to join regardless of whether they wanted to.

I tried to change the subject and talk about girls and my own problems, but Ralf wouldn't let me. "Willi," he said, "I feel it's very important to be informed about politics because they will eventually affect your life as well."

Ralf had become noticeably agitated. "The consequences of the wrong kind of politics can be extremely serious," he warned. "Under Hitler's guidance Germany plans to conquer the entire world. The Germans will start with the small, insignificant countries and work their way up to the larger and more powerful nations. In order to accomplish this they need everyone's support, including women and children. Don't think for a moment that you will be spared. No way! Once the avalanche starts, nothing can bring it to a stop." He lowered his voice and said in a conspiratorial tone, "I know through very reliable sources that Hitler is planning to invade my homeland, and then, my dear friend, I will have to shoot at you and you will have to shoot at me."

"I've never looked at it that way," I replied. "But regardless, I would never shoot at you and very likely many other Germans wouldn't either."

However, Ralf went on relentlessly. "When it comes to war," Ralf said, "it will be too late for politics." His feeling was that the Germans would have to stand up and oppose Hitler before that time arrived.

"I'm working at the Siemens factory here in Berlin," Ralf said, "and I can see for myself that not all Germans belong to the herd that follows the Nazis. The Germans sacrificed enough during the last war."

Ralf took out a handkerchief and wiped his forehead. Pearls of perspiration had soaked his face while he spoke.

"Have you read Hitler's *Mein Kampf*?" Without waiting for an answer, he added, "Before 1933 the German worker said: If the Nazis want a war let them put the weapons into our hands—we will use them on the true enemy because we know who he is. I've come to learn about this in the factories, where many blue- and white-collar workers think as I do."

He forced an uncertain smile. "I can already see how the sheep will be led to the slaughter, with all but a few following blindly. Don't think I'm prejudiced against Germans—quite the contrary. I think they're hardworking people. But as it is, bad elements usually have an easy target. Perhaps you have some idea now what politics can be and lead to. Keep your eyes and ears open, and don't believe everything you read in the newspapers or hear on the radio."

I had never heard anyone talk with such enthusiasm. I was very impressed with what he had said.

We kept on meeting for several months and became very close friends. Ralf spoke to me like a father would speak to his son and was the only person who treated me with respect and recognized me as an individual. When the subject was the Nazis or Hitler, his eyes would flare up and radiate a hatred that was almost frightening in its intensity.

Then suddenly, one day, Ralf told me he had to leave Germany. He wanted to give me his boat, but I explained that I wouldn't be able to keep up the boathouse rental. He was lucky and sold the boat the same day. In the evening he took me home, and we said our good-byes. Ralf patted me on the back as we embraced and said, "Take care, little friend; perhaps we'll see each other again someday." After he had left I felt very alone.

On my sixteenth birthday, Dr. Wischnevski gave me a copy of *Mein Kampf.* I read it carefully and found myself agreeing with much that Ralf had said. I decided to become more aware about what was going on, but I found it impossible to develop much of an interest in politics.

Then, on September 1, 1939, war broke out. I thought about Ralf and was happy not to be a soldier. As the first victories were announced over the radio, Dr. Wischnevski was ecstatic, remarking that the entire world would soon see how strong Germany had become. My boss was so excited that he gave me some money—one mark, to be exact—which was fine with me.

The next couple of years were uneventful. However, in the early spring of 1942 I received a notice to appear before the draft board. I had no choice but to go and was declared fit for duty. Dr. Wischnevski wasn't happy about it, but he had no choice either.

It did enter my mind to flee the country, but where could I go? I had no relatives to turn to. My grandfather had died in 1938, and my mother had come for his funeral just to collect his belongings, making no attempt to see me.

I had to report for duty and was assigned to a training unit in Spandau. I drew attention to myself on the very first day, but not in a positive way. During an initial drill exercise, when I was ordered to turn right I accidentally turned left, and I thought the sergeant was going to bite my head off. At each roll call I did something wrong, and the same sergeant ridiculed me in front of everyone whenever he had a chance; at times it became intolerable.

One day during an outdoor maneuver the sergeant screamed at me, "Even if I have to bring the water in your ass to a boiling point, I will do so to make a soldier out of you. I know your kind, you tried to dodge the Hitler Youth, but here there is no dodging and your stiff joints will be made flexible, I guarantee you that!" We were trained, had to obey, and were treated like dogs.

After living through eight weeks of barracks life I truly panicked and decided to escape. On my first Sunday furlough, I took a streetcar to the lawyer's house. I asked Dr. Wischnevski for the one hundred marks' salary he owed me and the five hundred marks I had inherited from my grandfather. I told him I needed certain things the army wouldn't provide. I went to talk to the old lady in the kitchen and told her how much I missed her good cooking. She fell for my compliments and packed a loaf of bread and some cupcakes for me.

I then went upstairs to my former room, where some other unfortunate victim had already moved in, but my belongings were stacked very neatly in a paper carton on top of the armoire. I removed a few things from the box—my passport, birth certificate, identification, and inoculation cards—and wrapped them in some clothes. I replaced everything else and put the box back on the wardrobe.

I took the streetcar out to the lake, sat down at my favorite spot, and wrote the letter of my life, a four-page suicide note addressed to Dr. Wischnevski. I said I was unable to cope with my life anymore. I gave him detailed information about my experiences in Spandau, about my upbringing without a mother's love, my grandfather's hatred toward me, and what I really thought of him. I requested that he inform my commanding officer about my death.

Late in the afternoon, I took off my uniform, folded it neatly, and placed the envelope with the letter in one of its pockets. I covered it with a rock so the wind wouldn't blow it away. Naked and carrying only my bundle of civilian clothes on top of my head, I waded about two hundred meters into the lake and stepped out again at another spot, put my clothes on, and took the streetcar back into Berlin. There at the railroad station I bought a ticket for Dresden and took the next available night train. In Dresden I changed trains and rode farther, toward the border of Czechoslovakia, where I got off at a small village about two stations before the frontier.

I walked into a wooded area and slept for a couple hours on the soft green moss. In the course of the next day I met some lumberjacks, whom I accompanied in the direction of the border. I had told them that I was looking for my mother, who was supposed to be living in this general area.

I had absolutely no problem crossing the border into Czechoslovakia, since no border patrol was in sight. After almost two hours of walking I arrived at a small village, where I boarded a train in the direction of Prague. Without difficulty I found my friend Ralf's house. He was very happy to see me but immediately told me that it was far too dangerous for me as well as his family for me to stay in Czechoslovakia.

"You are now a deserter," he said, "and as such you will be shot on the spot. This includes anybody who assists you. The Nazis have their spies all over the place, and they don't fool around. Upon their entry into Prague they shot and killed my youngest brother. What would be best for you would be to get out of here and into Switzerland and then to Sweden, where you'll be safe. I'll try my best to get you all the necessary papers, and in the meantime you can stay with a friend of mine who lives on the outskirts of the city."

We arrived at his friend's house around nine P.M., and Ralf instructed me not to step outside or to be seen at the windows. The friend was an older lady who hated the Nazis even though her parents were both of German descent.

Early the next morning, Ralf arrived with everything I would need for my escape. He had marked a map showing my route via Vienna to Innsbruck and along the Inn River across the Swiss border into a small town called Zernez. There I was to go to the only Catholic church and ask for the priest. "You tell him that you are the painter and show him this picture," Ralf said, handing me a photograph of a man I didn't recognize. "He'll welcome you, and only then will you tell him who sent you. He is our middleman and knows me well. He'll make all the necessary arrangements for you to go to Sweden. The priest is a kind old man, he wears wire-framed glasses and has a short grayish beard. This photograph you are carrying is of our former president, Tomás Masaryk. Keep it with you at all times; it will help you even in Sweden."

He next handed me a falsified tourist's pass and a Hitler Youth membership card made out in my name, pressed a couple of Swiss francs and some American dollars into my hand, embraced me, and wished me good luck. The old lady packed some food for me and put an overcoat that belonged to her son over my shoulders. With my map and directions I went on my way.

I encountered no problems in Vienna or on the way toward Innsbruck. There were no patrols around the border area, and I just kept on walking. As I passed a customs barrier, I saw a cornerstone with the Swiss emblem about fifty meters ahead. I saw that there was another barrier fifty meters behind me now.

Suddenly, a German border patrol guard appeared from nowhere and shouted, "Halt!" I was surprised but had figured this possibility into my plan. "Where are you going, and where are you coming from?" demanded the guard. I said I didn't know where I was and that I was lost. "You're in no-man's-land," he cautioned. Then he asked me for some identification. As I reached for my papers, the photo of Tomás Masaryk fell to the ground. The guard ignored the photo as I bent to pick it up. He returned my pass to me and said, "Everything seems to be in order; just walk back the same way you came."

I took a deep breath and was ready to start walking again when the guard called me back. "By the way," he said, "who was in that picture that fell out of your pocket? Let's have a look."

I had no choice but to show it to him, hoping that he wouldn't recognize it. I said that it was a photo a friend had given me in Berlin, but the guard snapped, "What? This looks like that bloodhound Masaryk to me." He turned it over and on the back saw a notation in Czech plus last Sunday's date.

"Now let's start all over again," he said in a much more official voice. "Who gave this to you? This story about Berlin can't be true."

"It's the truth," I pleaded. "I showed it to a guy on the train, who must have written something on the back in Czech. You have to believe me," I begged with my heart knocking frantically. He looked at me even more suspiciously now, and I felt my face turning red. He ordered me to come with him, and I trotted stupidly next to him, unable to speak or think. He stopped in front of a small customshouse and instructed me to wait until he got the keys. As he disappeared behind the house I felt a voice inside me saying "Run, Willi, run." But my feet felt glued to the ground. I wasn't able to move a muscle. Thinking about all this now, I'd like to kick myself for being such a coward.

After a few minutes the man came back with another guard. I noticed that the second man was wearing a different type of uniform. I was asked again to show my identification papers, and the other patrolman stepped inside the house to pick up the telephone. He kicked the door shut with his foot, so I couldn't hear who he was talking to or what he was saying. After ten minutes or so, he reappeared with a satisfied grin spread over his fleshy face. Turning to his colleague, he bragged, "We've caught us a big fish here. They're looking for him in Berlin." Turning toward me, he said, "You're under arrest. Please don't try anything foolish; otherwise we have to use our weapons. You're a military case, and we have to take you to Innsbruck."

My dream of freedom in Switzerland or Sweden had come to an abrupt end. The officers manacled my legs together, and I was put into a jeep and taken to Innsbruck, where we arrived late at night. I wasn't able to make out where they had taken me. Apparently it was some kind of prison. The guard there wrote down my name and put the word 'Deserter' next to it. He looked up at me and continued asking more questions. He did all the talking. I did all the listening and refused to answer him. "Listen, you!" he finally yelled. "I've been known to get people like you to talk." In his rage he picked up a piece of firewood from behind the oven and threw it against my head.

Angrily I protested, "You can't hit an unarmed man; I'll report you to the authorities."

"Report me!" he snapped back. "You bastard, you can start with me; *I'm* the authority around here." He got up from behind his desk, pushed the chair to one side, walked over to me, and punched me in the face, at the same time kicking me in the shin. In so doing he lost his balance and fell down. Apparently this was enough for him, because he decided to stop his harassment; he took me to another room with barred windows.

A few minutes later a man appeared and shaved all my hair off. I hoped to get something to eat, but no such luck. Toward dawn I contemplated suicide, this time for real. But how? There was a small lamp hanging from the ceiling, but the light burned all night, and besides the room was checked by a guard every thirty minutes. Around four in the morning I couldn't hear the tread of the boots anymore and it became quiet. Now is the right time, I thought. I removed my belt from around my waist, tied it to the window, made a loop, and placed it around my neck. As I slumped to the ground I felt the belt tighten against my throat, but it was just a blur of sensation as I couldn't breathe anymore and lost consciousness.

Unfortunately, that wasn't the end of me—obviously. The next thing I knew, someone was slapping my face. I awoke and looked at a man—probably a doctor—who felt my pulse. "Well, at least you're among the living again," he said. I wanted to say something, but my neck was swollen so badly I couldn't utter a sound. I was also having trouble breathing. As it turned out, someone had found me and cut me loose. What was left of my belt lay next to me on the sheet. At the foot of my bed stood a guard who eyed me as if I had come from another world.

A sergeant in uniform entered and inquired of the doctor if I was fit to be transported to Berlin. "Give him about two more hours; then he should be all right." They brought me something to drink, but I wasn't able to swallow it. Another soldier appeared and tied my hands behind my back. They put iron chains around my ankles and locked them together. I was loaded into a car and driven to the railway station. In a boxcar of an express train coming from Rome we rode toward Berlin, arriving at the Anhalter station in the late afternoon. From there I was taken to Tegel prison, where I was put into a solitary cell. Two days later I was interrogated by two officers in civilian clothes. After the information was written down, one of the men said that I needed an attorney, since mine was a closed case and death was the penalty for the crime I had committed.

I told them that I had no money, nor did I want an attorney. "Unfortunately, we can't go along with you on this," one of the officers said and they both left. Later I was summoned into a room where a man introduced himself as my defense attorney, Mr. Fuhrmann. "Who hired you, and who's paying for all this?" I demanded. "A Dr. Wischnevski has retained me to represent you," he replied. Probably Dr. Wischnevski's guilt had worked on him to spend the money on me, or perhaps my grandfather had left me more money than he had told me.

The lawyer placed a legal-looking document in front of me and asked me to read and then sign it. "It's an authorization for the court," he said. I asked him what court he was talking about, and he told me he was referring to the military court-martial in the Turmstrasse. "Am I permitted to write to the court or to you?" I inquired. "Yes," came the answer. "You have the right to do so while you are here in custody pending trial, so you'll have to be furnished with the necessary writing materials."

The following morning I received paper, pen, and ink with which I wrote a long letter to the court, petitioning them not to fool around with me too long. Go ahead and shoot me, I suggested, or hang me, or even behead me, but please don't let me live in a society where no one gives a damn about other human beings.

The response was swift. I was sent here to establish my sanity—or lack of it. Apparently the lawyer had convinced the court to have me examined to see if I was mentally fit. He argued that if I had been of sound mind, very likely I would have escaped at the border and certainly I would never have written this letter to the court. Dr. Wischnevski also provided some documentation that supposedly documented my mental state. What kind of documents they are, I'm to be told at the hearing. The trial is scheduled for right after Christmas, although I don't know the exact date.

"Well, guys," Willi said, "you heard it all. Everything I've told you is the unvarnished truth." He leaned back against the bench, obviously tired and waiting for someone else to speak, but we remained silent for a few minutes while we thought about the desperately serious case of one very unlucky young man.

Fritz was the first to break the silence. "Let's eat our supper, and then we can continue with whoever draws the next lot."

We ate our meager meal of bread topped with some sort of fish paste and drank the unsweetened tea. As soon as we were finished eating, we drew lots; Alex drew the shortest straw this time.

We had little to offer to Willi beyond a sympathetic expression on our faces. Could there be hope for a deserter in wartime? The question remained unanswered in our minds.

Alex removed his horn-rimmed glasses and rubbed his eyes, glanced around the room as if he wanted to assure himself that everyone was listening, and began to tell his story in his smooth, cultivated voice.

CHAPTER 6

ALEX KEMINSKI: THE DILETTANTE

Fundamentally, my life has taken quite a different course than Willi's. I was born in Moscow into a wealthy furrier's family in April 1910. My grandfather had established the business, which had affiliates in several European countries. Besides the fur business, we owned a novelty shop and boutique that was under my mother's supervision and that catered only to the very wealthy. Since my father traveled often, a Jewish gentleman named Kohn managed all of his affairs at home. My father employed several people, among them a German governess, who taught my sister and me everything we needed to know from grammar to etiquette. It was my mother's wish that besides Russian and French we also learn her native language, German.

My mother was a tall, elegant lady who ran her business with style. Only the aristocracy and the very rich patronized her store. Whenever my sister and I—accompanied of course by our governess—were allowed to visit the store, we would make ourselves comfortable in a corner niche where the customers were served refreshments, and we would sip hot chocolate and eat divine petits fours or miniature pastries. There were even colorful oil lamps burning during the daytime, projecting a cozy, elegant atmosphere.

It was around this time that the Great War with Germany broke out. At first, we were not affected, but soon the situation changed and became rather serious for us. When the revolution came to a boiling point in 1917, the entire family fled to Germany, where my mother had relatives.

It was exciting to go to Germany because my mother had told us wonderful stories about her native country and her family. We traveled through Finland and Sweden to reach Germany, where we were received with love and kindness and made very comfortable by my grandmother, aunt, and uncle. My grandmother and her younger sister, who was married to a Jewish cattle dealer, lived in a small village outside Berlin. This uncle had lost a leg during the 1871 war with France, but the handicap did not seem to interfere with his work. He was an extremely active man, and I certainly admired him.

Since we had left Russia in a hurry, there wasn't much we could bring, but my mother was able to save all her fine jewelry by sewing it into our undergarments. Later on, when we were out of Russia, she told us that we had carried more than a million marks' worth of diamonds and other gems on our backs.

My father joined us a little later by coming directly to Berlin, where he stayed with a business associate he had known for years. Herr Katz was a Jewish fur trader and had at one time been my father's best client. He was an older man who had never married and had no family of his own.

After a couple of months of their joint venture, a few German craftsmen who were talented professional furriers joined the business. Under Herr Kohn's supervision they made the most beautiful fur coats and jackets. Since mink and other precious skins were not available, the craftsmen used rabbit furs and came up with some exclusive creations that sold as fast as they were made. People had plenty of money at the time, but they didn't get much for it.

What happened to our family after the war ended should come as no surprise, but we were luckier than most people. For several months there were rumors that there would be a revolution. Everything was in chaos. Although we were able to survive the hunger that ravaged the country, I saw what hunger did to the old, the very young, and the weak, the ones most unable to go hustling for food. I remember the starvation, the sight of city residents desperately going into rural areas to exchange whatever goods they had for food. For the farmers and peasants, however, it was a golden age.

Since my uncle was in the cattle business, he knew where to get food, so we were personally not affected by the hunger that swept through Germany. Mind, I'm not telling you this to give you the impression that we took bread away from other people, but everyone had to look out for himself, and we were no exception.

Well, the rumors of revolution eventually ended and we moved to Berlin, living in an apartment in Herr Katz's complex that had become vacant. Because of ill health, Herr Katz sold his part of the business to my father for roughly two thousand dollars. Dollars were considered the most reliable currency. In return, he requested free room and board and a hundred marks per month as an allowance until his death. My mother sacrificed some of her jewelry, which my father took to Zürich to auction off through connections he had established there. Once again we had our own business.

But in 1922, when inflation soared and the money market dropped rapidly, we had to struggle to keep the business open. I remember that on the days when we sold an item, if we didn't immediately use the money to purchase something, that same evening whatever we had received had deflated to practically zero. However, since quite a few of our transactions were in dollars, we were able to buy almost anything—if not through regular channels, then on the black market. When the goldmarkade, or rentenmark, came into existence in 1923 or 1924, life changed for the better. The market escalated, and so did our business.

Primarily, my father did all his purchasing in Poland, but later on he went to Norway, Sweden, and even as far as Canada to buy only the finest furs. As Berlin once again became the cosmopolitan city it had been and its population began to catch up with what it had missed during the depression, our family business once again attracted wealthy clients.

Most of the customers, including quite a few Americans who patronized our store, always asked for Herr Katz. Since he so obviously was a well-liked and respected businessman, my father left the sign with his name, "Katz Fine Furs," hanging over the store entrance.

It seems insignificant now, but I remember how happy I was when my father was able to buy back my mother's jewelry, which had been auctioned off. But then, when Herr Katz suddenly died of a heart attack, our entire family felt the loss. His funeral at a Jewish cemetery was attended by many like us who thought the world of him. My father had a beautiful monument erected in his honor with the inscription "In memory of a dear friend and a fine human being, who was loved and respected by all."

A few weeks later Herr Kohn, who was now the head of our purchasing department, married a dancer, left our establishment, and moved to Leipzig to start his own business. Eventually, my father got tired of the constant traveling his job demanded, so he started sending his representatives to do all the selling and negotiating. Almost all of them were Jews, since they were well trained and were the best at this type of business.

By 1929 our business was booming, and my father decided to buy a large office building that had once housed a bank. The owners were close friends of my parents who wanted to emigrate to the United States because they were Jewish and felt that the situation in Germany was becoming too critical for them. They sold the building for a very reasonable price. We had a good safe place to store our valuable furs in the heavy basement vaults. As I recall, we paid about a million marks for the building. My father told us he bought it as an investment for my sister and me. She was already actively involved in the business, but I still had to complete my schooling before I could take part.

I must say, I was an excellent student at the local secondary school, always bringing home the best grades. Our parental supervision was not as strict as it had been in Russia; my sister and I were mostly left on our own with constant reminders that we were the offspring of respected businesspeople and should conduct ourselves accordingly. Then came the time when I had my first experience with a woman.

The secondary school I attended was a coeducational institution where the majority of the students were males. One of the few girls in my class was the daughter of a locomotive conductor. Her name was Margot Müller. She was a very attractive girl with a well-developed figure and a cute face that reminded me of one of my sister's dolls. Her ash blond hair, which she wore unusually long, was draped over her shoulders. Most of the other girls wore their hair pulled back in buns or braids.

One afternoon, Margot approached me in the schoolyard with a solemn, almost distraught expression. She asked me if I would consider tutoring her in mathematics. She explained that she had gotten too far behind and since I was the best math student I could help her. After looking into her pleading eyes, what could I say but yes? I told her she would have to find a suitable place for studying. She had already given this some thought because she immediately said we could do so undisturbed at her home.

The next morning, before class, she came up to me and said that she had spoken with her parents and they were glad that she had taken the initiative to get help. She inquired what my fee would be. I told her that since we were school chums I would gladly help her without pay. Our first tutoring session was scheduled for four P.M. Her house was within walking distance of mine, practically around the corner. My heart was pounding and my palms perspiring as I climbed the stairs to the third-floor apartment because I didn't quite know what to expect and how it would be to be alone with such a beautiful girl. I arrived punctually and rang the doorbell with such force that I heard the chime echo several times.

A middle-aged lady, short and friendly, opened the door and, after I had introduced myself, told me she was Margot's mother. She explained that Margot had gone out to run an errand for her but would be back shortly. Only a few minutes had passed when Margot entered the well-furnished living room with her hair flying. She radiated an abundance of energy that was catching. Without much conversation she went to get her math books, and we pulled chairs up to a small table in the corner of the dining room and started studying. Her mother peeked in on us occasionally, making remarks like "Margot can if she wants to; she's just too lazy sometimes."

Finally Margot pleaded, "Please, Mama, I have to concentrate, so stop interrupting us all the time." I was astonished at Margot's learning ability. She certainly knew more than I had imagined. Margot and I decided to meet three times a week until she had caught up.

As I was leaving, her mother asked me what my fee for tutoring her daughter would be. I replied that I had already told Margot that my services were free, considering that she was a school friend. This seemed to make the lady happy, and she thanked me for my kindness. She told me she was working to supplement her husband's income, because it just wasn't enough.

The next time, I arrived on the dot and was met at the door by Margot herself. She welcomed me with a big smile and escorted me straight to her bedroom. When she noticed my puzzled expression, she told me we could study more comfortably on her rug. The room was well lit by two large windows and had quite a different decor from the rest of the apartment. Margot's unconventional personality was reflected everywhere. Besides the high bed and wardrobe, there were a small desk, a chair, and an oyster-colored lambskin rug.

I asked her what her mother was going to say when she got home and found us in the bedroom. Margot explained that her mother was a very understanding person, and besides she wouldn't get home from work until around seven in the evening. Her father, however, who was away on business, would not tolerate her having friends in her bedroom.

We devoted the next hour to studying. As I was getting ready to leave, she stopped me at the door and begged me in a childlike voice, "Can't you stay a while longer? I get so terribly lonesome when I'm home by myself." She was blushing, and her dark blue eyes seemed to grow in size. Before I could answer she threw her arms around my neck and kissed me on the mouth. Half stunned, I blurted out, "Why did you do that?" She answered, "Because I love you. I've been in love with you for a long time, I just haven't had the courage to come out and say it. You're the first man I ever kissed."

"Well, that was my first kiss too," I mumbled.

"Kiss me again!" she demanded.

I enjoyed the kiss and her demands were not necessary for I placed my arms around her, drawing her closer, and kissed her, this time more passionately. "Please stay here with me," she whispered close to my ear. I followed her to the bed and sat down. "What are we going to do now?" I asked naïvely. "We're going to get undressed," she said.

She undid her skirt, and it fell to the floor. As I unbuttoned her blouse, I felt the blood rush to my head. Dressed in just her underwear and stockings, Margot came closer to me and embraced me. She gently removed my clothes until I stood in front of her completely nude. She now pulled off her undershirt and panties and pressed her young body against mine. I thought I would go insane with pleasure. We lay down on the bed, kissing each other again and again. She began caressing me in just the right places and started to rub my erection up and down between her thighs. She was moaning with pleasure and gave a quick scream as I came into her. We made love quickly and intensely.

Afterward, I became scared, thinking her mother might walk in at any moment, so I jumped up from the bed and got dressed in a hurry. Margot, however, was still lying on the bed, moaning, "So this is what it's all about! How wonderful, how utterly wonderful! You know," she continued as if she was a chaperone, "we shouldn't have done this. We're too young. But wasn't it marvelous?" She got up, still naked, and started to embrace me again, but I told her I really had to go.

Our tutoring sessions continued in this delightful fashion, one hour of mathematics and another hour devoted to lovemaking. Margot turned into a love goddess; she wanted to try out everything and every position she had heard of or read about. Whenever I didn't want to cooperate, she'd complain that I wasn't man enough for her. During school hours we stayed at a distance from each other so no one would suspect we were having an affair.

Without realizing it, I had also fallen deeply in love with her. I thought about her day and night. It got to the point where I couldn't wait to be in her arms or even be near her. But then, one day after school, she slipped me a note to meet her in the back of the building. When I walked up to her, I noticed that her lips were quivering as if she were about to cry. "I didn't get my period this month, and Mother noticed it," she said with a twisted mouth. "I had to tell her about our relationship. I'm forbidden to see you again. What are we going to do?" she wept. "I don't know," I said. This was a terrible blow for us.

After a few days she slipped me another note. She told me that her mother had given her something to drink made of red wine and a bitter herb that grows in graveyards. She had had to drink it three times a day for several days, but the concoction had brought on her period. Of course, I was relieved to hear the news.

Margot's mother changed her work schedule, and it became more difficult for us to meet. But when we did, our lovemaking was even more passionate than before since Margot had a doctor give her a diaphragm so she wouldn't become pregnant.

After our final exams and graduation, our school held a farewell dance. During the celebration Margot and I danced together constantly. Edwin, one of my classmates, asked me during the band's intermission if Margot was my steady. Still somewhat on the defensive about our affair, I lied and said no, not exactly. "That's good," was his answer, "because I've seen her on several occasions in the company of an older fellow. Just the other day I spotted them near my family's weekend bungalow in the Grünewald."

"That can't be," I said.

"Oh, yes," he replied. "She was even wearing the same pink blouse and blue skirt she always wears to school."

Although I wasn't convinced he was right, I became uncomfortable, recalling that Margot had been acting strangely lately. Her kisses had been less demanding, and her lovemaking had become less passionate. At first I felt like leaving the dance and going home to my room, but then I decided to keep on dancing with Margot. I didn't let her know of my suspicions. She was smiling as always and held me close while we danced. I tried to dismiss what Edwin had told me and thought that perhaps he had been mistaken. After the dance I took her home, and as I kissed her good night, I suggested that just the two of us meet on Sunday afternoon at the café around the corner to celebrate our graduation. With a smile, she agreed. I couldn't sleep that night. I kept on hearing Edwin's words over and over. They danced around inside of my head until the early-morning hours.

My mother looked at me over the breakfast table and commented on how terrible I looked. "You probably did a little too much celebrating last night," she said, smiling. The truth was, I did feel miserable and besides, I had an awful headache.

On the Sunday afternoon I met Margot at the café as arranged. I suggested we go for a walk in the Grünewald to discuss our future plans. She said she would rather go to a movie. When I kept insisting, she reluctantly agreed to go to the park. My plans were to take her in front of Edwin's cottage and confront her with what I had been told.

We took the streetcar and disembarked at the entrance to the park. As we strolled along the narrow gravel road, I noticed how uncomfortable she became. My heart was beating frantically from the anticipation of having to ask her this important question. As Edwin's bungalow came into sight, I asked her if she had ever been here before. She replied, "No, not lately," only as a child with her father. I stopped and turned, facing her, as I said, "Then tell me who the man was that you've been seen with here on several occasions." First she blushed; then all the color drained from her face as she looked at the ground. I saw her slender hands trembling as she kept denying having been here before. "Very well," I said, "then you won't mind if we go in and visit Edwin. I'll ask him again." As I tried to pull her in the direction of the house she broke down and screamed, "Stop it, I'll tell you the truth!"

"All right," I said angrily. "Let's hear it."

For a few seconds, Margot was silent. Then she pointed in the direction of a nearby bench. We walked over and sat down. She began. "When my father found out about our affair, I thought he would kill me. He kept demanding how I could dishonor my family by going around with a Jewish pig. He was referring to you."

"I'm not Jewish!" I interjected. She said, "Please let me continue. My father went on asking me whether I really was so stupid as not to know that the Jews were the Germans' downfall. I didn't have any idea what he was talking about. He said he would rather see me dead than have Jewish blood mixed with my own. I told him I had no idea that you were Jewish. His answer was 'All you have to do is read the inscription over their store's door, it says *Katz*. Every idiot knows that Katz is a Jew, and so are the present proprietors. They took off from Russia when they couldn't do business there anymore and came here to take advantage of us Germans.' Then he told me that your mother's brother-in-law is a Jew. Crying, I kept telling him I didn't believe a word. 'Is it evidence you want?' he yelled. 'I'll give it to you. Tomorrow I'll introduce you to a man who knows this kind of people, he'll give you all the evidence you need.'

"The next day he took me to the park to meet a man he introduced as Assistant Principal Pfeffer. My father took the streetcar back home and left me standing there with the man. He was about thirty years old, a blond, blue-eyed, tall fellow. Pfeffer told me that besides being a member of the Brownshirts he had connections to get information into the Keminski family's background as my father had asked. He said that Mrs. Keminski's brother-in-law is a full-blooded Jew. During our lengthy conversation he looked at me and asked, 'How can a nice German girl like you even think of having sexual relations with one of those inferior beings? You certainly are pretty enough to have lots of suitors.'

"I said, 'You still have not convinced me that all this is true.'

"'Very well,' he said with a smile. 'I'll bring you some documents tomorrow that will certainly prove I'm right. Can you meet me again at the same place?' I told him I would.

"The following afternoon he was waiting for me at the station. He looked really sharp in his SA uniform. We walked to the park, and he told me several times how beautiful I was and that he could easily fall in love with me. Then after a while he confessed that the documents he had spoken of were not available yet. I protested that this was a lie, but he interjected, 'One moment, young lady, you better be careful about how you speak to me. I know about your pregnancy and how you terminated it. Do you realize you could wind up in prison for such a horrible deed?'

"I know I blushed, not out of embarrassment but from rage. How had he found out? Had my father told him? Pfeffer continued, 'Besides you, your Jewish lover would also be in hot water.' He grabbed me by the shoulders. 'By the way, how does a Jew make love?' he asked. I tried to free myself, but before I knew what was happening we were on the ground and he was kissing me. I wanted to scream but remembered what he had said about the abortion. He pinned me down and got on top of me. Within seconds he had penetrated me without removing our clothes. I couldn't believe what was happening to me. He even asked me to marry him! He then ordered me to see him again, at which time he would bring the so-called evidence.

"When I arrived home that night, I was debating if I should tell you about all this or tell my parents what the man had done to me, but I decided to wait until I had seen the evidence.

"We met again the next day. Pfeffer was extremely apologetic about his behavior. He sweet-talked me for about an hour, telling me that my radiant beauty had forced him to act like an animal and that it would never happen again. He said he had adored me since the moment we met and was sincere about wanting to marry me. He never did produce the evidence he had on you or your family, but otherwise I really think he was honest with me.

"I don't know what else to tell you, Alex," Margot said with a sigh. She had composed herself. "I've decided to accept his offer and marry him. I'll be able to get away from my parents and not be a burden to them anymore. I also must admit, he's very handsome and built more masculine than you, and besides, he's a far better lover and knows how to please a woman."

Was this the intelligent girl with whom I had fallen in love? God, what an idiot I had been! I was angry; I felt bitter and humiliated. How could she betray me for such a cheap reason? "For God's sake, the man raped you, Margot!" I snapped at her. "And you call this being more masculine? Did you believe him when he told me I was Jewish? I'm as Jewish as he is." I wanted to leave her standing there, never to see her again, but she begged me to take her home. I had to go home the same way she did, so what did it matter?

On our way back she confessed that she had already made all the arrangements to marry her true-blooded German. She said she would write to me from Pomerania, where he had been offered a position as a teacher at a prestigious boarding school. As the wife of a senior assistant schoolmaster, she could certainly live a very comfortable life and raise a family.

Shortly before we got to the corner of her street, Margot actually wanted to kiss me "for old time's sake," as she put it. When I drew back, she said, "Oh, Alex, don't take life so seriously. You'll forget me in no time. Our relationship was childish and experimental, you know that." Well, I didn't feel like that, I had truly loved her. "Go," I said. "Get out of here. I don't ever want to see you again."

The weeks that followed were a torment for me. I couldn't eat, I couldn't sleep, and I lost interest in everything. Inadvertently, my father rescued me by introducing me to his business world, which served to distract me. Eventually, after concentrating thoroughly on my new assignments, I recovered from Margot and my heartache. My family and I decided it would be best if I continued my studies, and I decided to study law. I was accepted at the University of Leipzig after prolonged difficulties that arose because of my Lithuanian citizenship.

My paternal grandfather had originally come from Lithuania and had settled in Moscow as a young man. When I asked my father at one point if there were any Jews in our family, he replied, no, we were all of Protestant Christian stock as far back as he could remember. "Why these sudden inquiries about Jews?" I told him that someone in school had accused me of being Jewish because of the name of our store. "Does this bother you?" my father asked. "No, it doesn't," I said, "because I know that most of our friends and business partners are Jewish."

Then one day my father decided it might be to our advantage if we held German citizenship. My mother was a German by birth; therefore it was only my father, sister, and I who would need to apply. He commissioned our lawyers to take care of this matter with the immigration office. After a lengthy wait and lots of money spent, we finally received our citizenship papers and German passports. The lawyer maintained that we should consider ourselves lucky that my mother was German; otherwise even the front money wouldn't have helped us become citizens. Another suggestion the lawyer had was to remove the name "Katz" from our sign. My father reluctantly agreed to change the firm's name to read:

DEUTSCHES PELZGESCHÄFT
IMPORT AND EXPORT OF THE FINEST FURS AND
FURRIER'S WORKSHOP
PROPRIETORS: HUGO KEMINSKI AND SON

Although I was not yet an official partner, my father felt that I would be one day.

Through some former classmates I found out that Margot actually had married her SA fellow and had moved out of the area. That was the last I ever heard of her.

In the fall of 1929 I took my prelaw studies very seriously. It was the first time I had been away from home. I lived at the house of our friend and former employee, Herr Kohn, where I had a spacious room and bath. I ate my meals at the university cafeteria. I was on my own now and thoroughly enjoyed the freedom and the occasional weekend visits home. Meanwhile, my sister had gotten engaged to a Turk—a handsome fellow named Ali who worked as a manager at one of the many cafés at the Haus Vaterland. The engagement party was a festive, crowded celebration at my parents' house. A number of girls buzzed around me, but I was still apprehensive of starting a new relationship after having been humiliated and betrayed by Margot.

Shortly after the engagement party, my grandmother passed away and soon after her my favorite uncle, the cattle dealer, whom I loved like a father. His death hurt me deeply, and I became depressed and remained that way for several weeks. Then my aunt came to Berlin to live with us.

With my first semester behind me—and I'd gotten excellent grades—my father decided to take me with him on a business trip to Paris and London. He felt it was time for me to get to know some of his associates and clients.

That vacation was one of the high points of my life. During our stay in Paris we lived at the home of a wealthy friend of my father, a rich Polish Jew named Warschauer, whom my father had known since our days in Russia. This man owned two fur stores, one in downtown Paris and another in England. I had never seen anything as magnificent as his Paris store. It made me almost sad upon entering the two-story building, for it reminded me of my youth and the lovely store we had had to leave behind in Moscow.

The front façade was a single large smoke-colored glass panel. On entering, you sank into plush carpeting, and a stately mahogany staircase led to the second floor. There, a circular rotating bar served excellent coffee, mocha, hot chocolate, and even champagne to the elite customers. Ornamental gold-framed mirrors adorned the paneled walls. The display of the world's finest furs and accessories blended in with the elegant decor and the trilingual sales personnel, handsome young men and beautiful young women who were dressed in the latest fashions and looked as if they had just stepped out of a magazine. The atmosphere projected wealth and luxury, they oozed out of every corner of the store; even a haze of the world's most exquisite perfumes seemed to linger in the air.

The Warschauer villa, on the outskirts of Paris, was even more luxurious. While our family residence in Berlin certainly was not what I would call shabby, it was nothing compared with the splendor of this stately mansion surrounded by beautifully landscaped gardens. The rooms were decorated in different colors and different historical styles. Each bedroom had its own bath and dressing room; pink, rose, and blue marble tiles flanked the oval bathtubs, which were ornamented with golden fixtures.

After being formally introduced to the family, I noticed that there were more servants than family members. I met Monsieur Warschauer, his wife, a son named Pierre (nicknamed Pedro), and a teenage cousin who was visiting. Pedro offered me his friendship the moment we were introduced. He was what one would expect of a Frenchman, an elegant dresser, suave, sophisticated, and a hearty lover of women—as I soon found out. Pedro was able to converse not only in French but in German, English, and Polish, and his Russian was more fluent than mine.

It was Pedro who introduced me to the Paris of poems, lyricism, and cabarets. It was in a Paris club where I saw my first nude dancers. The girls with their gorgeous bodies, dressed only in a headgear of huge, colorful feathers and black patent leather boots, paraded around, ostentatiously displaying their charm and sensuality.

The spectators were the cream of Paris, and they all seemed to know one another. They sat around small tables, sipping expensive wines and champagne. I was fascinated by all this. Pedro with his friendly eyes, which always seemed to me to be laughing, was watching me as my eyes kept returning to one particular dancer. He touched my elbow and whispered, "She's yours, *mon ami,* if you want her, I only have to tell the waiter, and she'll meet you after the show." A sudden image of Margot leaped into my mind, and all my desire drained from my body. On our way back home, I told Pedro of my unhappy experience with her. He called me a moron for wasting the best years of my life without women.

After a scrumptious dinner of baked pheasant at the mansion, Pedro called me aside in the drawing room. "I have a splendid idea for how to cure the heartache you feel for your little German girl," he smiled. "I'm going to take you to the best bordello in Paris and let you get a taste of our French girls."

"Oh, I have to think about this," I said, recalling the whores who walked Berlin's red-light districts. As if reading my mind, Pedro assured me, "Don't worry, these girls are clean and healthy, they get checked periodically and are the finest. You'll see. Come on, let's go!"

We took a taxi, then walked the last part of the way, until we came to a fairly large house set back off the road in a parklike environment. We strolled along a narrow, winding road that led us to an ornamental iron gate, where Pedro announced us to the heavyset doorkeeper. We were taken to a sitting room decorated with red wallpaper and satin drapes. It was obvious that Pedro was well known here, since everyone passing smiled at him or said hello. The madam, a statuesque woman dressed in black lace, brought a portfolio of her girls and placed it on the coffee table in front of us. Apparently Pedro had already selected his choice for me, because with a wink he asked the madam if Gisèlle was available. He leafed through the book and pointed at a picture: "Believe me, she's a man's dream, and besides, she speaks German."

I really don't know what I had expected, but somehow I hadn't visualized that things could work so fast. Taking hold of the picture, I had to admit to myself that this girl was indeed very beautiful. After a while, the madam came back and, with a professional overtone in her voice, informed us that Gisèlle was mine for the asking. Pedro took me across the room to a French provincial desk and picked up the telephone, which he handed to me. "Here," he said, "dial eight, and Gisèlle will come down and get you. I'll meet you later on down here. Enjoy yourself."

I was left standing there, not quite certain of what I was doing; I followed Pedro's orders like a robot and dialed the number.

Soon a petite maiden appeared. She was dressed in a lovely shade of blue that blended with the blue of her almond-shaped eyes. What a rare beauty, and so very young, I thought as I followed her up the stairs. At the last door of a never-ending hallway, she led me into a bedroom that was painted pure white. A lush deep-pile purple carpet and satin drapes in subtle shades of peach and mauve decorated the otherwise small room, which was dominated by the bed. Fluffy pillows in the same hues as the drapes looked inviting against the spotless white bedspread.

She closed the door behind me and quietly proceeded to undress herself, shedding first her robe and then her negligée. She turned around and noticed I was still standing there like a fool. "Is this your first time?" she asked softly and somewhat puzzled. "No, no," I whispered back, starting to laugh. Why am I whispering? I thought to myself. That beautiful creation came floating over toward me like an elfin princess out of a fairy tale. I started to remove my clothes since I had become excited watching her sweet body and its tiny breasts move so gently. She went on her knees to the floor and placed the side of her face against my groin. With her lush mouth she turned to kiss and caress me. I started to push her away but pulled her closer instead. She was an artist with her mouth and tongue, and the pleasure became unbearable.

Somehow we wound up on the bed. I started to kiss her all over, somewhat unsure of what to do. Suddenly my little princess sprawled on top of me, turning into an insatiable wildcat.

She caressed my ears with her tongue, rotating it in and out while the rest of her body was busy torturing me into the most magnificent orgasm I had ever experienced. At the same moment, her biting and nibbling came to a stop as her body began to tremble with sheer pleasure, and she collapsed with a muted cry.

Gisèlle rolled over and sighed, still out of breath. "You're wonderful. You're the strongest man I have ever had." In the same breath she asked, "Was it good for you?"

So I was a good lover after all, and not a flop in bed, as Margot had said. I wanted to give Gisèlle the world; she had made me feel like a real man again.

Pedro was already sitting downstairs waiting for me. I asked the madam how much I owed and was told it had been taken care of by Monsieur Warschauer. I felt happy and carefree, and my thoughts kept lingering on what I had just experienced. When we arrived back at the mansion, my father told me we would be leaving for London soon since his business transactions had almost come to an end.

I was sad to leave Paris and my friend Pedro. On our last evening together, Pedro warned me that dark clouds were gathering over Germany. "Remember, *mon ami,* you and your family are always welcome here. The National Socialists are maneuvering for power. Don't be fooled by them, because if it they win an election, I guarantee that war is not far off."

We left Paris and headed for London with a profit of two hundred thousand marks. Pedro had bought me an entire suitcase filled with expensive perfumes and lotions. I was rather disappointed with London. Maybe it was the drizzly weather or the people walking about in their hats and overcoats and umbrellas, all with the same cold, stiff expressions on their faces. Or perhaps I just missed Pedro and his charming personality.

My father's London business associate was an Indian gentlemen who dealt mostly in wholesale products. My father sold him wolf and sable skins we had imported from Finland and Russia, and in turn bought sheepskins from New Zealand and sealskins from Canada. My father was very pleased with his transactions, and after a couple of days we returned to Berlin.

When I told my father about the impression I had had of the English, he corrected me. "Son," he said, "one has to get to know the English from the heart. They seem cold on the surface because they're correct and dependable people, but inside they're warm and caring. They're extremely proud of their king and their royal family, and very likely they will always remain that way. You cannot judge people by spending two days in their country."

Back home, with vacation behind me, I returned to Leipzig and university life. I was given a complete new wardrobe and extra pocket money, and my father told me I could take as much money from the bank as I wanted, provided I let him know about it and spent it on reasonable things. One of my classmates convinced me to enter the prestigious Germania student organization. I was given a green, white, and purple student cap and, later on, the traditional shoulder sash. It was customary to wear these in the streets so that everyone could see that one was a student at the university. The girls swarmed around us like bees. I lived by the motto "No day shall pass without a woman." Margot was but a faint memory. Both my personal and scholastic life were at a high point, and I felt very satisfied with myself.

It was during one of our periodic fraternity meetings that I first heard about Adolf Hitler. Not Hitler the man but his ideas and philosophies. There were discussions about the great German Reich, the courage and bravery of the Germanic race, and the spirit of the German people.

Most of the members of Germania were the offspring of well-to-do families of which the fathers were successful businessmen, professors, or high officials of the imperial government. Working-class students did not exist for us. Although there were a few Jewish professors among the faculty, none of the Jewish students was permitted to join our fraternity. Even then, before Hitler came to power, Jews were considered second-class citizens and suffered ridicule and constant harassment. It bothered me to have to listen to speeches about the evil, destructive Jews who were out to conquer and dominate the world. How wrong could they be? I thought, remembering my Uncle Sam, my friend Pedro, and Herr Kohn. They certainly didn't seem like world dominators to me. I must say, however, that most people didn't take Hitler's aggression toward the Jews as seriously as they were expected to.

Meanwhile, Germany had fallen into a pleasure-seeking frenzy. People went out dancing and drinking, filling bars and saloons. Imported dances—the Charleston, the tango, the fox-trot, and the ever-beloved English waltz—became part of the social scene. In every corner of the larger cities dancing schools multiplied, and their business boomed. Women cut their hair short and dressed in revealing clothes with hemlines above the knee. Long, flowing hair and dress tails vanished. Cinemas and theaters were filled to overflowing. People had work and felt good, earning excellent money. What else could a country ask for?

Our business prospered beyond our expectations and became too much for my father to handle alone. He came to see me one day just as I had completed my third semester at law. He asked me to interrupt my studies and help him out with the store. He reluctantly confessed that he had been under medical treatment for a heart ailment and just couldn't cope with all the pressures of the business as before.

In the fall of 1930 I joined the business. I was not yet a partner since I would have to be at least twenty-one to become eligible. I was inspired to be the businessman my father was, and watched him carefully during his negotiations. Besides our store, there was also the retail business, which consumed most of my time. People were buying furs like crazy. Our vaults needed to be expanded in order to hold the overflowing minks, ermines, and sables.

Meanwhile, my sister married her Turkish fiancé, Ali, and became Frau Clark. Ali had been born into a mixed marriage, his mother being Turkish and his father an Englishman. I liked my new brother-in-law, and we became good friends. He was a handsome fellow with black hair like mine and a French mustache. My sister would probably have never married him if he hadn't been so extremely polite and well educated.

As part of my sister's dowry my parents gave the newlyweds enough money to set up a café in the Kantstrasse. They called their place "Türkische Bar." The café was decorated to give it a Middle Eastern atmosphere. Soon after it opened, an expansion to the second floor became necessary. Most of the downstairs was taken up by a large circular dance floor, an area for musicians, a bar, and, surrounding the dance floor, tiny round tables with chairs. The upstairs, consisting of several apartments with a separate side entrance, was converted into a sultan's palace. A new staircase was erected to connect the two floors. Cozy, cushioned booths and separate small rooms served only the very special clients. My brother-in-law hired a housemaster whose living quarters adjoined the restaurant on the second floor.

Whenever time permitted, I would stop by and enjoy an evening with the interesting clients who patronized the café. Ali was a genius when it came to running his business. He had a natural instinct for how to attract the right clientele by offering only the finest exotic food and entertainment. His philosophy was that the middle-class customer would eventually stop coming when the world economy took a turn for the worse, but the rich would always come. He claimed that the 1929 bank failures in the United States would have a tremendous impact on all of Europe. And right he was.

Our business was not immediately affected by the sudden economic changes that took place, even though unemployment swept through Germany like the Black Plague. When I turned twenty-one, my father had my name entered as coproprietor in the commercial register. I was now a full-fledged business partner. The house we owned in the Kantstrasse was listed in my sister's name.

It was around this time that I met a young ballet dancer from the Skala, the prominent cultural center. Her name was Katja and she was of Russian descent but had lived most of her life in France with her grandparents. She had been accepted by the Skala because of her outstanding talent. My sister introduced us, and we started to see each other regularly. I brought her home to meet my parents, but she apparently didn't impress my mother much. She felt Katja was too fragile—and besides, a dancer didn't belong in a business environment. I assured my mother that although I had been intimate with Katja, marriage was not on my agenda as yet. One day my dancing butterfly informed me that she had received a marriage proposal from a very respectable gentleman at the French embassy and she had accepted. I wished her well, and within weeks she returned to France.

I didn't waste much time in replacing Katja with Brigitta, a blond sex kitten, twenty-three years old and married to a Swedish diplomat three times her age. I saw her husband only on one occasion at the café: an unusually short, heavyset man with a broad, bald head and the bulging eyes of a bulldog. I'm not exaggerating, that's what he really looked like.

One evening, she joined me at my usual table at Ali's café and told me that her husband had been called away on duty to India. She apparently had no interest either in the trip or in joining her husband. It was obvious she wanted to see me again. Smitten not only by her Nordic beauty but also by her sensuality, I agreed to a rendezvous without hesitation.

During our first date we mostly talked about insignificant things. I did, however, begin to understand why she had married a much older man. She explained that both of them belonged to wealthy old-fashioned families and her parents had arranged their marriage. We had been drinking steadily, and now we both started to giggle. Although slightly tipsy, I was able to take her home to her villa in the prestigious Charlottenburg area of Berlin. At the front gate, she asked me if I enjoyed sailing. When I said yes, she asked me to pick her up on Sunday to go to the Wannsee.

We met as agreed. The boat—or rather yacht, for it was a very large boat—that awaited us was fully equipped. Below deck was a salon, a bedroom with a double bed, and a kitchenette with a gas stove and a full refrigerator.

A cup of strong coffee set us on a cruise around the lake. Brigitta was an accomplished sailor. With her blond hair flying in the wind we sailed down the Wannsee to Havel and then back north to where we had started out. She pulled the boat into a narrow cove surrounded by tall reeds, disappeared belowdecks, and reappeared completely nude to sunbathe. Lying down on her stomach on the hard planks, she smilingly gestured for me to come and join her. Without a word I went below and took off my clothes. Looking at myself in the wall mirror hanging in the bedroom, I thought, no, Alex, you can't go up like this in your underwear. A seductive voice came from the doorway. "*Mein Liebling*," she said, "you are on a Swedish boat, and in Sweden we sunbathe in the nude."

What had started out as sunbathing turned into ferocious lovemaking. This lady was a barracuda! She didn't want to stop. After we had exhausted ourselves, she ran her fingers through my hair, telling me that I was the best lover she had ever had. "Oh, I knew I would fall for you," she whispered in my ear, "from the first day I looked into those mysterious black eyes of yours."

I took her home, leaving her a block from her house, for she thought it safer. She insisted that the servants all had one-track minds and loved nothing more than a good gossip. Back home, my sister, Elfriede, stopped by for a visit. She must have sensed that I had something going with Frau Hansen, as she referred to Brigitta. "The woman is a man-eater," she warned me. "She devours men and spits them out. Be careful, dear. Her love nest is a boat she keeps on the Wannsee. I've heard tales that she takes a new lover every weekend and at times two and three at the same time. I'm telling you this so you won't get hurt as you did with Margot."

She continued, "Ali says that her husband knows about her affairs but leaves her alone because he pursues women of his own. Ali is right when he says people like this are good for business but not to have as friends."

That was the quick end of my affair with a married woman.

All my physical and mental abilities were now directed and devoted to our business, as the dark clouds Pedro had predicted were indeed starting to gather over Germany. Unemployment was out of control. Crowds and mobs gathered in the streets demonstrating either against the National Socialists or against the Communists. It got to the point where people attacked and beat one another to death. The police were powerless. It wasn't unusual to have to replace broken windows or doors. The Communists accused the Nazis of being warmongers, capitalistic pigs, proletarian trash, vulgar herds, scoundrels, and pimps. The Nazis counterattacked with slogans like subhumans, brutes, criminals, and traitors who had been hired by the Bolsheviks to do their dirty work.

The Nazis paraded around displaying signs: "Germany Awake! Jew Croak! The Jews Are Our Downfall! Germany: Don't Buy from a Jew." My family experienced some of this new hatred. Arriving at the office one morning, I was appalled to see the words "Jewish Pig" smeared in black ink above our store's main entrance. Either the scrawlers were referring to my aunt, or perhaps they thought Herr Katz still owned the store.

It was my father's idea to remove all the furs from the display windows and replace them with less expensive leather coats and jackets.

My brother-in-law, Ali, used some of his connections with high-ranking Nazi officials who patronized his café to look into the incident at the store. The following morning a local SA group leader appeared to tell us that his people had not been responsible. He suggested that the Communists had been the villains. Two days later, two other Brownshirts stopped by and asked us for a donation for their organization. I got angry, but my father, being wiser, gave them fifty marks. They returned to collect every four weeks. My father's intuition was right, and we were not bothered anymore.

My father, in the meantime, had bought a small but elegant villa in the Dahlem district of Berlin. The previous owner, a Jewish client of ours, sold it at a very reasonable price because she had moved to France to be with her daughter. The house, which was completely furnished, was to be the domicile of my aging parents.

I was struck by how political circumstances always turned out in favor of the Nazi party. Our friend Herr Kohn, who lived in Leipzig, sold all his property and also moved to Paris. Quite a few Jews we knew emigrated shortly before the Nazis' climb to power. My father and brother-in-law advised all their Jewish friends and clients to do the same. A neighbor of ours, a Jewish jeweler, and the Samuel brothers, who owned a store across the street from us, decided to stay. The jeweler's wife and daughter, however, did move to Switzerland, where they had a summer chalet in the Alps.

Then came the year 1933. The power struggle had ended, and the Nazis had won. Berlin was in turmoil. Some people cheered triumphantly while others wept. The Nazis' slogans became edicts: The Jews, the Communists, and the Socialists are to blame for all evil. The Führer is the savior. He will redeem us. Almost everyone was eager now to join the victorious Party. Anyone favoring the Left or disagreeing with the Party was arrested and sent to newly established concentration camps for rehabilitation. The SA raged through the streets like madmen, terrorizing people.

My brother-in-law managed to keep attracting more and more Nazi officials to his bar. The women of this new society wanted to dress elegantly and therefore were sent to our store to buy furs. Our business was doing well, if not better than before.

In 1935, when military service became compulsory, I was over the current draft age. Signs suddenly popped up everywhere saying: "Hitler Wants War! War and Corpses, the Last Hope of the Reich!" Unfortunately, all these early warnings were in vain, for no one heeded them. And why should they have? People had work, everyone ate well and was promised a bright and secure future in a country with a powerful leader who knew exactly what was best for his nation.

One evening while our family dined, my mother brought up the subject of emigrating to either France or Switzerland. My father wouldn't hear of it. He said he was too ill to move, and besides, he had no intention of starting a new business.

But how disappointed and helpless my poor father must have felt when, soon after, he saw his best friends, the Samuel brothers, dragged from their homes into the streets with mobs spitting at them and insulting them.

Among the attackers were the parents of children whom the brothers had fitted in their first pair of pants. For as long as I can remember, actually every Christmas, these kind men had clothed about fifty of Berlin's needy children even though they themselves weren't Christians. Now they were being rewarded for their kindness and generosity by mob violence.

When our neighbor the jeweler, a man of sixty and at one time a well-respected member of the business community, was pushed into the street with a sign hanging around his neck, "I Am a Jewish Pig," and beaten to death, my father suffered a massive heart attack. He never recovered. In the spring of 1936 we buried him. My mother was devastated. Fortunately there was my aunt, who, with her warm personality, was a consolation to her. I now ran the family business, which employed about thirty-five people.

In 1938, when Austria was annexed into the Reich, a party was held at Ali's café to celebrate and honor this historic event. It was there when I first laid eyes on a Major Kramer, a sophisticated-looking gentleman in his mid-fifties. He was employed at the Ministry of War in the Wehrmacht's conscription office.

In the course of time I became acquainted with several other high-ranking officers, whom I assumed were all good friends of Major Kramer. A few of them patronized our store, buying fur coats and stoles for their wives and girlfriends.

But the quickening movement toward war seriously disrupted our business. When the occupation of Czechoslovakia took place, trade with France, England, and Norway was interrupted and eventually came to a halt. Later on, when Poland was attacked, all my import and export business resources were exhausted. But as I was about to give notice to all my employees, I received a large order for sheepskin coats from the Wehrmacht's office.

I was called to the draft board, as the upper draft age had been raised, but I was given a deferment since my firm was fulfilling a military contract.

During one of our meetings at the bar, Kramer asked me why I had never married. I confessed that I actually didn't think much of women. He just smiled and said he wasn't married either and felt the same way as I did.

Then one day he invited me to join him in an intimate group meeting. He asked for my word of honor not to repeat to anyone where these meetings took place. He summoned his driver, who drove us to a three-story private residence in the Friedrichstrasse. As we sat in the backseat, Kramer, while talking constantly, placed his hand on one of my legs, stroking it back and forth. At the time I didn't think anything of it. I just assumed he was an enthusiastic talker who had gotten carried away.

Upon entering the room, I saw several officers sitting on plush sofas and easy chairs, drinking liquor and smoking cigarettes. The room was decorated with expensive Persian rugs and fine oil paintings. A cheerful conversation was taking place. Some young civilian men mingled among the military brass. Sounds of a piano being expertly played came from an adjoining room.

After a while, I noticed several men leaving in pairs, disappearing behind closed doors. It wasn't until then that I realized where I was. I found myself among a group of homosexuals. Kramer, sitting next to me on the sofa and watching me, asked if I would also like to go upstairs. I told him not today, for I had a headache and wasn't in the mood. "Well," he said with a smile and a hungry look in his eyes, "there will be other days for us."

When I told my brother-in-law about my rendezvous, he called me a naïve, stupid jackass for not having realized that Kramer liked other men. He warned me that it would be dangerous to retreat and that I risked being murdered, for I knew too much already. Although I never had any relations with Kramer, I did become his lover in name only.

All this happened while the war was getting more ferocious on both the eastern and western fronts. The war with Russia came in June 1941. My Wehrmacht contracts were not renewed, and within a couple of weeks I was drafted. I was to report to Spandau. I approached Kramer about my dilemma. "My dear sweet boy," were his words, "don't you worry your pretty head about it. I'll have it taken care of in no time." I handed him my draft notice, and within two weeks I received another deferment that excused me for the reason that my sister was not in a position to take care of my business.

My life went on in the same rhythm. Hours turned into days and days into weeks. Then one August morning, shortly after I had opened the store, two policemen walked in and arrested me without explanation.

I was taken to Moabit, where I became deathly sick with dysentery and consequently was brought here to Buch. My business lawyer told me that there was no indictment against me as of yet; however, I was involved in a very serious affair. Apparently Kramer, several high-ranking army officers, and an attorney were being charged with receiving money in return for draft deferments. Two hundred and thirty-two cases were known, and in each case individuals had been charged a fee of ten thousand marks for a deferment. Besides that, most of the accused were involved in homosexual affairs and charged with indecency.

My case was still being investigated. My lawyer wasn't certain if I would be tried by a court-martial or at the special Volksgerichtshof [People's Court]—where no appeals are possible—once I was indicted. He also said the case was being treated as top secret and the death penalty was practically assured if I were tried with the Kramer group. My sister and brother-in-law are running the store and are deeply concerned about my well-being. Those were the last words I spoke with my lawyer; I haven't heard from him since. Before I was transferred here to Buch I had to sign a document swearing to secrecy.

All I have left now is time and this endless waiting.

Just as Alex finished speaking, the lights went off. All of us were wide awake, for we had listened attentively. Once again it was Fritz's voice that broke the silence. "Alex," he said matter-of-factly, "you are a naughty man of ill repute." No one laughed.

Christmas Day 1942 had come to an end.

The next day was Saturday, and once our usual routine, which included cleaning our cell, was behind us, Fritz began drawing the lots. Richard was chosen. He sat on a chair close by the window, obviously uncomfortable at having been selected. Insecurity was written all over his freckled face.

CHAPTER 7

RICHARD WELDER: THE "GOOD GERMAN"

I can't tell you my life story as Alex did. One could write an entire novel about his experiences. Just take into consideration that Alex had a higher education and I only attended a one-room village school with one teacher and thirty-two pupils.

I was born on December 28, 1903, in a small village in the highlands of the Black Forest mountains. My father was a tailor, and my mother worked as a maid for local farmers. She worked during the spring, summer, and fall but was always at home with us during the long, harsh winter. Together we went out into the forest and chopped firewood. Although it was hard work, I enjoyed being outside in the crisp mountain air among the majestic firs and pines. My father never joined us, for he was of a small build and far too weak to perform this type of manual labor. My mother brought home most of our food from the farms where she worked, and we kept several chickens and rabbits to supplement our needs.

It was not often that my father was able to practice his profession; the local farmers were not wealthy and did not need many tailored suits. Mostly they just brought their slacks or shirts to be mended, so we very seldom had any money in the house. The only better-off people were the minister, the schoolteacher, one of the farmers, and the forester, whom I admired tremendously. It was my dream to become a forest ranger. Every time I walked by his log cabin, I longed to be him. When I expressed this desire to my mother, she would sadly remind me that there were no funds available to study forestry.

Village life was always the same. The only excitement was the yearly parish fair. Musicians would come from neighboring villages and play a piece of music in front of every house or cabin. Then, in the late afternoon and evening, they'd continue playing while the village folks danced on a wooden platform. A booth was also set up where sugar candies and a rasp-berry-flavored drink were served. This was a great treat for us children. The greatest excitement, however, was staying up late and listening to the happy music and watching our parents and neighbors enjoy themselves.

Changes came about in 1914, when the war broke out. All the available village men were drafted, even my father, who at the time was not very young anymore. With each victory the pastor would ring the church bells and our schoolteacher would dismiss us from classes. Then the letters and notices bearing sad news began to arrive: "Your son or your husband has given his life for the Kaiser and his fatherland." The mourning crowd would assemble in church and pray all day. Even our family was not spared. My father died on the eastern front. The letter said he had contracted pneumonia. In reality, as we found out later, a bullet had penetrated his left lung and he had bled to death.

My mother felt there was nothing left for us in the mountain village and decided to move to Stuttgart, where she had a sister and a brother. Apparently, it was there that she had first met my father while he was trav-eling from town to town. My aunt managed to find us a place to live in an old but clean gray stone apartment building. The third-floor flat consisted of one room adjacent to a tiny kitchen with one skylight as a window. The only problem was that the entire building had only one toilet and wash-room, which was located on the first level. Well do I recall some hot sum-mer nights when it was impossible to go to sleep. The only ventilation was the tiny skylight and the door, and we had to keep the door shut because the odor from the toilet would penetrate all the way up to our room. During the winter months the cold became unbearable at times. The walls of our flat would be coated with ice even though my mother fired up a small iron stove that she mostly used for cooking.

My mother finally found work at the post office as an assistant letter car-rier. She worked twelve hours on weekdays and eight hours on Saturdays for a meager salary. Between her income and the food stamps we were enti-tled to, we could just make ends meet. We had brought several containers of smoked meat from the mountains, and we traded them for other items such as sugar or flour or dried fruits. It was my job to pick out the tiny worms from the fruits before we cooked or ate them.

In 1917 I graduated from elementary school. It was my mother's wish that I become a barber or hairdresser. She felt that men always needed to have their hair or beard cut and I would therefore always have an income. I bowed to her wishes and went out looking for an apprenticeship. I walked around the town for days and weeks, but to no avail.

In desperation, I took a job weaving wicker baskets for ten pfennigs an hour. The workplace was a run-down community center. Mostly women worked there, weaving baskets that would be used to hold grenades. My job was to sort the withes and then soak them in water so they would become more flexible and easier to handle. It certainly was boring and very tiresome at times, but at least I had a job and brought home some money. Even so, we were barely able to survive. Many of the older folks died of starvation.

Times were difficult for us, especially since we had very little to barter with. My mother started making purses out of material my father had left behind. She would sew every Saturday evening and all day Sunday until she had made about twenty purses. Then we would go out to sell them door to door and take whatever we could get for them. But the plight of the people became more severe as time went by. The police got involved and waited for hoarders to arrive at the train stations with their goods. There they were ordered to empty all that they had collected onto the station floor, and whoever tried to salvage anything or get away was shot at. Quite a few people lost their lives this way. Due to the interference of the police, people stopped using the railroads.

Instead, all transactions were made on secret walkways or in back alleys. Often I'd see a beautiful sterling silver set being exchanged for a pound of flour or beans. The laws became stricter, and whoever was caught with more than three pounds of food was sent to jail.

When we were down to our last piece of bread and last pound of potatoes, I decided to go to the mountains on a hoarding trip. My aunt lent me the money for the train fare. The farmers recognized me in the village where I had grown up, and most of them spared me a chunk of bread and some other food. I felt so good that day, being able to return home with a small rucksack filled with food. I had gotten some eggs, smoked meat, flour, lard, and even fresh butter and dried fruits. What else could I possibly ask for? On my trip back home I got off three stations outside the city limits, where the restrictions were not quite as severe. I walked home via hidden paths. After about three hours I arrived at the house. I ran up the stairs, not feeling the blisters and sores I had gotten from walking so long. When I opened the door and emptied my rucksack onto the kitchen table and watched my mother's eyes light up, I was the happiest young man on earth.

Immediately, my mother prepared a feast by cooking several slices of the smoked meat with flour dumplings. Never in my life had I enjoyed a meal more than on this Sunday afternoon. Usually we had only watery soup and bread that couldn't even be called bread anymore, since it was mostly made out of sawdust. Although the food lasted several weeks, it didn't last forever. Since Germany had lost the war, conditions now became worse. I went on hoarding trips on several other occasions but always came back empty-handed. So we went back to eating the soup, which now consisted of boiled water with a shredded potato in it. Only on rare occasions could we add an egg or a couple spoonfuls of flour.

When the men began returning home from the war, my mother lost her letter carrier job. There was a laborer job opening for road construction, but when my mother went for the interview she was told she was too fragile. It was true; we were both nothing but skin and bones. Then my aunt's husband came back after being a prisoner of war and suggested I go to Switzerland, where he had a brother who owned a barbershop. I didn't want to just leave my mother behind, but when she finally found another job as a streetcar conductor and then encouraged me to leave, I decided to go.

When I arrived in Switzerland, I thought I had landed in Paradise. There was an abundance of food and merchandise as I had never seen before. All this happened shortly before the inflation of 1921. Herr Schad, my uncle's brother, welcomed me with open arms into his home and shop. He told me to call him and his Swiss wife aunt and uncle. He had a small shop in Andermatt, where I was to work. On the day after my arrival, he took me shopping and outfitted me with a nice suit and a white smock, which I had to wear at work. I learned fast and became a good hairdresser in no time. The excellent food served in their home made me strong and healthy. After three years of apprenticeship I passed the state licensing examination and was now a professional hairdresser.

I remained with the Schads for another year but then went out looking for another position. The shop was really too small to justify two salaries. Since I had worked only for room and board and no wages, it had not made any difference up to this point. My uncle agreed with my decision and reluctantly let me go. I found a position in Brunnen, not very far from Andermatt. The manager and owner was an older man who, together with his wife and sixteen-year-old daughter, lived in an apartment above the store. The entire Heberlein family was kind and friendly toward me and Germans in general. Fanni, the daughter, was sent to Luzern and Zürich to take some courses in hair styling. But one day while she was still in Zürich, Herr Heberlein suffered a stroke and became partially paralyzed on the left side of his body. I had to take over the management of the shop and did so gladly. Fanni came back immediately after she heard of her father's illness. One evening, while we were dining together, Herr Heberlein looked at me and then at Fanni and said, "It wouldn't be a bad idea if you two got married. You are both nice looking, and you seem to like and respect each other."

Fanni and I just sat there speechless, with flushed faces. Herr Heberlein continued, "Richard, I've observed you carefully, and I think you're a decent, hardworking fellow whom I wouldn't mind making my heir." I still didn't know what to say. Frau Heberlein got up and, supporting her husband out of the room, left Fanni and me by ourselves. Fanni turned to face me and said, "Probably Father is right. I do like you, and this might be the sensible thing to do." I answered that I felt the same. She continued, "We can try it out." She stood up and prepared to leave the room. I reached for her and tried to kiss her. She stopped me gently and said, "I didn't mean to try out *this*—at least not yet."

Early the following morning, Herr Heberlein asked me if Fanni and I had thought his proposition over. I said that we had and would get married as soon as possible. This made him very happy. That same afternoon Fanni and I went to the jewelry store to buy our engagement rings. The owner smiled at us and said that we had certainly kept a low profile of our intention to get married. We smiled back at him, but not for the same reason. We celebrated our engagement amid family members. Three weeks later, we had our wedding. Herr Heberlein went all out and rented an entire floor of a local hotel. Everyone we could think of was invited. Unfortunately, my mother was unable to attend since she had fallen ill, but my aunt came in her place. Fanni and I spent our wedding night, which was also our first night together, at the hotel. Neither of us had any experience with intimate relations, and we consummated our marriage awkwardly.

Otherwise, little in our life changed. I was a happily married man now and looked forward to having children. Alfred, our son, was born just about nine months after we got married. Now I felt my life was complete. I enjoyed reading German newspapers and listening to German radio stations, and I was fascinated by Adolf Hitler and his ideas of ending the misery in Germany. Most of our clients supported Hitler since he wanted to stop Russian communism from infiltrating his beloved Germany. But there were others who opposed the Nazis because of their well-known and well-advertised anti-Semitic actions.

In 1933, when Hitler came to power, my father-in-law and I regularly listened to the newscasts and, in particular, to Hitler's speeches. What a leader this man was, I thought, he was showing the people that there was a way out of their rot and that Germany could look forward to a bright, secure future. Even though I had no conception of what the Nazi ideology was all about, I was proud to be a German and let everyone know it. When Swiss newspapers started to criticize Hitler's actions, in particular his attacks on the Jewish population, this didn't faze me the least. What did I know about the Jews? Why should I care about their well-being? They meant nothing to me. Perhaps what Hitler was saying was correct, that the Jews were indeed agitating countries to fight one another so they would have the upper hand. How well I remembered Germany's people suffering during the last world war. When Hitler said that if the Jews succeeded once more in helping to organize another war against Germany, their extermination throughout Europe would be inevitable, I believed it had to be so. I was of the opinion that Hitler was a peace-loving man, since he emphasized peace in all of his speeches. So why should I have thought otherwise?

But then refugees from Germany began arriving with their tales of horror. They spoke entirely differently of Hitler and the Nazis. They claimed that Hitler was preparing Germany for the ultimate war and anyone who dared to oppose him or criticize the Nazis was being thrown into concentration camps. I heard that the Brownshirts had arrested massive numbers of Social Democrats and Communists, after beating them half to death, and had thrown them into camps from which they never surfaced again. It was said that in each larger town or community the SA had set up its own torture chambers. One woman told me that she would never forget the agonized screams of the men who were being tortured.

I listened to what was said but didn't believe a word. How could this be the truth?

I decided to visit my mother in Stuttgart and find out for myself what the situation was. My mother told me that these so-called concentration camps had been set up as training centers for people who didn't want to work, or drunkards and Gypsies who needed to be disciplined. Only once in a while were opponents of the National Socialists taken there. A couple of Jews disappeared here and there, and announcements were made not to patronize Jewish establishments. SA members would occasionally stand in front of Jewish businesses and encourage people to stay away. If people didn't obey, their names were written down. What happened afterward, my mother said, she really didn't know. She said she never bought merchandise at Jewish stores anyway, because they were known to take advantage of people and always charged much higher prices. She was of the same opinion as I that Hitler knew what he was doing.

I couldn't help but notice the enormous changes that had taken place in Germany since I had left. There were newly constructed, beautiful autobahns and new housing developments for people who otherwise couldn't afford to build their own houses. The unemployment that had plagued the country had vanished. Families were encouraged to have many children, and those who did received government assistance. Young couples received state money to build their own houses. Prosperity had returned, and no one was going hungry as I had been when I had left Germany. The labor service was employing and training young people to perform productive tasks like draining swamps and marshlands or helping the farmers with their harvest. Discipline and order were established everywhere. What I heard and saw on this visit convinced me that Hitler was doing a great job in getting Germany back onto its feet.

On my return to Switzerland, I had some difficulty at the German border, but after a four-hour wait and a thorough check of my papers I was given permission to cross. Back at the shop, I informed our clients of what I had seen and experienced in Germany, but later events heightened the debate. The annexation of Austria into the German Reich was not received well by the Swiss. When Czechoslovakia was occupied, I felt happy since many German settlers there wanted to come home to their Reich. The Swiss, however, didn't share my opinion. The local newspapers warned that Hitler was indeed aiming to start a second world war.

Then came the invasion of Poland. The Swiss shook their heads in disbelief over Germany's nonaggression pact with the Soviet Union. I was of the opinion that Hitler had signed the treaty so he could have a free hand in Poland to run out bolshevism. When France and England kept their word and supported Poland, things in Switzerland changed. I dared not mention the name of Hitler anymore. Everyone needled me to go home to Germany and fight for my country like any decent citizen would, not sit around in another country like a traitor. I certainly didn't want to be called a traitor, and Germany was, after all, my fatherland. So I decided to go back home. My wife tried very hard to convince me that my home was now with her and our son in Switzerland. However, my father-in-law thought, as I did, that it was my duty to serve my country.

When I crossed the well-patrolled Swiss border one of the officers remarked that I was the first German living in Switzerland to volunteer to go back to Germany to serve in the military. He thought I was insane. I was well received at the German border. The only question the patrols asked me was where I was going. I went to Stuttgart and went to see my mother, who was still living in the same apartment building, somewhat renovated with a couple more bathrooms.

My mother didn't want to believe it was me when I arrived on her doorstep. "Are you crazy?" she said when I told her of my decision. "Son," she continued, "you should have let me know before you came. Things have changed since your last visit. All the prosperity you saw was the Nazis' way of preparing for war. Initially, the Nazis said that a woman belongs at home with her family and housewives were placed on pedestals. Now women are being forced to work in armament factories and do a man's job for low pay. The authorities even wanted me to work for them. Luckily, my doctor said otherwise. I was fooled just like you. The Nazis are out to conquer Europe, or at least most of it, and I wouldn't be surprised if they actually start a war with Russia. I don't think they will touch Switzerland, because then America would interfere, but for you to go back now is impossible."

I completely ignored what she said.

The next day, I went to register for the draft. At the draft board I was told also to go to the citizen registration office. There I had to fill out several forms detailing where I had lived in Switzerland, my marital status, and how many children I had fathered. I also was asked if I was of Aryan descent. For that I needed proof. I had to get some sworn documents from my mother to satisfy the authorities.

Approximately two weeks later, I was called to go and report for duty at Schwäbisch-Gmünd, not very far from Stuttgart. At the barracks there I went through a physical examination and was declared fit for the infantry. I had visualized being placed with an armored outfit or with the mountain infantry but was told that I was already too old and the training would take too long.

In the spring of 1941, with about thirty other men all about my age, I was transported by train to the south of France, now under German control. There, at a training center far removed from any settlements, we prepared to become soldiers. We slept mostly outdoors, which wasn't that unpleasant since it was almost spring. Nevertheless, I was sore all over my body from the rigorous exercises and the constant crawling around on the ground. Besides, our meals consisted basically of cauliflower, which gave us the nickname "Cauliflower Division." I took everything in stride; after all, this was war, and war is never pleasant. Most of us thought we would be stationed in France as occupation troops. How wrong we were! After about four weeks had passed and I had just barely learned how to handle a rifle, I was transferred to Angoulême. There I was placed with troops who were waiting for their orders. After another physical screening I was assigned to a special detachment.

On the following morning, fifteen men, a corporal, and I were put on a train headed east. It took us four days and nights to cross France and Germany and finally into Poland. In Lódz, we received some additional training in combat against partisans. The instructors at the camp were SS men. All day, every day, we were told about Polish pigs, scum, murderers, and subhumans. The Poles were dirt and had to be eliminated. It didn't take me long, however, to find out that the Poles were also human beings and not inferior or scum as we were told. They loved their fatherland with the same intensity as we did. During our indoctrination, "fatherland" and "love" were never mentioned by the SS. The only words used frequently were "destruction" and "killing."

After a couple weeks of training, we were assigned to a post in a small village outside Warsaw. There I was placed with a commando unit to fight partisans. We were quartered in a spacious farmhouse, where we also ate big meals and slept. Our immediate orders were to arrest any suspicious-looking Pole and bring him to our headquarters. What exactly was considered "suspicious" was left to our own discretion.

On our three-man patrols, we didn't encounter any suspicious Poles; the villagers went about their own business, and the peasants were busy plowing their fields.

But one day, a couple of German patrols who had arrested two men were shot at in a nearby wooded area. The two men fled, leaving the patrols behind. This incident created chaos at our headquarters. The telephones kept ringing all day long. We received orders to occupy the village nearby and not to let anyone in or out of the area. Within a couple of hours reinforcements came, and together we set up posts around the village.

The following morning, a high-ranking SS officer appeared and ordered us to arrest all the men in the village between the ages of fourteen and sixty-five. The command was carried out immediately, and all the available men were herded into a vacant courtyard on the outskirts of the settlement. Altogether there were fifty-six of them. The strongest-looking ones were handed spades and shovels and told to dig a ditch. In the late afternoon, five of them had to stand facing the ditch and were shot in the back so their bodies would fall forward into the hole. They screamed and pleaded that they were innocent, but the killings continued regardless. One of the men, a handsome blond not more than eighteen years of age, yelled out before he fell, in excellent German, "You goddamn murderous pigs, may you all burn in Hell." He had barely finished when a bullet ended his young life. As I watched this senseless slaughter of human beings, I became sick to my stomach. When it was the turn of my commando unit to be the firing squad, I refused.

The SS officer came up to me and hissed between his teeth, "Do you know what it means to refuse a direct order?" I was trembling and shaking so badly that all I could say was "Sir, I can't do it." The officer noted down my name and told me to report to him in the morning at headquarters. The killings continued without mercy until all fifty-six Poles lay dead in the ditch.

Flashbacks of the horrendous happenings kept me awake the entire night. On the following morning, I walked with still-weak knees down to headquarters. Several of the other soldiers who had participated in the massacre were there when I arrived. The SS official was praising the men for the loyalty they had shown in performing their duty. When he noticed me he called me forward. "And you!" he yelled so everyone could hear. "You belong in front of a firing squad for not following my orders! Consider yourself lucky that I am exercising mercy instead of righteousness, otherwise I wouldn't let you get away with a minor sentence. Your punishment is two weeks of solitary confinement so you can meditate about your stupidity and cowardice. Next time you will be shown no mercy. Believe me, there isn't a court-martial to be found that would not give you the death sentence for refusal to obey orders at the front."

I spent the next fourteen days on bread and water in a cellar under the guardroom. I overheard some guards saying that the village women and girls had been ordered to fill in the mass grave where their husbands, sons, and brothers lay slaughtered.

Even though I had never said a prayer in my entire life, I called on God that first night. I prayed with an intensity I didn't think was possible; I wanted to be taken away from this insane, nightmarish place. I also wondered if the Führer was aware of these injustices. When I expressed my concern to the other soldiers after I had gotten out of confinement, they laughed in my face. One of the men said, "Do you think we enjoy what's going on? But believe me, it's even worse at the front. You'd best keep your mouth shut and just obey orders. Going around questioning your superiors will just get you court-martialed. Anyway, the Poles deserve this. If we don't show these sons of bitches our strength, they'll stab us in the back."

As if the Lord had heard and answered my prayers, I was transferred back to Lódz in late April. There I was assigned to kitchen duty, which suited me fine. After several weeks had passed, I received orders to join up with a commando unit patrolling a railroad junction near the Russian border. Most of the patrols there were composed of Austrian nationals about my age or older. When I told them that I had come from Switzerland of my own free will to join the military, one of the men remarked, "Well, if the jackass has it too good, he jumps on the ice and dances until he falls."

What seemed to concern the men the most was that if Hitler were to start a war with the Soviet Union, we would be the first victims, as we were so close to the border. I was told that the nearest German troops were about twenty-five kilometers behind us. Our orders were to guard the railroad station even though there was no activity anywhere around. One of the Austrians said to me, "Do as we do, come and have a good time. We eat well and drink vodka and let the stationmaster's wife bake us bread and cakes every day." This carefree bunch of Austrians even managed to find musical instruments, which they played loudly and long. Close to the station house they had set up a wireless broadcasting station, which was operated by three young women. One of them was a Viennese who also served as vocalist for the band.

In early June of 1941, we received orders to return to Lódz. The women were ordered to disassemble their equipment and return to Germany. We concluded that maybe Hitler had come to an agreement with the Soviet Union and we weren't going to be the first victims after all.

But back in Lódz we noticed many changes. Heavy tanks and more troops arrived and were unloaded. However, they didn't waste much time there; instead, they headed east. The Austrian outfit was summoned back to the Reich. I was placed with an infantry unit that practiced sharpshooting daily. The company commander praised me for being a good marksman and promoted me to private first class. I became a member of the first squad in the first platoon. I was very surprised to receive a promotion, considering that I had an arrest record.

Then came the blow! Hitler ordered the attack on Russia. Already in the early-morning hours we had to advance east. We were transported straight to the border on trucks. Along the way we passed some burned-out villages, but otherwise there was no war activity. The leading German troops had already penetrated into enemy territory.

Our assignment was to secure the roadway and bridges and eliminate any partisans we could find. The few Russian settlers who lived in the area escaped into the forests. Then we arrived at the Soviet border. The villages and settlements looked like ghost towns. There wasn't a man, woman, or child to be seen anywhere. Russian tanks, ammunition, and equipment littered the streets and ditches. We marched around for about three weeks without any contact with the enemy. During the fourth week, my commando unit made a flanking movement toward the south. Now the enemy was nearby and bullets started whizzing around our heads. We had to advance at a faster pace and for many more hours at a time.

Since we were held up at almost every village because Russians would hide and fire at us, our supplies always caught up with us and consequently we were never short of food or ammunition. However, the deeper we penetrated into the south the more ferocious the attacks became. The Russians defended their settlements to the last bullet, and when we would finally enter a town, there wouldn't be a single one left. We suffered more and more casualties.

Then the rains came and the roads turned into muck. Our supply trains had difficulty keeping up with us.

Now we lacked food and ammunition. The little food the villagers and natives had left, we took away from them. When the Russian troops withdrew, they would blow up their food stores by soaking them with petrol and then igniting them. Autumn was quickly turning into winter, and we were not prepared. We set up quarters in a small town. The entire area was snowed in and iced over within a couple of nights. The cold remained. We had no overcoats, boots, or gloves. We took the peasants' sheepskin coats and felt boots so our guards would not freeze to death.

The little furniture we found in the houses, we used as firewood. Smaller houses that could not be dismantled were torn down, and we burned the doors, window frames, and floorboards to keep ourselves warm. Almost every soldier had a cold, a fever, or a cough. Although we had a physician with us, he could do nothing, as he had no medicine or medical supplies. The cold became fiercer by the day.

Then suddenly new orders came for immediate withdrawal. Everyone, including our company commander, cursed and wondered how we were going to survive a long march in this ungodly weather.

So there we were, muffled-up, shivering figures, half frozen and without anything to eat on our way back to the West. For three days and nights we fought our way through hip-deep snowdrifts and iced-over roads. On the fourth day, around noon, we came to a Wehrmacht camp, where we stuffed ourselves with anything we could find to eat. As a consequence, every one of us contracted diarrhea—in this cold and with no enclosed toilets! But we had to keep going. Whoever stayed behind or couldn't go on out of weakness was certain to die.

We used every imaginable curse in the German language, but they did little good, as the bitter cold raged in every nerve and bone of our bodies. I wasn't spared either, as I lost my right big toe to frostbite. However, I considered myself lucky, because many men lost all their fingers and even some whole limbs.

When we arrived in Minsk, we quartered in a school building. An army infirmary was set up in a large hog pen whose floors had been covered with straw. The only furnishings were a couple of round iron stoves that stood against the walls. The doctor had about thirty-five infantrymen under his care, most of them frostbite victims like myself. The doctor told me my toe had to be removed. About thirty minutes later I had one less toe on my foot. I spent three days in this amputation factory and then was transported to a nearby church. All the benches and icons that must have adorned the walls at one time were gone. They had been used as firewood to keep the room warm. Once again we were bedded down on the floor with straw for a mattress. All the wounded men were made to believe that they would soon be shipped home. But we had to stay and were then told that there was no possibility of getting transport. The infantrymen who had lost limbs received war service decorations, which they sarcastically referred to as "frozen flesh medals."

Everyone cursed Hitler and his war strategy. It was said that he had mis-calculated enormously with Russia. Apparently he had thought the Soviet Union could be taken as easily as Poland. What a bad miscalculation! One of the soldiers predicted that Hitler's armies would be defeated at Moscow's doorstep, as Napoleon had been. In any event, he added, if it weren't for modern technology, we would have lost this war a long time ago.

Despite the loss of his hand, the soldier who had made this statement was arrested two days later; we never found out what had happened to him.

It was six weeks before I was able to get my foot back into a shoe. Initially I thought my foot had become permanently stiff, but through daily exercise it started to feel normal again. I left the infirmary grounds and started walking around the city. The population didn't seem to be hostile toward us. Anyway, what choice did they have? Their city was occupied by Germans. I also saw quite a few Jews, who—as in Germany—had to wear the Star of David on their chests. Although I'd never thought much of the Jews, I couldn't help but feel sorry for these men, women, and children who walked about the city streets like ghosts.

I couldn't imagine that these people had been responsible for the war, as Hitler had so often stated. Perhaps the rich and powerful Jews, but certain-ly not these harmless creatures. I wondered now what Hitler's real reason was for his intense hatred of these people. These poor souls with their hol-low cheekbones were starving to death. They weren't even allowed to beg or to approach anyone who was not Jewish. They had to step down off the sidewalk when passing a gentile.

One afternoon as I walked through a side street I noticed a young Jewish boy leaning against the wall of a house. With his glassy eyes he didn't have to say a word, I saw hunger written all over his face. I thought about my son back home, who was about the same age. I approached the boy and told him to stay where he was and that I would come back. Apparently he understood. I went back to my quarters and took half a loaf of bread from the mess hall. I hid it under my jacket and walked back to the side street. The boy was still standing where I had left him. I handed him the bread. He looked at me and took off, quickly disappearing into a courtyard.

The following day, our second lieutenant in charge at the church infir-mary informed me that the chief of staff wanted to see me. When I asked why, I was told he didn't know. I walked over to the pigpen and announced myself. The chief of staff appeared, accompanied by an SS official. He then asked the SS man if I were the person in question. The SS man confirmed this by nodding slightly. The doctor said, "So it was you who gave a piece of bread to a pig yesterday, right? Didn't you notice the Star of David on his chest?" I replied, "Yes, I did. But I also saw the kid's begging eyes."

The officer snapped, "You are hereby sentenced to four weeks' arrest. That should be enough time for you to think about your mistake. Dismissed!"

I couldn't believe my ears. After all, it had been my own ration that I had given away.

Back at the church I was locked up in the vestry to serve my sentence. The room was not heated, and my clothes and one blanket were not sufficient to keep me warm. My entire body trembled day and night. After three weeks I developed a high temperature and severe pains in my stomach. I started vomiting and got diarrhea. A young doctor was summoned, and after a quick examination he told the lieutenant that I had to be hospitalized immediately. Within minutes an ambulance came and took me to a genuine hospital on the outskirts of the city. However, instead of the hospital I was taken to a garden shed on its premises. There were already three or four men lying there with active jaundice. Although no one told me, I knew then that I had contracted typhoid fever.

During the weeks that followed, I was delirious from the fever and kept hearing the agonized screams of the dying Polish peasants. Alternatively, I would see the Jewish boy's eyes staring at me, and then again I would hear the bullets and screams. My nightmares didn't seem to end. When I finally awoke and was able to think more clearly, I noticed that two of the other men had died. My mind was functioning again, but I was still too weak to speak or feed myself. Another week passed, and I debated whether I should write to my mother. I decided against it since this would just worry her. To send notification to Switzerland was out of the question because mail was not being delivered there. Also, I was not allowed to receive any mail.

I remained in the garden shed for three months. I now had plenty of time to think about my stupidity. I became so frustrated at having ignored both my mother's and my wife's advice. I had lost a lot of weight, and the first day I looked into a mirror, I was scared; I looked like death warmed over. I was all eyes, ears, and cheekbones. The only contact I had with the outside world was our Polish nurse, and she didn't speak a word of German. Once in a while we saw a doctor, who never told us how the war was going.

When the birds started singing outside our window, I knew spring was just around the corner.

One morning, a sergeant told us that we would be taken to Lvov. Within an hour we were taken to a hospital train and loaded into the last wagon with other typhoid cases. Two first aiders joined us as we went away and then changed to a regular passenger train that took us to Berlin.

I was sent to an infirmary at Kreuzberg, where I remained hospitalized for an additional four weeks. I was transferred again to a hospital, which had once been a schoolhouse, in Tempelhof. Aside from the constant bombardment by English planes cruising over Berlin as if it were their own territory, this was a good time for me to recuperate.

By the middle of April 1942 I was discharged and got permission to take sick leave for an undetermined amount of time. I took the next train to Stuttgart to visit my mother. When I knocked on her door, she opened it but didn't recognize me at first. When I said her name, tears shot into her eyes and she screamed, "My God, what has happened to you?" She repeated the words over and over. In fact, I was a pitiful sight, with my jaundiced face and body of skin and bones. So there we stood in the doorway embracing and crying. After we went inside I asked if she had any news about my wife, Fanni, and my son, Alfred. She said she didn't. I now had to find a way to let them know I was still alive. But how? I took the train to Schwäbisch-Gmünd to pick up my civilian clothes at the barracks where they had been sent.

I stayed with my mother for a while and was able to regain my strength. I gained some weight and looked and felt like myself again. Between the food stamps and additional ration stamps I received because of my illness, and my mother's food, we lived pretty well. I was invited by one of the farmers whose farm my mother had worked at during the summer to spend some time there. The farmer lent me his son's bicycle, and on it I pedaled around the lovely Black Forest mountains.

On the outskirts of Henner, a small town nestled in the mountains, I stopped because of the spectacular view over the entire area all the way to Switzerland. As it happened, I also had a flat tire. I stopped at a farmhouse to ask for help since I didn't have a repair kit with me. An old man, who told me he had lost both his sons in the war, helped me get the tire fixed.

When I told him of my experiences and where I had lived before, he pointed in the direction of Switzerland and said, "You could be living there now in peace with no one bothering you. I hope you've learned your lesson like we all have. No one believes Hitler anymore, nor the authorities who speak of victories. They should really be announcing defeat after defeat."

I had to fight back tears when I looked toward those majestic mountain ranges. When I reached the foothills and eventually the valley, there was only the Rhine River between me and Switzerland. I continued until I was at the shore, where I got off my bike and sat down on the bank. My intention had been to ride up to Waldshut and then return to the farmer's house. However, as I sat there, idly throwing tiny pebbles into the water and watching them disappear, a sudden thought entered my mind: Jump into the water and swim across. All your stupidity will be rectified once you are on the other side.

It was just about noon, and there wasn't a soul to be seen anywhere. As if under a spell, I hid the bike under a bush and walked back to the river, where I jumped into the water fully clothed. I had always been an excellent swimmer and therefore had no doubt I would make it across. I had gotten about halfway across when I heard the engine of a boat with three border patrol guards in it approaching. My initial thought was to dive and never come up again, but I changed my mind and swam back to where I had jumped in. As I got out of the water, I was arrested by the guards, who had followed me to the shore. I was taken to the town of Säckingen, where I was interrogated and confessed to the longing I had to see my family. After about a week I was taken back to Schwäbisch-Gmünd, where I was interrogated once again.

Apparently, my story was not believed, and perhaps they needed a spy to hang. I was given permission to write to my mother. I don't know if she ever received the letter. I had to put on my uniform again and was sent to Moabit and then on to Tegel, where I was officially charged with desertion. The only lawyer I talked to was one who came to see me in Tegel. That was the last I've heard about my case.

Richard arose from his chair and walked the few steps to the table, brushing his right hand over its surface as if he were removing dust.

"So here I am in this damn place dwelling on my own stupidity with the hope that some miracle will happen and that, someday, I'll be a free man again. Only the good Lord knows what will happen next," sighed Richard with only a faint touch of optimism in his voice.

Richard suddenly appeared older than his thirty-nine years. He desperately needed someone to tell him everything was going to turn out all right—but no one in our cell would tell him that for it would not be the truth and would therefore betray our friendship.

"You should have kept on outswimming those bloodhounds," quipped Willi, leaning over Richard's shoulders.

"Oh, shut up, look who's talking," came Fritz's voice from his bed. "Food will be brought soon, and somebody has to help me to get out of this damn bed before someone reprimands me."

Fritz was right; shortly thereafter food was brought in, potatoes cooked in their skins and some sort of tomato sauce, a slice of stale rye bread, and unsweetened black tea. When we had finished, an almost eerie unearthly silence again prevailed in the prison halls.

Otherwise the day had passed uneventfully, punctuated only by meals. The grayness of the day turned into darkness and the lights came on. It was nearly six P.M. Looking up, Alex asked, "Shall we hear another story tonight?" We all decided against it. "Tomorrow is Sunday, and we can continue then," said Fritz. "But after the holidays we may not have the opportunity to do so, so it has to be tomorrow."

That night we all fell asleep quickly, and for once there were no sirens or the crashing of bombs to awaken us.

On December 27, the following morning, Fritz drew the lot. Earlier, he couldn't wait to tell us his story; but now he seemed oddly quiet, almost withdrawn. He finally spoke, focusing on Richard, who was sitting across from him: "Have you had enough now of the Nazis' clever clichés and deceptions, or do you still have faith in the Führer?"

"You know very well how I feel about my stupidity," Richard defended himself, pulling his chair closer to the table. "When I told you my story, you must have realized that I look at myself as an idiot and the most ignorant man who walks on God's earth. But apparently I'm not the only one who fell for the Nazi line."

Fritz crossed his arms and leaned back in his chair, his injured leg extended in front of him. "We all swore to tell our stories unvarnished, and I will do the same. I'll tell you everything I can. There is, however, certain information that I must keep from you until after my sentencing, as I took an oath to keep silent. I'm probably one of the few among my comrades who has a chance to convey this knowledge to others, since the majority are in solitary confinement. I will only mention the names of those unfortunate souls whom the Gestapo already know and who are imprisoned as I am. With some people I can name only first names. I hope you all agree to that. It's not that I mistrust any of you—but you have to understand my situation."

Alex interjected quickly, "Fritz, we do understand you, and I don't think any of us wants to complicate your or your friends' lives in any way."

Glancing at Willi, Fritz said, "Willi and I are both Berliners, born and raised here, although our lives developed quite differently." Fritz paused briefly before telling us about his life and the events and circumstances that had brought him to this cell.

CHAPTER 8

FRITZ RÖMER: THE SOCIALIST

I was born in June of 1921 in the Münzstrasse in a rear flat together with my sister, Waltraud. Around that time, my father was working as a laborer at the Siemens factory and my mother cleaned house for well-to-do people. Our flat was rather small but cozy.

As the years went by, my father, an ambitious man, climbed the ladder of success and became foreman in his division. When I was about five years old, we moved to another apartment, this time in the front of a large city house in the Harzerstrasse. The rooms were sunny and spacious. My father was extremely proud of our new apartment, especially since our old apartment had been in a notoriously run-down neighborhood.

My mother was a deeply religious woman with a strong faith in God. At every opportunity she would speak of "Jesus, our Savior." My father, on the other hand, was a materialist who believed only in what he could hold in his hand, or what somehow might produce profit for him and his family.

From the day I entered school in 1927 he encouraged me to study hard and learn as much as I could, so I could eventually attend secondary school. I was a good student, and my father was very proud when I passed the final examinations with honors. That was in 1938. Since he always said he wanted a better life for me, he insisted that I attend university and study economics. His dream was that I would become one of the directors at Siemens, where he was working. Even though this was primarily his idea, the thought of studying for and working in this particular profession appealed to me.

My father didn't pay much attention to the political life around him. My uncle, however—my father's older brother—was just the opposite: he had strong political convictions and was extremely outspoken. I often visited him since I liked him as a person.

Uncle Oskar lived not far from our house and was employed in a machine-tool factory as a foreman. He didn't get along with my father too well. He felt that my father was an opportunist and had been an egoist even as a child. Whenever my uncle's name was mentioned at home, my father described him as a grumbling know-it-all who would eventually get himself into hot water with the government because people like him would not be tolerated. Otherwise, being brothers, the two seemed to compromise in their relationship with each other.

I had quite a different opinion of my uncle. I felt he was a person who had a clear picture of our society and of his fellowman. As a socialist, he believed a practical system should be developed in which all people would be happy. He explained that rationalism and education alone wouldn't accomplish this goal—it could be achieved only by force.

As an inquisitive young person trying to understand the world, I spent many hours listening to him. During one of our discussions I also promised him that I would think carefully about his philosophy. The next time I met my uncle, he asked me if I had given his ideas any thought. I told him I had and that I had several questions for him. "Ask as many questions as you like, I'll answer them to the best of my knowledge and with honesty," he assured me with one of his generous smiles.

Needless to say, I devoted most of my spare time to discussing political issues and philosophies, religion, and the ever-increasing problems facing our nation and society.

In all honesty, I can't tell you in detail everything my uncle tried to convey to me, but a few things he said seemed to coincide with some of the comments made by my history teacher, Professor Sommermann. He too had ideas that were not found in our history books. I recall the professor saying that war is not the last instrument of politics but the end of politics, and that reforms are more easily carried out after a lost war. My uncle's ideas were very much the same. Once, while we were studying England, our professor mentioned the word "warmonger." I took notice of this immediately, for my uncle used this word quite often when he spoke about Hitler or the Nazis.

On one occasion, I asked my mother whether she knew that Jesus was a socialist. My father must have overheard us, because he became outraged and told me right away that this sounded like the kind of rubbish my uncle Oskar would put into my head. He also told me that he was not sending me to the university to fill my head with absurd ideas and insisted I stop seeing my uncle. "Believe me," he warned, "your uncle's clichés have long been out of style."

At this point my father thought it might be a good idea if I joined the Hitler Youth. By then almost 90 percent of all young people aged ten and older had joined this Nazi-dominated organization. It was relentless in its propaganda tactics, and it was easy for young people to be persuaded to join. My father insisted that he would somehow come up with the money to pay for the membership fees and uniform. "Just remember," he threatened, "I'm sacrificing a lot to put you through school."

When I mentioned to my uncle what my father had said, he shook his head and said harshly, "Your father is a miserly parvenu who has lost his class consciousness and is crazy in the head. My son, never forget that you are from the working class, and be proud of it. Everything you hear nowadays about our safe and sound world in films and documentaries is misleading propaganda and has to be considered rubbish. A person becomes unhappy when he leaves reality behind. Only a chosen few gain by what the capitalistic world promises, and then only at the expense of the masses—the working class. My own belief is that when men exploit one another, it is a criminal act and should be punished accordingly. To join Hitler's youth movement, whose most popular slogan is 'We are born to die for Germany' and whose overriding purpose is to brainwash our nation's young into becoming zealous followers of Hitler—that should be your decision alone, not your father's. He cannot force you to give your time and energy to an organization that indoctrinates the young to wind up as cannon fodder for the Nazis. But," Uncle Oskar added, "if you do decide to join, you need not come by to see me anymore, since you are aware of the strong animosity I feel toward Hitler and his goons."

I decided against joining and told my father that it would be far too time-consuming and leave me too little time to devote to my studies. I continued to see my uncle without my father's knowledge.

Meanwhile, I enjoyed school. It felt good being liked by Professor Sommermann because the feeling certainly was mutual. I admired the man and what he stood for. He was a bearded man, tall, and a casual dresser who gave the impression of being a kind yet assertive person. Once he approached me in the corridor to ask me what my father's profession was and what I wanted to be. I told him that my father was working as a foreman at Siemens and that it was his wish as well as mine that I should study economics. He smiled and agreed that it was a good choice as economics was definitely a profession of the future. Then Professor Sommermann took me completely by surprise by asking me to come visit him at home. He told me Sunday afternoon around three P.M. would be a good time and gave me an address in the Treptow district.

Sunday was also my eighteenth birthday, and Uncle Oskar had invited my sister and me to a festive luncheon. I thought I could leave early and be at the professor's house by three o'clock.

Sunday arrived before I knew it, and Oskar—by now we were on a first-name basis—served a gourmet meal consisting of sauerbraten, dumplings, a salad, and an exquisite chocolate mousse. Afterward, we all enjoyed a glass of red wine. Oskar was a fantastic cook. He explained that his wife, who had passed away eight years earlier, had taught him all his cooking skills.

When I mentioned to Oskar that my history professor had invited me to his house, my uncle told me that this was a great honor, since it was not common for professors to invite their students to their homes.

The wine had worked its way to my head, so I went happily on my way to Treptow. I had no difficulty finding the professor's villa. I found the whitewashed stone house surrounded by aged oak trees very attractive. As I opened the black wrought iron gate and strutted down the walkway, I straightened my tie and cleared my throat. I rang the shiny copper door-bell. Professor Sommermann himself opened the door for me. I was surprised at the elegant interior of the house: the marble-tiled foyer alone was larger than our entire apartment.

The professor led me into a library whose glass-fronted cabinets were filled with books in all sizes and colors. He invited me to sit down in one of the four brown leather chairs surrounding a beautiful mahogany table.

"First of all, I want to congratulate you on your eighteenth birthday," he said, as a tall, attractive young woman entered the room carrying a tray with three wine goblets and a bottle, which she placed on the round table. The professor smiled at her and introduced her as his wife. She also wished me a happy birthday. I was surprised because I didn't expect him, a man of about fifty, to have such a young wife. I guessed her to be not more than twenty-five.

He filled the three glasses with a heavy red wine, explaining that it was a product of Tyrol, his wife's homeland. "I met my wife during a holiday right after my first wife had died. I invited you here today because you remind me so much of myself when I was young, and if I had a son, he could be just like you. My wife and I don't have any children," he explained.

The complimentary remark and the side effects of the delicious wine increased my self-confidence. Never having traveled at all, I asked him about Tyrol and its people. Professor Sommermann told me that Tyrol was a German-speaking territory of Italy, but that the natives felt they were true Germans and didn't want to belong to Italy. Many uprisings for free-dom had taken place in this region. "And now, Hitler of all people, who always talks about expanding the great German Empire, has given this region away to Mussolini," he said. "I assure you, the name 'Hitler' is not very popular there. I am personally very interested to find out what the end results are going to be."

I thought to myself that the professor must have a tremendous amount of confidence in me to speak with such candor. I also realized that he had not, as my uncle did, asked me not to discuss his comments with anyone else. First it crossed my mind that perhaps it was a trap, but this fear soon vanished when Professor Sommermann told me I could ask him anything I wanted—and that he would answer my questions without reservation.

The only stipulation he now made was that I should not mention to my fellow students that I had visited him at home, because they might be jealous. He then invited me to come again the next Sunday.

When I told my parents about my visit and the fact that I had been invited to come back, they, especially my father, were very happy and agreed with Oskar that such an interest in me by the professor was a good sign.

Late in the afternoon on the following Sunday, I went back to the Sommermanns'. It was a beautiful day, and I felt good, anticipating a visit with people I enjoyed. This time the professor's wife opened the door. She looked rather chic in her bright-colored Tyrolean native attire, which made her look even younger. She escorted me into a spacious, well-furnished room—I guessed it to be the parlor—and asked me to make myself comfortable, explaining that her husband was momentarily occupied.

In the semidarkness of the room, in a corner chair, a young lady sat reading. When she saw me enter, she arose and came slowly toward me. Frau Sommermann introduced her as Fräulein Gitta Balser. As she extended her slender hand I stared at her in amazement, for I had never been introduced to a more beautiful woman. With her powerful, intelligent eyes fixed on me, her voice was clear and assertive as she said, "So you're Herr Römer. We're colleagues, you know. I'm also attending evening classes at the university, studying political economy." I was able to stammer a few words to the effect of "How very nice to meet you."

Meanwhile, Frau Sommermann excused herself, saying she was going to prepare some coffee. Fräulein Balser turned and walked across the room toward the window. I followed her and was able to get a good look at her. Her appearance struck me as that of a classic beauty. She had penetrating dark blue eyes, a well-formed mouth, and deep golden, almost auburn-colored hair, and she was wearing a dark blue pinstripe suit that accented her well-shaped body. Although she was probably younger than me, somehow she seemed more mature. She spoke in a clear, high German that didn't sound at all like a Berlin dialect. I felt numb; I had never seen such an exquisite woman. I didn't even dare to look her straight in the face.

Entering the room through a double door from the library, Professor Sommermann attempted to introduce us to each other. Fräulein Balser smilingly interjected to say that we had already met. The professor opened the paneled wooden door to the library all the way and asked us to join him for a cup of coffee. Frau Sommermann had already placed the gold-rimmed fine china cups on the table and soon appeared with an aromatic coffee cake.

Aside from some polite chitchat and exchange of formalities, the professor led the conversation. He told me that Gitta was an enthusiastic political economy student, and very quickly the conversation proved to be an interesting and instructive discussion on the world economy.

The professor made himself comfortable in his chair and said, "Let's discuss what possible economic relationships Germany might have with other countries." In his opinion, the greatest possibilities for development were with Asia, including the Soviet Union. He elaborated on his ideas, and I was very impressed at how Gitta joined easily in the discussion. Compared to them, I felt like a flop.

While it would take too long to give all the details of our conversation, I did notice that both the professor and Gitta, just like my uncle, showed a partiality for Russia, especially in economic matters.

After several hours of vigorous discussion, it was time to go. I spent several minutes working up the courage to ask Gitta if I could walk her home. Finally, my attempt was successful. She told me that she lived near the Kurfürstendamm and asked if it wasn't too far out of my way. I wanted to tell her that where she was concerned nothing was too far out of my way, but instead I only said, "Of course not."

Since that was the first time in my life I had escorted a young lady home, I felt fantastically inadequate and clumsy walking next to her. Even so, I dared to ask her whether she would join me for a cup of coffee. While I was waiting for an answer, I surreptitiously counted how much money I had in my pocket. By feeling the coins I knew I had two marks, eighty pfennigs on me, barely enough to pay for two cups of coffee. She agreed and told me once we got off the subway she knew of a small, inexpensive café very close by. Sighing with relief, I said, "Let's go there." Instead of coffee, we decided to have a glass of white wine. We talked for almost two hours. I told her everything I could think of, without stopping. Gitta listened attentively.

After we left the café, it was only a short walk to her house. We said good night, and I hoped she would notice my amorous feelings. During the course of the evening I had tried to bring up the subject of attraction and love but somehow hadn't been able to find the right words. Perhaps she knew what I was feeling, since she glanced at me teasingly with a flirtatious look in her eyes. Impulsively, I asked her if she would join me for a dance the following Thursday in a café in the Potsdamer Strasse. To my surprise and sheer delight, she agreed without hesitation.

Until Thursday, I was unable to function. My thoughts were about Gitta and Gitta alone. I had become oblivious to the world around me. I ate, slept, dreamt, and thought Gitta. I told my uncle Oskar about her. He said he wanted to meet her. Both my uncle and father now gave me a small allowance of three marks a week each. At the time that was a lot of money for me. Since I did not smoke then and had hardly any other vices, I thought I'd be able to take Gitta out often.

With more than cheerful anticipation, I was at the café an hour early for our rendezvous. I could hardly wait for the moment when I would see Gitta again. For the first time in my life, I felt I had genuinely fallen in love. Never before had I experienced a feeling like this, not even for my uncle, whom I thought I loved the most.

I waited for her in a circular room, illuminated by a large mirror-inlaid crystal ball that hung suspended from the ceiling. Colored lights reflected off it and onto the glass dance floor in the center of the room. The fantastic illumination of dim colored lights and the cozy niches around the edges made it an idyll for young lovers. All the walls were covered with dark red velvet, and the cubicles had heavy satin drapes that could be closed for a more intimate atmosphere. The walls inside the cubicles were adorned with exotic pictures.

The waiter came and asked what I wanted to order. I told him I was waiting for a young lady and that I would order later, when she arrived. He gave me a puzzled look, murmured something, nodded his head, and left. Anticipation made me restless, and restlessness made me perspire. I pulled my handkerchief from my trousers and dried the tiny pearls of water that had collected on my forehead.

The long-awaited moment was here. She appeared at the agreed-upon time, wearing a yellow flower-print dress that looked great on her perfectly shaped body. She saw me immediately and came across the dance floor to meet me. While I had visualized myself saying wonderfully clever things, when I came face to face with her all I could say was "I'm so happy you kept your promise to come."

"Well, of course, I always keep my promises," she responded with a hearty laugh.

The waiter, with a spotless white linen towel draped across his left arm, returned, and we decided on a bottle of wine for 2.80 marks. Soft background music sounded from invisible loudspeakers. Gitta asked me if I knew how to dance. I did not. Somewhat frustrated, I recalled how often my sister had insisted I learn how to dance. Unfortunately, I had never had any particular incentive to do so until then. Gitta told me that she didn't know how to dance either, but she was willing to learn.

Looking at me inquisitively, Gitta asked me what my opinion was of Professor Sommermann. I told her I admired him as a teacher and as a person. We agreed to visit him together, and she also expressed an interest in visiting my uncle.

At this point during our conversation, a couple sitting across from us closed the heavy drapes to their booth. Turning to Gitta with a hot face and searching her eyes, I said, "It's not hard to guess what those two are doing." What I said brought a blush to her lovely face. With her eyes fixed upon mine, she smiled and whispered close to my ear that if I wanted to I could close our curtains also. Without a moment of hesitation I stood up and pulled the drapes, knocking over my chair in the process. She gave a quick laugh and said, "Not so impetuous."

I sat down next to Gitta on the small sofa. She didn't seem to mind. I reached for her hand, hesitantly put my arms around her shoulders, and kissed her gently on the lips. Pulling her closer to me, I kissed her harder and told her how much I had loved her from the first moment I had set eyes on her. Still holding her hand, I felt an overwhelming amorous feeling rush through my body, and I became the happiest man alive when Gitta confessed her love for me.

Our faces were flushed and our lips had turned crimson from kissing. We drank the wine, held each other close, and talked endlessly, as young lovers do, forgetting about space and time.

Sleep never came to me that night. I kept thinking about Gitta and fantasized about my future with her.

That café and the small velvet sofa in its corner became our favorite meeting place, and there we spent the most beautiful days of our courtship. Once in a while, we even braved the dance floor and swayed to the music. Gitta always insisted on splitting the bill. She said she had sufficient money and definitely more than me with my modest allowance.

It was during one of those evenings when she told me that she was half Jewish. She watched my face intently as she explained that only her mother and herself knew about this. I took hold of her hand and looked straight into her eyes. "Whether you are a Jew, a half Jew, or who knows what else is of no importance to me. What is important is that I truly love you and that you love me. Everything else is irrelevant," I assured her.

Gitta let out a deep sigh, the tense expression left her face, and her usual radiant glow returned. Her words rushing out of her, she confessed,

"I was born out of wedlock. My natural father was a successful Jewish businessman who frequently came to Berlin. His permanent home is now in London. At the Bureau of Vital Statistics and the Youth Welfare Office, I'm registered as the daughter of a traveling salesman, whose name my mother had forgotten. My mother and father agreed that this would be best since he was already married."

Gitta explained further that her father had bought her and her mother an apartment house to give them some financial security. Now Gitta was living with her mother and her new stepfather.

At one point Gitta had thought of joining her father in England, after the death of his wife, but had changed her mind. One of the reasons was her strong opposition to the Nazi regime. She felt that Hitler and his thugs had to be disposed of before she could enjoy a life anywhere else.

Gitta had joined the resistance movement organized by Professor Sommermann because of her deep conviction that the Nazis had begun an outright war against the Jewish population. She felt that as a half Jew she would have to fight with her entire existence and at the risk of her own life against the hate-filled killers of a people she was part of.

Her warning that I was endangering my life through my association with her and the movement fell on deaf ears, for I had my own convictions. Besides, her life and her well-being had become the most important thing in my life.

One afternoon we decided to visit my uncle. He met us with a delicious cherry soufflé, which he had prepared in Gitta's honor. She thought his gourmet cooking skills were quite inspiring. The two of them got along well from the start.

My uncle asked Gitta why she had chosen to study economy. She told him that she enjoyed the subject and felt a career in this field could only be beneficial to her. Oskar told her that he was a devout socialist who was convinced that life was only worth living through this philosophy. He idealized the Soviet Union, for he felt that a serious attempt was being made there to make socialism a living reality.

On the other hand, our frequent conversations with Professor Sommermann usually revolved more around the possibilities of an economic relationship between Germany and the gigantic East. Once when we discussed my uncle Oskar's opinions, the professor said that he would like to meet him. At first Oskar was reluctant. He insisted that professors were not the kind of people he normally socialized with, but he changed his mind after Gitta persuaded him.

On a very pleasant Sunday afternoon all three of us arrived at the Sommermanns' house. My uncle was still somewhat distrustful, and I could sense how uneasy he felt. However, when the professor told him that he agreed with my uncle's philosophy that only the Communists could change mankind's direction and that he admired them as individuals since they were energetic opponents of imperialistic wars, Uncle Oskar relaxed. The professor and my uncle agreed that quite a few other people thought as they did.

The professor said, "Hitler's politics will lead all of us into a deep abyss from which deliverance will be impossible. Hitler is a warmonger of the most malevolent kind. He speaks of peace but means war. Warmongers enjoy misusing the word 'peace' for their own purposes, especially when they are mobilizing for a war. The Nazis' rhetorical clichés of a superior Germanic race only serve their war preparations. Hitler knows just as we do that a superior race does not exist, certainly not in a nation whose entire objective is war. It is well known that many people are subjected to social and economical hardships, but just because they're uneducated and forced to live in primitive or impoverished conditions does not make them inferior." The professor became excited as he continued. In the meantime, his wife interrupted by offering us all tea. He thanked her and went on.

"Let's take a good look at what kind of people the Nazis have brought to power. They're nothing but shady characters and fame-seeking braggarts. Of course, there have to be some exceptions. Nevertheless, let me say that most of them are puppets who were pushed forward and backed by capitalism. They're being rewarded splendidly and even glorified as heroes, when in reality they're nothing more than parasites who don't give a damn about their fellowman.

"They've succeeded in forcing people to believe their demagogic clichés by creating artificial unemployment, which in turn caused economic woes and hunger, which compelled people to join them. Many powerful capitalists heaved Hitler onto his throne. This was done to further their own expansion plans and to get them out of the threatening labor upheaval.

"Nevertheless," Professor Sommermann continued, "the day will come when their charades will be revealed and their boastful roars will be silenced. Then, my friends, we will see a piteous sight of what is left of those who called themselves superior human beings.

"A war cannot be initiated or led without a motive. Hitler, of course, recognized this and started his diabolic campaign, first against the Communists. When he realized that this was not sufficient, he targeted the world's Jewish population. For Germany's destitute economic plight he blamed everyone from the French to the English to the Communists and, last but not least, the Jews.

"Up to now, Hitler's war of aggression has had some success, but he is treading on very dangerous ground because once the slowly grinding wheels of other nations gain speed, Germany's collapse will be inevitable.

Therefore, it is our duty to step in and demonstrate that there are Germans who do cherish peace among nations and are willing to fight for it.

"We Germans should really look toward the East, not with the same eyes as Hitler but in an economic sense. The Soviet Union has so many great expanses of land that need to be cultivated and mineral resources that are just waiting to be tapped, but it has neither the means nor the skilled manpower to utilize them.

"This can be a good goal for our politics. A good long-term marketing strategy would be to provide them with industrial goods, anything from agricultural machines and tools to sewing needles, in return for which we would receive foodstuffs and raw materials. By doing this we would be helping that country build up its own industry."

When Gitta, Oskar, and I left the professor's house we all felt we had broadened our knowledge. Our next meeting was the following Thursday. Professor Sommermann introduced a gentleman by the name of Werner who was a professor of linguistics and an expert in international affairs. We now decided that from now on we would address one another by our first names only, primarily for security reasons.

My uncle Oskar brought a bright young man who called himself Eric, a lab technician and a genius of sorts, who was working for Telefunken, where he had already invented several unique things.

In the course of the evening, Professor Werner gave a lecture on Africa and South America.

We decided to name our group "The Circle." It was soon expanded by four new members: a baker named Hans, a city inspector named Theodor, Theodor's daughter Mathilde, and her fiancé, a medical student by the name of Heinrich. Our small group now had a membership of eighteen. They were all politically well informed, intelligent individuals motivated mainly by one concern, the future of our country.

During our periodic meetings we discussed mostly our own ideas and strategic concepts of Germany's future.

Then it happened. One night after returning home from one of our meetings, I found an induction notice from the army notifying me to report for active duty. Since an objection or refusal would have been out of the question, I would have to continue my studies after the war. All able bodies were needed at the front.

A secondary school principal who had recently joined our circle had said that any conscientious objection petitions submitted to the Wehrmacht were useless, since it was inevitable that sooner or later everybody would be drafted—even minors. The schoolmaster explained that he had thought out a plan for coming out in public and fighting for our principles through action.

Professor Sommermann immediately disagreed with him and warned that any premature action would make future success impossible.

"I agree with you, Professor," said Eric, "and I want all of you to know that I am working very hard on an invention that, if successful, will benefit us in many ways. However, before I go into detail about it, I have to conduct several more experiments to ensure that it works well."

"It might not be a bad idea for some of us to become soldiers," said Professor Werner. "I've developed a code that can be worked out by only one of us." He handed out several sheets of paper containing tables of numbers and asked us to memorize them as soon as we could. Then he warned us to destroy the notes.

As the time approached for my departure, Gitta and I met in our little "love nest" in the Potsdamer Strasse for a farewell dinner. We ate our one-course meal in silence, though neither one of us was very hungry. We kissed long and passionately and held each other close. Somehow this eased the pain of our upcoming and inevitable separation. Shortly before we left the restaurant, Gitta unclasped her hands from mine and reached for my face. Gently she turned it toward her and gazed at me with sad, tear-filled eyes. She managed the most beautiful and tender smile that I will never forget. My heart was pounding frantically as she whispered close to my ear, "Fritz, promise me that when things get really bad out there, you'll cross over. Don't be a hero for Hitler. I'll meet you wherever you decide to go."

As we walked home that breezy summer night, arm in arm, both of us remained silent. Although we were absorbed in our own thoughts, the agony of our mind and spirit was evident when we held on to each other desperately, neither one wanting to let go,

The following day I went to say good-bye to my uncle. He also had several pieces of advice for me: "First of all, son, never volunteer for anything. When someone shoots at you, throw yourself onto the ground or find the nearest ditch to crawl into. Stay there, keep quiet, and don't move. An enemy doesn't shoot at something he can't hear or see. Never get too involved in other people's affairs or worry too much about them—that could cost you your life. I tell you all this from the experiences I had in the last world war. Forget words like 'hero,' 'bravery,' and 'fatherland'; they will only get you killed."

He walked me slowly to the door, laying his arm around my shoulders. Turning to me, he said tenderly, "Fritz, come back in one piece. Know that I love you as a father loves his son. Always remember what I've told you."

We embraced, and he patted me reassuringly on the back. I left his apartment feeling drained of all my energy. I guess all good-byes are hard to take, and it was no exception with my relatives, especially my mother.

My hope was that I would be sent to an army base at Spandau for training, which would keep me close to Berlin. What a fantasy! After only a few days of drilling—one could not call our workouts training—we were shipped out with a signal corps to Bohemia, where I was trained in communications.

Furloughs were out of the question. We weren't even allowed to receive visitors from Germany. The only contact I had with home and Gitta was by mail. I now realized how much she meant to me and how much I missed her. She also suffered from our separation and told me so in her many long letters. But of course she never mentioned our circle.

In the late summer of 1941, I was transferred to an outfit bound for the ongoing invasion of Russia. At this point the war was proving to be a great success for Hitler's army. I was promoted to private first class and became the first communications operator in our outfit. Under my command was a second operator and an alternate who carried all of our heavy radio and communications equipment, which weighed close to eighty pounds.

I was eager to find out what Russia was really like, and whether my uncle and the professor had been correct. We advanced so rapidly that I didn't have much time to pursue my thoughts or interests. Mostly we detoured around cities and advanced through the rural areas of the country. I was overwhelmed by the sheer size of Mother Russia, whose population lived mostly in the country and, indeed, under very primitive conditions. Primarily, our mission was to advance in the direction of Moscow, but orders now came to split up the advances. I was assigned to an armored outfit that was withdrawn toward the south. Apparently, we were going to push forward to the east and, in a pincer movement, cut off the Russians' escape route behind Moscow. I was getting this information from encoded commands that I received from divisional headquarters to pass on to our regiment commander.

Winter broke out unexpectedly early in all its fury. The snow piled up quickly by the meter, and the icy winds lashed mercilessly at all living creatures. Not only our soldiers but the Russian people themselves were surprised by the fierceness of the bitter cold ravishing their country. Regardless, our armored unit shivering in their boots, we moved steadily south in the direction of Gomel. There was hardly any resistance from the Russians at this point. South of Gomel, at the river Desna, my unit was attached to an artillery outfit. It looked as if we would be able to pass the winter there. The three of us made ourselves comfortable in an isolated farmhouse. A farmer lived there with his wife, five or six children, and two old women—probably the grandmothers—who shared his meager surroundings. The eldest son spoke some German. He told us that German was a mandatory subject in school and therefore many people in that area spoke the language.

Their windowless house, an oblong structure, was built of dry clay. Upon entering through a shabby wooden door without handles or locks we saw that there were at least two rooms. A wall with a wide opening in the center separated the rooms. We realized that one served as the living and sleeping quarters while the other half was the stable for the house animals. We saw and smelled a cow, three goats, two sheep, several noisy geese, and multitudes of chickens in a variety of colors and sizes. There was no electricity or running water. A well in the front of the house was the water source.

Since we had occupied the so-called living quarters of the house, the two old women and two of the young girls moved in with the animals. They didn't seem to mind. They bedded down on straw in a dark recess of the stable, where they huddled together to sleep. The remaining family members slept in an alcove surrounding a huge tiled wood-burning stove. The sparsely furnished room had only a wooden table, two wobbly benches, a trunk filled with a few personal belongings, and one single bed with only three wooden legs. Clay bricks piled on top of one another took the place of the fourth leg. It seemed that one of the old women had slept there until two of us took it over. One of us was always on guard. The family took our presence for granted and didn't seem to be annoyed at all. They spoke very little to one another and mainly attended to their chores. There was plenty of wood to heat the stove, which kept the house and us warm. The army field kitchen kept us well provided with food.

I observed that all the Russians I had met so far truly belonged to their land. Their entire character seemed to be molded around the soil they tilled and cherished. The Russians usually ate only once a day. Their basic diet consisted of milk, goat's cheese, eggs, dried fruits, wild honey, peppermint tea, a sort of hard bread, and some kind of flat noodle. To please us, they killed a goose, coated it with clay, and hung the bird in the oven. After several hours of baking, they smashed the lump and took out a deliciously baked goose. It was a feast for all of us. Our radio operator brought some potatoes from the field kitchen, which we baked in the ashes of the oven. We even had a dessert that day, prepared by the peasant women from yogurt, honey, and vodka.

The Russian farmer wore a cap on his head night and day, removing it only during mealtimes. The women and girls wore white headscarves that they kept immaculately clean, even though we never saw them use any kind of soap or detergent. This puzzled us since they washed their laundry with a mixture of ashes.

Shortly before Christmas, our dream of spending the winter in this primitive but comfortable farmhouse vanished. We were called out and attached to a transport and engineering unit. So once again we had to pack our gear and equipment onto a truck that moved us south through ice and blizzards toward the Ukraine. We passed over never-ending flat terrain, swampy marshlands, and the vast and wide-open steppes. Whenever we went by a village or settlement, the people would greet us with a cheer: "Stalin kaput, Hitler good!"

Without the friendliness and hospitality of these Russian peasants, we probably would have died of starvation or frozen to death. The roads—provided there were any—were almost impassable due to the heavy snowfall and icy conditions, which made it extremely difficult for our backup troops to catch up with us. We advanced at a slow pace, and our situation became more desperate by the hour.

Our orders were to build a bridgehead on the river Bug near Vinnitsa. Together with the engineers we established ourselves in the sheds and coops of an abandoned chicken farm. The livestock and feed had vanished. There were several stoves around, but no firewood. An old man who had been left behind told us that the Russians had butchered about fifty thousand chickens and transported them out of the area, leaving not even a single egg behind. He told us there wasn't any food left at all. This was indeed devastating news. Our field kitchen was forced to rob the peasants of their meager food supplies and livestock.

Our rations now consisted mainly of a thin rice or noodle soup and no solid food whatsoever. Our bodies shivered from the cold and trembled from the nausea and accompanying diarrhea. Fortunately, however, our distress calls were heard, because rescue came by air. Several planes parachuted enough provisions down to keep us going for a couple of weeks. In the meantime we stripped the houses of their rafters, sawed them into pieces, and burned them to keep warm.

After a couple of days we received new orders to break camp and head east, but no specific destination was given. The orders simply called for an advance of thirty kilometers per day. The drudgery of marching in the fierce cold started all over again; at times we had to knock the ice off our vehicles constantly. On other occasions, everything melted and we got stuck in the gray slough.

The farther we moved on, the more we were fired at, and eventually we were bombarded by Russian artillery. At times we suffered several casualties every day.

Our next objective was to cross the Dnepr River near Cherkassy, but the bridge had been blown up and completely demolished. Our only choice was to transport our vehicles over a very unsafe-looking railroad bridge that was still more or less intact. Moving all our equipment was a laborious and extremely difficult and dangerous task in the intense cold and over the savage currents of the river below. In addition, we had to be on constant alert against grenade attacks. With the icy winds lashing us mercilessly, our guards, their faces blue and covered with frost, had to be relieved every fifteen minutes to keep them from freezing to death. We had barely made it across the river when several Soviet planes swarmed high above us, dropping bomb after bomb and damaging the bridge considerably. However, since the structure was made of iron it was not an easy target to destroy by air. It seemed to us as if the bombing lasted all day.

Our engineers' next orders were to remain at the bridge and perform makeshift repairs. Our communications team had to stay with the transportation detachment. We knew that eventually we would continue advancing to the east—it was just a matter of time. One of the messages received over the radio said that a Russian army was encamped near Kharkov and had to be destroyed.

We took up quarters with our staff in a railroad signal-box shed. The icy winds blowing off the river made staying outdoors almost impossible. The artillery bombardment never seemed to cease. Later the planes returned in low-level attacks and hit us with machine guns.

One Saturday noon it was my turn to get the food for our men. Our field kitchen had taken up shelter in an old barn about five hundred meters from the bridge. I had walked only a few meters when a shell hit directly next to me and knocked me to the ground. A splinter tore up my knee. For a moment I thought my entire leg was torn off. I didn't feel any kind of pain, only the impact, and, strangely enough, my thoughts at that moment were only about Gitta. I vaguely recall that three soldiers appeared and carried me to the kitchen. A corpsman bandaged me up. The first spoken words I remember hearing were that my leg would have to be amputated.

Later that evening, a doctor arrived and gave me an injection because by then I was in unbearable pain. The corpsman wrapped me up in a horse blanket that our cook had found somewhere. My blood-soaked pants were shredded to pieces, and the blanket was my only protection from freezing to death. During the night four of the soldiers carried me over the shaky planks of the bridge. Fortunately, it was a full moon that night; otherwise I don't think we would have made it. The river at this point was almost a kilometer wide. When we reached the other side, they placed me in a hut together with two other wounded soldiers.

In the early dawn of the next morning we were loaded onto an ambulance truck heading toward a small town whose name I have forgotten. We were transported to a church, where a makeshift field hospital was set up. In the late afternoon two medical officers appeared. One of them told me bluntly that my leg would have to be amputated below the knee. Helpless and in desperation, I looked up at the other doctor, who said, "If you think you can bear the pain, I'll put you on a hospital train to Poland." The other physician shrugged his shoulders but did not disagree.

Along with fifteen other severely wounded soldiers and one medic, we were loaded onto a freight train. The windowless boxcar's floor was covered with straw, where we bedded down. In the middle, a small stove gave off some heat, but otherwise the car was empty. We waited. Time seemed to stand still. Finally a train pulled by a huge engine appeared out of nowhere. Our cars were hooked to the train, and very slowly the wheels started rolling toward the west.

A doctor made his rounds, giving injections to ease the pain. The orderlies certainly had their hands full, changing blood-soaked dressings and bandages.

Several times we had to stand around in the middle of nowhere waiting for a shipment of coal to arrive so we could continue our journey. Whenever there was a shortage of coal for the engines, trains transporting troops had top priority.

The wailing and moaning of the injured became worse as the days went by. The doctors ran out of painkillers, and the corpsmen ran out of bandages. The stench of the wounds and the groans of the wounded became intolerable. Besides that, we didn't have any firewood left for the stove. Whenever we stopped, it was in open terrain, because the constant bombardments made it too dangerous to stop at depots.

After two to three weeks of sheer misery we finally arrived at Lódz. We had to remain there for a while, because the tracks were all overloaded. We noticed that troop and material transports passed, one after the other, heading east. Apparently the battle in Kharkov was going to be decisive. Our entire train was unloaded, with the exception of those who had died; they were left on the train.

We had been told that our destination after Poland was to be Germany, but instead we were transported to a university building that had been converted into an infirmary. I stayed there for almost three months. Upon arrival and examination by the doctors I was told that my leg would have to be removed. I begged them not to amputate. There was a constant discharge of bone splinters and pus, and the wound just did not want to heal. But somehow I hung in there. Since crutches and supports were not available, I started to jump around on one leg, biting my tongue to ease the pain. Finally, toward the end of March 1942, I was told that I was fit to travel and I was put on a transport train heading toward Germany. I considered myself very lucky, for I was brought directly into Berlin to Lazarett No. 122 military hospital in Kreuzberg. Aside from the miserable, nagging pain, it was a wonderful feeling to lie in a decent bed and be cared for by

Red Cross nurses. The trip had been difficult for me, and I was bedridden for several more weeks.

I had my parents and Gitta notified immediately where I was. Of course, they already knew of my injury through my letters. The morning following my arrival, Gitta was the first to arrive. When she saw me she practically ran across the room to my bed to embrace and kiss me passionately. Tears ran down her cheeks while she repeated time after time how happy she was to see me. I held her as close as I could, trying to wipe the tears from her face, and then I also broke down and cried with her. We remained in this embrace for a while; then suddenly Gitta pulled away, reached into her handbag, and produced a small, dark velvet box. I noticed a gold band on her left hand. She opened the box carefully and took out an identical gold ring. "This is for you, my love." She took hold of my left hand and placed the ring on my finger.

I forgot to mention earlier in my story that we had become engaged by mail before I was wounded. Gitta kissed me again and kept looking at me. I admired her so much and thought that she was more beautiful than ever. I felt this immense inner happiness to be able to call her my own.

Before noon the next day, my mother and sister came to visit. My mother said, "The good Lord has heard our prayers and brought you back to us." My sister embraced and kissed me, something she had never done before. They had already known about my engagement, and, as he told me when he arrived later on, so had my father.

Gitta came to see me every day between her classes, and my sister always visited in the late afternoon after work. I was happy to be back home and in the company of the people I cared for most. My uncle Oskar stopped by on weekends, always bringing me a newspaper or some other reading material. Gitta said little about our circle, except that it was still in existence. Whenever I inquired about details, she would say, "Your curiosity has to be tamed, my dear. You must get well first. We will talk about this later."

Once she asked me why I hadn't deserted. I told her about all my experiences and explained that there had never been a good opportunity even to think about desertion. "I'm so happy it turned out the way it did. At least I have you back with me," she said with a gentle smile.

Several weeks went by before I was able to get out of bed. My leg remained stiff, but it was still part of my body. I needed several operations, and I must say that these doctors really tried everything. First I walked with two crutches and later on I only needed a cane to get around, but the wound still did not want to heal.

I was moved to another military hospital in the Tempelhof district of Berlin. The rules were not quite as strict there as in the first infirmary; I was allowed to leave during the day, as long as I was back by ten P.M. When

Gitta finished her classes at the university, she came to pick me up. We usually went straight to her mother's apartment. Gitta's stepfather was working for a pharmaceutical company whose corporate offices were located in Munich, so Gitta's mother had bought another apartment there and their Berlin apartment was at our disposal. It was an elegant place with a stylishly decorated interior. Gitta and her mother were financially well off since both had an excellent income from the apartment houses they owned. Gitta never bragged about her wealth—quite to the contrary. She always said that if she had a choice, she would like to go with me to England to join her father.

We lived and loved like husband and wife and made the most elaborate plans for our future. On one occasion when I asked Gitta about the circle, she said that perhaps it would be best if I got out. "You still have an opportunity to do so. For me," she continued, "it's too late, and even then I don't want to give it up. It's far too important to me."

"My sentiments are the same as yours," I told her. "I want to share your life, and that includes every part of it, even if it means going to Hell. When the Nazis find out who you are, they will kill you without a trial. Your death would also mean my death, for a life without you is no life. By being active in the group, we will give ourselves and probably many others a chance to become free again. I could easily have gotten killed in Russia. But what for? For Hitler's glory? No way!"

Gitta studied my face carefully for a long moment. "If you really feel that way, I'll take you to our next meeting on Thursday. But I must warn you, things have changed drastically in the last few months. All of our meetings are clandestine and our situation has become extremely risky, since we're all involved in a very dangerous business."

That Thursday we took a streetcar to the Friedrichstrasse and walked a few blocks to a brick office building. She pointed to a sign that read "Dr. Helmut Ritz, Psychiatrist." We walked up two flights of stairs to an office with a ornamental glass door. Gitta pointed to a doorbell on the right side of the door. "We turn this all the way to the left and then depress it. That way it produces a certain chime and they know it's one of us. The doctor doesn't have office hours on Thursday afternoons." After a few moments, the door was opened by a middle-aged woman with gray hair who merely nodded her head and asked politely, "What do you wish?" Gitta looked up at her, then at me, and said, "This is Fritz." The woman acknowledged by welcoming me. "Please come in."

Upon entering, Gitta explained that the code word to gain entrance was "What do you wish?" in case someone other than a member accidentally turned the doorbell in the code. "There are a few other safety measures that I will explain to you later."

Olga, the doctor's housekeeper, led us through a padded door into the doctor's consultation room. She walked briskly over to a recess in the room where two white supply cabinets stood side by side. She pushed one of the cabinets to the side and exposed a hidden doorway through which we entered a windowless room. "You are the first to arrive today," Olga said as she turned on a couple of electric lights mounted on the white wall. At the opposite end of the room was another door, smaller than the one we had entered through, which led to the doctor's private living quarters. The room was almost empty, with the exception of a couple of exercise mats spread on a well-polished oak floor.

We took off our coats, laid them on the floor, and sat down on the mats. Gitta leaned over to me and continued with her security lecture: "No one knows who you are, except a few people whom you met before. Professor Sommermann will introduce you to everyone by first name. This is for your own protection. As a front, and to conceal our true identity, we meet under the pretext of being a meditation and discussion group interested in the psychological welfare of the human mind and body. We do this so we're capable of argument in case it should ever come to an interrogation. Professor Ritz will give you a few books on the subject that you will have to study. At one time or another you will be used as a go-between. All discussions are of a secret nature and are classified as such. Under no circumstances should they ever be revealed to an outsider. No one—except if he has the permission of the entire assembly—is allowed to talk about his business, his work, or the other members. We have to be careful not to make any derogatory statements, and it is of vital importance not to debate politics outside these four walls. Of course, within these rooms you are free to express your thoughts to the fullest. It might be a good idea if you were to tell the untarnished truth about what life was like in Russia as a soldier in Hitler's army. A few others before you have given their accounts."

Gitta's expression suddenly changed. She said gravely, "Whoever violates our bylaws for any careless or irresponsible reason has to count on severe punishment. This is not a game we're playing; it's far too important to all of us. The information we're producing is vital to many people and could even save their lives. You won't be able to meet all of our people today. We usually meet in small groups so as not to draw suspicion. A large resistance movement is backing us financially. Only our leaders and a few selected individuals know who they really are. Your uncle Oskar is the leader of yet another resistance group. By the way, he won't be coming today. But Eric, whom you've met before, will be here tonight. That man is really a genius. Professor Sommermann will go into detail about his inventions. Basically, we're the agitation and propaganda division of the resistance movement that I mentioned to you.

"We distribute the material given to us by our leaders. Usually they're leaflets and handbills informing the public of the truth on the western and eastern fronts. Some of the handbills, usually only ten to fifteen, are printed, and Mathilde and I distribute them at various spots in the city. Hans, the baker, has a small printing press set up in a room behind his ovens, where he prints the material. The group members pick them up and take them to be reprinted in large quantities. Then they're distributed by the thousand."

Our conversation was interrupted when several people arrived, one after the other. I saw Hans, Theodor with Mathilde, and Heinrich walk in. Professor Werner arrived a few minutes later with two men whom I didn't recognize. Finally, Professor Sommermann appeared and came over to embrace me. "What have they done to you, my friend?" he exclaimed. "I hope your leg will heal soon and the consequences of your injury are not too severe."

After the professor had said hello to everybody, he took me aside and escorted me into the consultation room. "Come, I have to talk to you. Has Gitta told you about what has happened while you were gone? Has she explained our basic rules and our different assignments?"

"Yes, she has" was my answer.

Eric arrived in the company of a young woman. In passing he said hello and walked on into the salon.

"By the way," Sommermann continued, "did Gitta mention anything to you about Eric?"

"She did briefly, but she said you would go into detail about it."

"Well, let me tell you about him. He's one of our best men. He made an invention that surpasses all our efforts. Probably you yourself have heard the genius at work. Over the German broadcasting network during the evening news a voice in the background always maintains the contrary of what the newscaster announces. Of course, it's always the truth."

I nodded in surprise. Once, while I was still in the infirmary, a fellow had brought in a radio and we had been able to hear a voice interrupting the newscast—although not very distinctly, since the newscaster spoke continuously. Unfortunately, when the radio broke down we had had no other to take its place. And, to tell you the truth, at that time it hadn't meant much to me and I hadn't paid much attention to the broadcasts.

"Let me go on," Sommermann said. "Eric keeps a weekend cottage and a small boat on the Zeesener Lake near Königswusterhausen. Directly across from there are the big antenna masts of the German radio network. He built a small transmitter that feeds directly into the same wavelength as the network antennas. Since the input waves are able to reach a distance of only three hundred meters and can be turned in only one direction, the network has not been able to detect where the transmitter is actually located.

"The girl who came in with Eric is Monika, his fiancée. She usually stays in the cottage during the day and has agreed to destroy all the equipment and kill herself if anything goes wrong. Eric is also working on something even more spectacular, which will assist our efforts even more. He's a devout and fanatically convinced Communist, and so is his fiancée, whose father was executed by the Nazis at the Buchenwald concentration camp."

Professor Sommermann paused and looked up. Two men approached us. One was dressed in a white smock and the other was wearing the uniform of a lieutenant colonel in the air force. They shook hands with Professor Sommermann, and he in turn introduced them to me as Dr. Ritz and Comrade Beesen. The lieutenant colonel came closer and said, "So you're Fritz. Gitta has told me a lot about you. Actually, you were one of the founders of this group. Very well, let's go and get started," he said, and we all went into the salon.

Gitta was waiting for me with a radiant, almost proud smile on her face. She whispered, "You're astonished, aren't you? The lieutenant colonel is our leader. He's a close confidant of Hermann Göring himself. He controls the private radio and wire installation and service in the Reich's Ministry of Aviation. He speaks Russian and English fluently. His father is a high-ranking officer in the navy. His wife is also an active member in our group, although I have yet to meet her."

Professor Sommermann introduced me to the congregation of about twenty people. Four of them were wearing a uniform like mine. A couple of them apparently lived in Dr. Ritz's building. The ones I didn't know from before were introduced by their first names. The lieutenant colonel proceeded to start the meeting. He informed the group that there were no particular problems and things were running smoothly. The text of the next handbill was completed and ready for Professor Sommermann to edit so Hans could print it.

The lieutenant colonel informed us, in a voice that projected conviction, that our goal was not far off. "The Russians will attack very soon. Our troops, and in particular the Sixth Army, will feel one hard blow after another in the Don River bend. The Freies Deutschland Committee in Russia, which is mainly composed of immigrants, German Communists, imprisoned officers, and deserters, will eventually take over power in Germany. The Americans, with their might, are not far behind. The Nazi leaders are well aware that this war is lost. Their insane dream will disintegrate before their eyes. They would like to draw the entire German population into destruction along with them. Their motto is 'After us the flood,' but let's not forget that we are here and there are many more like us. It's important that we remain strong and keep our cool when things get tough. Our work has to continue as it always has. We have enough clear minds and specialists among us who know their work and have the mental and physical capacity to form a workable administration. Even civic resistance groups have come forward and offered their assistance. But then there are those others of whom we have to be very careful."

The air force man continued in a strong voice, "By the way, even Göring is suddenly showing an immense interest in foreign news. He constantly demands to hear the news bulletins from abroad. Our goal won't change. We have to continue working with the Russians. It's the only chance we have to take control. Hitler and his generals have badly miscalculated in Russia. Even if they continue to win, they'll eventually run out of matériel to fight their battles. Our airplanes are running out of fuel now, and the troops are short on ammunition.

"However, if we don't succeed, it won't take long for the warmongers to get the upper hand once again. As far as the Russians are concerned, they're eager to help us in any way they can.

"Peace and freedom will not be handed to us on a silver platter," he said. "It will have to be gained by force."

The lieutenant colonel continued in this fashion for about two hours. Then we all departed. Professor Sommermann called me aside and told me that he would not use me for any activity or assignment until I felt better. We left and went straight to Gitta's place. Without saying anything she made coffee for me. She sat down and joined me at the table but didn't pour any for herself. "Coffee upsets my stomach lately, maybe I'm pregnant," she said matter-of-factly. "I've also stopped menstruating. What are we going to do if that's the case?"

Clearly, this was not the best time to bring a child into the world, but the thought of having a part of me growing inside my beloved Gitta made me very happy.

"Easy," I said. "We'll get married. Go to your doctor first and see if your suspicions are right."

Back at the infirmary that night, I developed a terrible pain in my leg. The doctor on duty told me that the next morning they would definitely have to operate again. Once again I lay bedridden. Gitta and my sister came to see me every day. Meanwhile, Gitta had found out that she was indeed pregnant.

It was at this point that the sergeant, who was after my sister, denounced me for making remarks about Russian weapons. I was also charged with purposely concealing a previous conviction. While at the Russian front, I had remarked that the roads were bad indeed, but looking at it from a military standpoint it was to the Russians' advantage, since it slowed down our advances considerably. I had also added that it would take several generations for them to build roads like ours in Germany. These statements had led to a confrontation with our company commander and six days of detention. There's very little left to say. Several hours later, as soon as I was able to stand on my own two feet again, I was arrested by two Gestapo agents. They took me to a police precinct at the Alexanderplatz, where I received a short hearing about my remarks. Not realizing that the consequences could be serious, I admitted to making the statements. I was informed by the Gestapo officer in charge that I had to remain in custody. Their staff physician examined me because I complained about my leg. Afterward he told me he would have me transferred to Buch, where I've now been for four weeks.

Obviously, I was not allowed to notify anyone of my whereabouts or where I was going to be. I had heard of Buch but had always thought it to be an insane asylum instead of a prison infirmary.

After a couple of weeks I was called before a different pair of Gestapo agents. They told me that I would have to go before a court-martial for having made antagonistic and adversary statements against the German Reich by showing favoritism toward the enemy. One of the agents looked at me with a cold, ironic smile as the other one told me that an even more serious charge was pending against me. He rested his arms on the table in front of him and looked at me. Then, in a slow, deliberate voice he said, "I must inform you that your fiancée, a Professor Sommermann, and quite a few others whose company you have been known to keep are in detention." He waited for my reaction.

Of course, when I heard this, my stomach turned upside down. All the color must have drained out of my face. It was a terrible blow. Trying to collect myself as best I could, I told these hoodlums I didn't know what the hell they were talking about.

"Don't worry," the Gestapo man sneered, "we'll get to you yet, once you've heard us out. We're well aware of what was going on with this group of yours. If you confess now, your chances for a milder sentence are assured."

They continued to interrogate me in this manner day after day; to my astonishment, they seemed to know everything I'm telling you now.

My so-called trial is set for after the Christmas holidays.

Fritz paused for a moment and wiped his forehead with his hand. His eyes watered as he went on. "The last time I spoke with the Gestapo, I was told that I was being accused of high treason, aiding the enemy, and demoralization of the Wehrmacht. I am to stand trial for each accusation, and the death penalty is mandatory for each individual indictment. The relationship I had with Gitta I will have to explain before a People's Court, and I won't be able to see her until then.

"Well, friends, that's my story."

At almost the same moment that Fritz stopped speaking, the lights were turned off, but the room was not as dark as usual. A full moon illuminated the milky windowpanes and outlined our faces, haggard and tired from listening to Fritz's story.

"Doesn't anyone have anything to say?" Fritz's voice came out of the dark.

Alex lifted his head from his pillow and spoke for all of us. "Fritz, that was a long story, and we're all tired. Rest now. We'll continue tomorrow, and hopefully we can listen to Franzl, Gerhard, and Erich. I had really hoped we could finish today. Perhaps tomorrow it will be quiet like today since most of the guards are still at home for the holidays."

Franzl said comfortingly, "Dear Fritz, I will say a prayer for you and your Gitta tonight. It is still our Lord's day."

Like the other prisoners, I was tired but had trouble falling asleep. I turned restlessly, feeling the ever-nagging pain in my hand and arm, no matter how I lay. I thought about Fritz and his Gitta, about my wife and child, and about my "loose tongue," which basically was the thing that had brought me here. Finally, after an hour or so of listening to Franzl's mumbled prayers, my mind slowly succumbed to sleep.

CHAPTER 9

INTERLUDE

Morning brought the same routine: get up, wash, walk the circle, eat breakfast. The only noticeable difference was that today it seemed very quiet and things moved at a much slower pace.

Shortly after breakfast, Phillip arrived with his medical tray. "Who needs to be bandaged?" he asked. Fritz and I raised our hands simultaneously. Phillip ordered Fritz to come with him. "I'll be back for you later," he said to me.

After a few minutes Phillip returned for me. As we walked next to each other down the empty corridor, he explained that he was allowed to take only one person at a time to the examination room. Apparently, the doctor was at home with his family enjoying the Christmas holiday, because an inmate who also served as an orderly was waiting for me when I entered through the double door. The chill of this particular room always made me shiver. Phillip closed the door behind us.

"Good morning," I said politely, introducing myself to the pale-looking orderly as I gazed around the room. The man's face was forlorn, and he stood close to a metal table that he was wiping off with a white dish towel. He barely looked at me when he lethargically acknowledged my greeting. I thought to myself that he must be a shy person and he probably felt just like I did, longing to be free and to be at home.

"Are you ill?" I asked the man. "No," he said, "but I feel so goddamn depressed. I was left in a cell all to myself with nothing to do except think about my wife, my children, and my grandchildren." His face fell into lines of deeper sadness when he confessed that he had almost lost his sanity. "This was the worst Christmas I've ever spent in my entire life."

While he unwrapped my bandages, the orderly asked me how we were managing to get through the holidays. I told him that we were passing the time by telling each other our life stories and why we were in this place. I noted Franzl's sermon.

"Let me tell you," he whispered, his eyes blinking nervously, "it seems as though everyone in your wing is a goner. Take Gerhard—or, as he used to be known, the Count von Silkenaski. He is accused of being a traitor to Germany by showing favoritism to and collaborating with the Poles. After he was unmasked he tried to flee to France in a stolen general's car. He was caught near Kaiserslautern, when he hit a horse-drawn carriage and received a severe head injury. Initially he was taken to Bruchsal; I'm not sure how long he spent there or if he's been convicted yet, but eventually he was brought here to Buch. A psychiatrist and neurologist are treating his mental condition. They want to find out if he was responsible for his actions at the time of his offense. His files are all labeled top secret and confidential."

The orderly paused. "Sit down here," he said, pointing to a stool near a clean-scrubbed metal table. "Please don't mention what I have just told you to anyone, Erich." He forced a sad smile. "Someday I hope to be able to tell you about myself and what I know. But right now I can't."

The man bent down and began working intensely on my injury. "I recall one fellow, a lieutenant in the Wehrmacht, who had an injury similar to yours. He joked around among his friends and sang these lines:

> Everything shall pass, everything will go by
> In April dies the Führer and in May the Party.

"Those lines of musical poetry cost the fellow two years in jail and a demotion to private. This happened quite some time ago; he was lucky. Now, of course, the courts are much stricter. But with a little luck you'll get a decent judge who will view your case leniently. Being the recipient of the Iron Cross and several other decorations might be an asset to you."

I listened to him as he talked and treated my wound. It was apparent that he knew about everyone's offense, including mine. Only a few minutes had passed when Phillip returned for me and took me back to my cell, where Fritz was sitting at the table next to Gerhard. It looked as if they were waiting for my return; Gerhard had drawn the lot to tell his story.

"Now that we're together again," began Fritz, "Gerhard can tell us all about himself.

"You can tell us the truth, Gerhard," he encouraged, "or are you really touched in the head, as rumor has it?"

Actually smiling, for whatever reason, Gerhard remained seated with his hands folded, twiddling his thumbs as he stared aimlessly into the room. Fritz repeated impatiently, "Come on, Gerhard, cut it out. No more game playing. I know you're as sane as I am."

Gerhard remained silent. We waited.

CHAPTER 10

GERHARD VON SILKENASKI: THE ARISTOCRAT

Without uttering a word, Gerhard reached into his left trouser pocket and produced several sheets of paper that looked like letters. Carefully, he placed the papers, still folded, on the table in front of him. Alex got up from his bed, picked the letters up, and began to study them. Gerhard's eyes followed his every move. Alex unfolded the papers and said, "There are two letters here, one dated May 1, 1940, and the other September 1, 1940. May I read them out loud?" he asked Gerhard. Gerhard didn't move; he remained silent, as if someone had sealed his lips.

The letters were written on exceptionally heavy white stationery. The engraved letterhead showed two horses and a coat of arms in red ink. Underneath was the year 1404 in roman numerals. From behind his glasses Alex peered at the mute figure. "Tell us, does this mean that you actually are a nobleman?"

I myself had been debating whether I should mention what the orderly had told me. I decided against it but said, "Perhaps you're even a count." Gerhard turned toward me but remained expressionless, recommencing his thumb twiddling. Fritz joked, "At times he does look like royalty, but when it comes to food and drink he acts and thinks like the rest of us."

Alex interrupted again and told everyone to be quiet so he could read the letters. Slowly he read the first one.

Lyck, 1 May 1940

Dear Brother Gerhard:

This is my fourth letter to you without receiving an answer. I am so deeply concerned about your welfare. I know you are receiving the letters, otherwise they would have been returned to me.

Mother is still bedridden, and she seems to get worse by the day. She is almost completely blind. The doctor insists it is a nervous condition and says that, medically speaking, there's not much he can do. Apparently she cannot get over the death of her sons. Day in and day out she talks about you and wants to know when you will be coming home.

I myself am so overworked that I don't know whether I am coming or going. Even Baron Lutz was called to duty last week. He was the only man left around here to give me business advice. Since Jan was drafted, the women have to attend to the horses, do the field work, and drive the tractors. I remember so well that you used to say girls were good for nothing. You should see the girls and women in action around here—you would choke on your own words.

Do you remember Liesel? She's the only German left now. She wants to stay with us. The other women and girls are all Poles. I'm happy they're here. A few new ones arrived last week. They had been chased out of the Warthe district.

The heavy field work is behind us, and most likely we'll manage to get through the harvest as well. If only I could hear a word from you.

Your favorite mare, Fuchs, gave birth to a beautiful colt a couple of days ago. Liesel insists that it is going to be the best riding horse in our district.

Unfortunately I don't have the time to take the horses out for long rides like I used to. At least they can roam around freely in the enclosures.

Liesel has asked me to send you her regards. Yesterday afternoon, she, a Polish girl, and I went fishing down by the lake and caught a gigantic pike, which we ate for lunch today.

I'm writing this letter from the tower room overlooking the green pastures below. I hope you'll come home soon. This war can't last forever, although at times it seems as if it will.

I went to the office of the district president to have you declared indispensable as a farmer, but they wouldn't even listen to me. I was told that the army was in dire need of officers.

I had two pictures of our brothers Karl and Wolfgang enlarged and put together with one of our father. I placed them on your desk. I know you will like them there.

My dearest brother, I hope the Lord will keep you from harm and bring you back to us soon. Please write or let someone else write for you if you are unable to do so. I just imagine the worst.

Your loving sister, Maria

Alex put the first letter down on the table after refolding it neatly. He then picked up the second letter, which read:

Lyck, 4 September 1940

Dear Brother Gerhard:

I can't sleep, the moon is illuminating my room and I am sitting here at my desk writing you my sixteenth letter. I have not given up hope that eventually I will receive some news from you.

Your unit commander wrote to inform me that all my correspondence has been forwarded to you. It was up to you to write me your address since he was not permitted to do so. I really don't understand any of this. Why don't you answer me? If for some reason you cannot write, isn't there anybody around who could do it for you? I hope we are still living in a world that knows some human compassion. My last hope was the Red Cross. I wrote them a long letter over à month ago and so far have not received an answer.

Since our dear mother passed away, I have been terribly lonely. If it were not for Liesel, I think I would have gone insane by now. I used to ask Uncle Egon for business advice, but since his son Horst was killed in action he can't seem to relate to anyone. His estate has deteriorated completely.

We managed to get the harvest in. Only the potato and turnip crops are left.

Liesel moved from the guest house into the manor house to take a room close to mine. At times I get scared.

One of our outer barns needed a new roof. It rained in on several occasions and damaged some of the feed. I hired a man from the village to make the necessary repairs at a reasonable price. Besides that I have bought a new bull. It's a handsome animal, and although it cost 3,000 marks, I think it is a good, solid investment. I know you'll be proud of me when you see him. Perhaps I have some business instincts, after all.

I am getting tired now. Please, dearest brother, write to me soon. I am desperately waiting to hear from you.

With kindest regards and warmest love, your sister Maria

Alex looked at Gerhard, who in the meantime had seated himself on the bench. With a compassionate look in his eyes, Alex asked, "Gerhard, are you aware that your mother died? Why didn't you tell us about these letters before?"

There was no answer. Gerhard was oblivious to all that had been said, or at least it seemed so to us. He did mutter something to himself while rocking his head back and forth.

"Do you have any more letters from your sister?" asked Alex. "Do you have an envelope? Can you give us your sister's address so we can write to her?" Again, no answer. Gerhard's lips remained sealed.

Fritz got up from his chair, limped over to the night table, and opened Gerhard's drawer to see what else he could find.

Suddenly Gerhard jerked and jumped up like an animal disturbed during a sound sleep, grabbing the two slices of bread that were hidden in the drawer and pleading, "No, no, they're mine!" He held them tightly against his chest and sat down on the bench with them.

Fritz was startled, and so were we. "Perhaps he really is touched in the head!" Fritz exclaimed. He returned to the table and sat down.

Alex suggested we find out Gerhard's home address so one of us could answer his sister. "Phillip mentioned to me once," continued Alex, "that all of Gerhard's files are treated as highly confidential. Apparently he was a spy for the Poles."

Meanwhile Gerhard returned to his seat and slid into the chair like a punished child. He continued to stare with the same indifferent expression, leaving us wondering what was behind his mask.

Before lunch was brought, the draw of the straws dictated that Franzl tell his story next.

Author Friedrich in 1935 at his sister Irma's wedding. He stands next to his fiancée Hilde; his parents are seated.

At home with his wife, daughter Renate, and sister-in-law Ilse during the summer of 1940.

Friedrich's class at the military training center in Taus (Domazlice), Czechoslavakia, in 1942. He is seated in front on the right.

Here, and above right: German troops on the Eastern Front. Friedrich was a mach gunner in the 673rd Regiment of the 376th Infantry Division. *National Archives*

Friedrich *(left)* recovering from his wound at the Bad Tölz military hospital in 1944.

Nürnberg as it appeared to Friedrich in 1945. *National Archives*

Berlin toward the war's end. *Novosti*

Haus Vaterland (Fatherland House) at Potsdamer Platz, a popular Berlin entertainment center consisting of cafés, restaurants, and movie theaters. It was here, after Friedrich's release from Buch, that he tried to find Alex Keminski's family. *Staatsarchiv Berlin*

Haus Vaterland at war's end. *Staatsarchiv Berlin*

Father and daughter
in 1952.

NOW

Friedrich and his daughter visited Germany in 1994. This is a partial view of the Wehrmacht prison infirmary at Buch, where Friedrich and his six cell mates were held. Now a psychiatric outpatient clinic, its outer appearance has changed little since the war. Bars remain on the window, and massive walls still surround the complex.

Buch: The two windows of cell number 7 are on the right side of the second floor.

Emotionally drained, Erich Friedrich stands in front of the wall that once kept him prisoner at Buch.

One of the gates to the individual cells at the Brückenkopf prison in Torgau, where Friedrich served out the remainder of his sentence. Occupied by the Russians at the end of the war and now abandoned, it is soon to be demolished.

One of the cell blocks at Brückenkopf.

CHAPTER 11

FRANZL REITHAMMER: THE JEHOVAH'S WITNESS

I was born in 1904 and raised in the beautiful Austrian Wachau region, near the old and charming city of Melck. My native village, a small community of about two hundred and fifty residents, was nestled amid rolling hills covered with vineyards, lush green meadows, fertile fields, and an abundance of fruit trees. There was one Catholic church, one inn, one chaplain, a teacher, and a municipal government consisting of one person.

Apart from a few men who worked at the nearby quarry in Krems, most of the villagers were vintners who also kept some livestock and tended a couple of fields. Our household was no different from the others. During the spring, summer, and fall we got up early and went to bed late. There was always enough work to keep everyone in the family busy. During the winter months the whole family helped my father weave wicker baskets, which we sold to the rural farmers. We had plenty of food to eat, and we lived a happy, hardworking life. Since our community was somewhat isolated, we had very little contact with the outside world. Most people read a newspaper only on Saturdays, and usually it was only the local news that interested us.

My family was Roman Catholic, and like most people, we attended Mass faithfully every Sunday. The chaplain paid close attention to everyone's attendance. If anyone missed a couple of Sundays, he would come to the house and inquire. The chaplain and the municipal officer were the most important men in our community. Any decisions involving the sale of wine and crops or the leasing of property had to be approved by them. They also set the prices of the wine, and so on. Nobody questioned their authority; that's just the way it was, and we accepted it. Once in a while we heard about unrest and revolt in Vienna, but somehow it never affected us. Vienna seemed so far away.

One day, during a pilgrimage to the monastery of Melck, I met Resi, a young, pretty woman who lived in a nearby village on the other side of the Danube River. I would walk to Melck to see her, which took me about one and a half hours. Eventually, all this walking became too much for me and we decided to get married. Shortly after the wedding, Resi moved in with my parents and me. We shared the house with my sister, Wally, my brother, Kasper, and an old uncle from my mother's side of the family. The house was large and spacious, and even if my sister and brother had decided to get married, we all would have had plenty of room to live together. My brother was thirteen at the time, and my sister was about fifteen. In 1931 our daughter, Mariandl, was born, and a year later our son, Lothar, arrived. Our house was filled with joy and children's laughter that we all enjoyed, especially my dear mother.

At the time, the son of one of our neighbors—we called him "Cheese Pot" because of his pale complexion—was very active in the Nazi party. He stated publicly that Hitler wanted to reunite the German empire, which included Austria. A couple of days later, some constables came to arrest him, but he had already escaped to Germany along with a few other young men from our area. But these events did not affect us directly; we had our own problems to think about.

My brother, Kasper, had developed a growth on his neck. My mother tried to treat it with homeopathic medicines without much success. At the chaplain's advice, I took Kasper to Melck to see a doctor. He told us that the growth was a tumor and would probably have to be removed surgically. The doctor then sent us to the University Clinic in Vienna, where it was confirmed that the tumor was malignant. Since we had no medical insurance, paying for the operation and the follow-up treatments presented a tremendous problem for us. My father scraped together his entire savings of two thousand schillings to make a down payment on the operation.

One of the physicians at the university clinic, a surgeon named Channek, took a special interest in Kasper. He performed the surgery and watched over Kasper day and night. When the head of surgery told my mother that Kasper's condition was very serious, Dr. Channek was there to console her with kind words. He told her that between my mother's and his prayers and the skills of the attending staff, Kasper would be well in no time.

The hospital bill cost us a fortune. My father had to borrow money from relatives and the remaining amounts from a kind and generous store owner. Dr. Channek, being aware of our poor financial situation, had provided his services for free. My mother, to express her gratitude, invited him over for a weekend dinner. She also asked him to bring his wife. He accepted the invitation but told my mother that he was not married.

Dr. Channek arrived on a Saturday afternoon in an older-model Opel. I guessed him to be in his early thirties. He was an attractive, well-built, well-educated young man. Dark brown hair outlined a face with a healthy reddish complexion and deep-set dark eyes. On Sunday morning Kasper and I showed him around the vineyards.

"The Wachau certainly is very beautiful—Paradise on earth," Dr. Channek said. "Such serenity," he sighed. Both my mother and I had to agree with him. We told him that we loved our home and the land that surrounded us. Somehow we got into a conversation about religion. He asked us if most of the people in the vicinity were Catholics. I told him that all the people we knew were Catholics and no other faith existed in our area. "The Catholic church certainly knows its business well," he said. Kasper and I just looked at each other but didn't quite understand what he meant. We thought perhaps he was a Protestant who thought a lot about praying, since he had mentioned it to my mother so often while Kasper was hospitalized.

That Sunday afternoon my mother prepared a special dinner in his honor, something she usually only cooked on holidays. We had stuffed Bavarian dumplings and roast beef. When we sat down at the table, Wally, as always, said grace. During the meal, my mother asked us if we had been to church in the morning. Dr. Channek answered for us, "No, but we attended the biggest and most beautiful of churches, namely Mother Nature. I haven't been inside a church for many years now," he added.

"Are you of the Protestant faith?" inquired my mother. "No," he replied, "but I am a true Christian, or at least I try to be." My mother stopped asking questions, and we finished our meal. Later that afternoon, the doctor returned to Vienna. He invited Kasper to visit him in Vienna, giving directions to his apartment at Tulpengasse No. 9, in the vicinity of the courthouse and not very far from the hospital. He then gave Kasper fifty schillings for the train and streetcar fares.

Kasper left on the following Saturday afternoon and came back on the train early Monday morning. When he arrived home, he couldn't wait to tell about his first trip to Vienna by himself. Apparently he had had little trouble finding the doctor's residence and had been welcomed by a nice older couple named Feichtlbauer, who rented out two upstairs rooms to the doctor. They had offered Kasper coffee and cake and asked him to wait in their parlor until the doctor returned from the hospital. They had referred to the doctor as their brother and seemed to be very religious people.

Later in the day, the doctor had finally arrived and apologized for his delay. He had explained that there had been one emergency after another, which was why he had been detained at the hospital so long. They had gone up to his study, and he had begun to tell Kasper about himself. He had explained that he was Hungarian by birth and had studied medicine in Vienna. Both his parents were dead, and otherwise he had no living relatives.

In the late afternoon Dr. Channek had suggested that they go out for a bite at a nearby restaurant. Kasper had felt completely out of place in the elegant surroundings, even though I had lent him my Sunday-best outfit. Everyone had been dressed in fine, expensive-looking clothes. They had dined on wiener schnitzel and drunk red wine, but Kasper had noticed that our local wine was better tasting by far than the one at the restaurant.

After dinner the doctor had asked if Kasper would like to go to a church service with him. Kasper had been stunned, for he had never heard of going to church late in the evening. But then he had thought, why not?

Dr. Channek had explained that the congregation did not meet in "pompous cathedrals or palaces" but rather in a simple hall that served as the ground of worship. "We call our meeting place 'Kingdom Hall,'" he had said. "Have you ever heard about it?" Kasper had answered, "No."

This marked my brother's introduction to Jehovah's Witnesses. As he told it to me and my family, it is through faith and by studying the Bible together that Witnesses believe the end of the world is soon to come. The register of sins is overbooked. Everyone is running after the golden calf, trying to get a bit through various methods and means. Even so, man is an individual who needs to be part of society in order to live, and the better the society lives, the better will be the life of the individual. The churches and their parsons have totally forgotten these basic moral principles, because they think only about their own enrichment. What is left nowadays is nothing but idol worship: "As soon as the coins hit the collection box, the soul has permission to enter heaven," that's their motto. However, the traditional churches and their parsons accuse Jehovah's Witnesses of being heretics and would like to burn them at the stake if it were permitted.

Then Kasper repeated Dr. Channek's explanation that orthodox Christianity is well aware that the Witnesses preach the truth about Christianity. "It is said that what we preach is impossible. So why do they call themselves Christians, if what is written in the Bible is impossible? In any case, our firm belief in the truth of the holy Bible is justified. Not one word that we teach is of our own making," Dr. Channek had said.

Meanwhile Kasper and Dr. Channek had taken the streetcar across the channel to the Augartenstrasse, where they had gotten off and walked through a narrow alley to a large building that had once been a nail factory. The interior was, as Dr. Channek had described it, a large assembly room illuminated by several ceiling lights.

They had been received with overwhelming friendliness by the people present. The Feichtlbauers had arrived earlier and greeted Kasper as if he were a member of their family. The crowd had seemed to be in a cheerful mood, and the atmosphere in the place had been happy and joyous. How different from our own serious and conservative church services! An older man had played a small portable organ, and the entire congregation had joined in by singing songs that were also of a merry nature. There was a desk in the front of the room where a few of the men and women had taken turns in reading from the Scriptures, always followed by a brief discussion. This had all been done in layman's language so that everyone could easily understand. Kasper had noticed how well informed these worshippers were about the Bible and its contents. The last man who had spoken had quoted from the revelation to John: "Be thou faithful unto death, and I will give thee the crown of life."

The doctor and Kasper had left together with the Feichtlbauers for the trip back home. Dr. Channek had asked Kasper how he had liked the gathering. He had responded that he had enjoyed it, especially the happy atmosphere that had prevailed. "That's one of our goals," Herr Feichtlbauer had said with a smile, "to make people feel good about themselves."

My brother turned to me and said, "The next time I go see him, I want you to come with me, Franzl, and Wally also. The Feichtlbauers have already said you two can sleep at their apartment."

Somewhat concerned, my mother interrupted, "I've heard a lot about these Jehovah's Witnesses, but I really don't know if what they are preaching is the truth. On the other hand, the doctor is no fool, and I don't think he would join a congregation unless there was something to it. After all, they do believe in God and Jesus as well as the Holy Scripture, and there certainly is nothing wrong with that. Just don't mention any of this to our chaplain, you know how he reacts when people don't do as he says."

Kasper put his arm around my mother and said, "Well, Mother, these people are not at all like our chaplain. They express genuine love and respect for one another that comes across very strongly during their meetings. They don't curse, nor do they talk negatively about other religions.

Their only complaint seems to be that Christianity has been getting farther and farther away from the true faith."

My brother began to go to Vienna more often. A deep and solid friend-ship developed between the doctor and our family, and especially my sister Wally. It was obvious that those two liked each other. Whenever Dr. Channek came to visit us, we would sit for hours debating about the Bible. He was a skilled orator and had answers to all the questions we asked, no matter how complex they were. As the years went by, the chaplain began to notice that Kasper, my father, and Wally missed Mass more often than usual and eventually stopped going entirely.

That brought the chaplain to our house. He demanded to know what was going on in our lives. As I recall, my father told him, "We're the same Christians you've always known; we love our Father and our Lord Jesus Christ, but we've decided to say our prayers at home with our family and friends."

The priest's response was what we expected. "Do not commit these sins against the Holy Roman Catholic church," he warned. Speaking directly to my father, he continued in an accusing voice, "The Church is the house of God that supports the moral foundation of our lives. It is through the Church that one learns the values of life and the moral principles to guide oneself by. Otherwise you might as well live like an animal."

After listening to this diatribe, my wife and I became doubtful and dis-traught about who was right and who was wrong. In a way it's true: the Church does not make murderers or thieves out of people, it does try to lead people in the right direction; but, on the other hand, why does it per-mit the use of cruelty and unethical means to enrich itself?

After the chaplain left us that evening, I must confess, our whole family was confused. After that initial visit, the priest returned twice more before he gave up on us. A few weeks later we received a written request to appear at the abbey in Melck. My mother decided to go on our behalf. Upon her return she told us that initially the priests had been very friendly and had asked her when we would start attending church again. When she had been concommittal, the priests had changed their tactics and made my mother feel as if she had made a pact with Satan himself.

Shortly thereafter, we received notification that the lease on our land, which was partly owned by the abbey, was being terminated. This abrupt and unexpected action hit us very hard, especially since we leased more than half of our workable land from the Church. We were also notified by the municipal official—who was the father of the boy who had escaped to Germany—that we were now responsible for selling our own wine and that we should not rely on the abbey's assistance in the future. This meant that we could sell the wine only to buyers who were not sent by the abbey—and there would be very few of those, if any—or buyers who wanted to pay next to nothing for the wine.

My brother had often warned us that this kind of harassment might take place. Kasper went to see the chaplain in person, telling him that these actions by the Church were not very Christian.

The priest warned, "You're the one who is to be blamed for all this. It is you who is ruining your family's life, because you are being possessed by the Devil. My ears are deaf to Satan's words." With this, he practically threw Kasper out the front door.

This created a major crisis in our lives. We had no choice now but to turn to our newly acquired friends, the Jehovah's Witnesses. The village people shunned us, and our life in general became unbearable. We were left with only a small piece of land, which was not enough to support our growing family.

Hearing of our plight, Dr. Channek immediately offered his help by getting Kasper a job as a hospital attendant trainee. He bought a bicycle for Resi so that she would be able to go to her family's place and help out with the harvest. Life started to improve again. We did not suffer the destitution that the Church had meant for us as a punishment.

Meanwhile, Kasper had moved to Vienna to pursue his job. He shared a room at the clinic with another hospital worker. Every four weeks the entire family would go and attend divine services with our friends. Usually we stayed with the Feichtlbauers. Kasper completed an instruction course on how to preach and lecture. When he gave his first sermon, we all went to hear him speak. What a proud day for all of us to see what a fine person Kasper had become! He bought us three new Bibles and sent us all kinds of literature relevant to our faith. We now spent our evenings reading the Bible and then discussing what we had read. Our religious life was now completely severed from the Catholic church.

Kasper also became outspoken on political issues, giving several public speeches warning his native Austrians not to fall for Hitler's rhetoric. During one of his speeches he said loudly and clearly, "We cannot permit the Nazis to force us to submit to them. Fascism has taken over Germany, and many innocent people are being victimized and thrown into prisons. We are all Austrians, and our country has to remain free. A repeat of the insurrection of 1934 cannot be tolerated."

Even though Kasper was only eighteen at the time, his speeches made the newspaper headlines on several occasions. In his talks, Kasper warned that the Germans under Hitler's guidance were planning a war. Hitler wanted to unite the two empires, not because he wanted to help Austria economically but because he wanted to use Austria as protection against invasion from the south and its people for cannon fodder. These were pretty strong accusations against the popular Hitler.

Naturally, people in our village read some of these statements. Our municipal officer accused Kasper of slander and radical behavior. He also warned Kasper to keep a low profile and if possible to stay out of sight for his own protection. A couple of days later, someone smeared the word "Judas" all over the front of our house. On my mother's request, Kasper kept his distance. However, we now went to Vienna more often, and at one point my father suggested that we sell our piece of land and resettle in the Vienna area permanently. My mother, my wife, and my sister fought this because they felt that the children should be raised close to the land.

In early 1938, Hitler forced our chancellor, Kurt von Schuschnigg, to sign an agreement giving him virtually a free hand in Austria. Although von Schuschnigg tried to repudiate the agreement by announcing a plebiscite on the question of the *Anschluss* with Germany, Hitler immediately ordered Nazi troops to occupy our country. As the Germans marched into Vienna, we were hopeful that its people would revolt against them. Instead, the opposite happened. The crowds cheered Hitler enthusiastically as he spoke of freedom and liberation, which, after all, were the dreams of every Austrian. Shortly after this triumph, Hitler set out to carve up Czechoslovakia.

"Cheese Pot" had returned from Germany and was greeted and treated like a king. He appeared in our village, strutting along the narrow streets in his SA uniform. He marched from door to door, visiting everyone— except our family. We were not strongly politically oriented, but we did see the warning signals in the distance.

As 1939 approached, Kasper received his induction notice to join the Wehrmacht. Upon receipt of the document he burned it and wrote a letter back stating that he was not about to commit murder or support a ludicrous venture like Hitler's, which would only lead to destruction of his country. He mounted a copy of his letter on the bulletin board of Kingdom Hall. About three days after he had sent this letter, a couple of plainclothes Gestapo men came to the clinic where he worked and arrested him. We have not seen or heard from him since. Nor were we ever told who had arrested him and where he was taken to. The only rumor we heard was one spread by Cheese Pot that Kasper had been convicted of subversion and treason and executed accordingly.

At the time, it had occurred to us that perhaps Cheese Pot knew more about Kasper's disappearance than he acknowledged. We had assumed that Kasper had been killed by a mob, since we never even received an official notice of his arrest from the authorities.

Kingdom Hall was forcibly closed down, and our services were prohibited. Our entire family was being harassed to the point that we were accused of being American or Russian spies.

It wasn't long before the Vienna draft board sent me an induction notice. We debated what to do next, since I was one of the few men in our area to receive one. Kasper's disappearance made us feel insecure about our own lives. We even thought of seeking refuge in Hungary, but my mother stood fast. "Let's not be afraid, the Kingdom of our Lord is not far off. Franzl, you go and tell the authorities the same thing your brother told them. You are not a murderer, you are a Christian and a conscientious objector, for you don't believe in killing innocent people.

"I'm certain," my mother continued, "that Kasper has found eternal life. He refused military service and told the authorities so. We have to be firm with our convictions as well. They will try to lead us into temptation; therefore we have to be extremely strong. What is this earthly life anyway, what can they do to us? We will continue to live by our rules and without sin; only then can we expect to receive the promised crown of life. No matter how difficult things get for us, we will never, ever consider taking our own lives, because that would be the greatest sin of all. Franzl, we'll pray for you day and night."

I told my mother that she was right and that I would go to Vienna and expect the obvious, that I would be prosecuted for refusing to fight.

The next morning I left for Vienna by train When I arrived at the barracks, there were just a few men waiting to be drafted. When my turn came, I told them right out that I was refusing to serve in the war since it was against my religious principles to kill another human being. I was held for two days without food and water before I had a court hearing. I explained to the judge that no one could force me to carry a weapon. "I am a conscientious objector, and my religion does not permit the act of killing," I said to the judge. I then quoted the Bible, "Thou shall not kill" and "Love thy enemy as thyself." It was obvious that the judge was annoyed when he asked me, "So, what you're telling us is that you refuse to serve in the armed forces." "Yes, that is correct." "The law," he continued, "is not on your side, and we are here to enforce the law. I'm considering your case leniently, and therefore I hereby sentence you to two years' imprisonment to be served in Germany."

Without being able to notify my family, I was sent to Straubing in Bavaria and later transferred to Magdeburg, where I remained for several weeks. My worst time, however, was spent on a prison ship on the Elbe River, where the rats almost ate us alive. I was forced to live among murderers and rapists. I don't want to go into too much detail about that now. After that I was taken to a lice- and flea-infested concentration camp in the marshlands of northern Germany. I spent about six months there. Our job was to dig ditches in the swamps so the water could be drained into canals. There again, most of the prisoners were hard-core criminals who'd kill their own mothers without blinking an eye. Escape was impossible since the swamps were covered by thick underbrush and there wasn't a village or settlement in the vicinity.

Then one day it was decreed that prisoners who had been imprisoned for refusing to serve in the army could petition for release. Whether or not I was willing, I was once more declared fit for the draft. Had they not fed and treated me fairly well in the hope of making a soldier out of me yet, I probably would have vanished in the marshes. Their attempts, however, failed. I stuck to my convictions and refused to let the authorities turn me into a murderer.

During my imprisonment, my faith became stronger. I prayed constantly to the Lord to help keep me sane and survive these ordeals.

Handcuffed like a common criminal, I was taken to trial in a courthouse in the Turmstrasse in Moabit. There I was sentenced to death for subversion of the Wehrmacht. I was informed by the judge that I was permitted to file a clemency petition. My court-appointed lawyer advised me to do so. I flatly refused. I told them that the day would come when they would have to beg for mercy in front of a much higher court. I am not the only person who is being prosecuted because of his faith. Hundreds before me have had a similar fate. But each one of us will gladly sacrifice his life, because through our suffering we enter the eternal kingdom of our most holy Father.

Now I'm here, waiting to be told if I'm sane or not. Those were the crimes I committed. But you see, my case is already closed. I'm a convicted man. Now it's just a matter of how and when I die.

Alex interrupted Franzl. "Tell us, Franzl, I've heard that you were set up for a mock execution once. Is there any truth to that?"

Telling us his story had visibly exhausted Franzl. His face showed lines of weariness, and a deep sadness came over him as his eyes filled with tears. "Actually, I didn't want to go into that. It arouses very painful memories. Yes, it's true, I was taken to Plötzensee and prepared for execution. On the day of the execution, a minister came to me and tried his best to convert me. He said that all I had to do was obey their commands and all this agony would be avoided. I remained firm.

"The chaplain had barely left the cell when two husky-looking men appeared, took me by the arms, and led me down a long corridor. Near the end of the corridor stood my wife, Resi, and my two children, with their eyes and noses red from crying. Seeing them standing there so utterly hopeless was a pitiful sight that will be etched in my memory forever. At that moment I wasn't sure if I could endure this ghastly cruelty much more. My legs gave way, and I would have fallen to the ground if those two goons hadn't held me up. I had made a resolution to end my earthly life and already saw myself happily in the eternal life with our Father. What an agonizing moment!

"Resi came running toward me with her arms stretched out wide, screaming. 'You look terrible!' she cried out. 'What have these people done to you? Oh, my God, please help us, don't forsake us.' My children followed close behind her and embraced me, crying and sobbing.

"My wife was trembling but was able to tell me between sobs that they had dragged her and the children here to convince me to change my mind. 'But, my dear Franzl,' Resi said between sobs, 'I tell you one thing, they don't know how strong our faith really is. You do what you feel is right. Your mother says the same. Even if we have to lose you, we know you'll be in our Father's hands.'

"Resi held out her hands to me and said, 'I love you, but if our faith dictates that I must give you up—I will.'

"Just then one of the soldiers who was standing around pulled Resi away from me and asked if I had come to my senses and would be willing to serve the Fatherland. Quickly I answered, 'The Lord is my Shepherd, and he alone will lead me. I say no to you.'

"Barely had I spoken these words than the two men grabbed my arms and pulled me away from my family. My children's screams didn't have the slightest effect on them. They took me back to my cell, where I had a nervous breakdown and lay unconscious for several days. No one can know the agony I suffered, and that's why I didn't want to tell you about it," concluded Franzl.

An uncomfortable silence fell over us again. Each of us probably had the same thought: How can human beings treat a fellow human being in such an undignified and cruel way by putting him through such terror?

Fritz, as always, managed to break the silence. "I tell you, I'm not going to ask for mercy from these subhumans in judges' robes. I realize it will be immensely difficult, but I feel I can endure it.

"Do you know," he continued, "that now they've decided to rid the world of the entire Jewish population? Just imagine—we're talking about millions of people, innocent people who have never hurt anyone. There has been no crime as heinous as this in the history of mankind. And these individuals call themselves 'Germans,' products of a nation of world-renowned philosophers, poets, and scholars, who besides that claim to be the descendants of a high-minded super race."

Fritz had become so exasperated that, pounding his fists on the table, he yelled, "I tell you, these are criminals of the worst kind, for whom a fitting punishment has not yet been invented!"

"Calm down, Fritz, we're all tense," interrupted Alex. "Let's not get into any discussions now, we can do that some other time. Now it's Erich's turn to tell us his story. Maybe we can get finished today."

Alex turned toward me and said, "Well, friend, let's hear what crimes you've committed that could justify the death penalty."

I supported my aching arm and leaned forward to look into Alex's face. "Before I begin to tell you my life story, I need to emphasize to you how strongly I believe that the justification of the death penalty is built upon the existence of fascism and dictatorship."

"All right," piped up Fritz from his bed. "Let's hear what life has offered you."

CHAPTER 12

ERICH FRIEDRICH: MY STORY

I was born in 1911 in an old stone mill house in a fashionable health resort in the foothills of the Thuringian Forest. The spa was world-renowned for the therapeutic radium baths that attracted nobility from all over Europe, especially the Russian nobility, who were frequent patrons there.

My grandfather, a noble man with dark straight hair and a well-groomed mustache, was the official bathmaster of the spa. He was fluent in both French and English and was well respected in our community.

When the Russian revolution broke out in 1914, the princes, counts, and dukes stopped patronizing the spa; this had a drastic effect on our lifestyle. Wealthy German and Austrian clients also stayed away because in the meantime a porcelain factory had opened, and its tall smokestacks were polluting the once clean, crisp air.

My father, mother, and grandfather were soon unemployed. After only a few weeks of idleness, my grandfather took a job in an insane asylum, but he didn't enjoy the work and resigned shortly thereafter. As a young man he had studied at a mining college in Freiburg, Silesia, where he had earned his degree and subsequently worked as director of a silver mine. A mining accident had taken the life of one of his closest friends; this in turn had prompted him to leave the area to come here, where he had taken the position as head bathmaster at the spa. Now he decided to get back into practicing his old profession, and he was lucky enough to be offered a position as managing director of a slate mine in the nearby small town of Lehesten.

After the First World War began, he relocated his family, and my parents were forced to move into an apartment of their own.

Shortly after my sister, Irma, was born my father was drafted and my mother went back to work as a hairdresser, only now she styled the hair of dolls that were manufactured in the porcelain factory.

I must admit that I can't remember much about the war years. I spent most of my preschool years with my grandparents and uncles in Lehesten, where they had bought a picturesque old stone house situated in a beautiful scenic valley where a mountain stream drove a large wheel to produce electricity for the house and nearby mill. The slate mine's owner turned the entire management of the mine over to my grandfather.

The year 1918 was eventful: I started school and was permitted to visit my grandparents only during summer vacation; my brother Ernst was born; and my father was severely wounded in action on the western front. Some Moroccan soldiers had cut his throat, and he had almost bled to death. Through sheer luck he had survived, and only a scar that stretched across his entire neck remained of this terrible incident. He had not come right home after the war ended, but instead had remained in the service, where he had been promoted to officer's rank and at the end to captain. In 1921, when all officers of the newly created Weimar army had to commit themselves for longer periods of duty, he was released due to his previous injury. Partially due to his own ignorance, and very unfortunately for us, he relinquished all his rights to any compensation.

In the meantime our family grew as my brother Adolf was born and my mother took in an orphaned girl named Irmgard. Now we were five children to be fed, and each one of us felt the pinch. As an artist, during times like these, my father would have starved. Fortunately, he got a job at the porcelain factory as a pattern painter and only then because he had been in the Reichswehr.

It was during this period that companies and factories frequently experienced strikes and disturbances. Then inflation hit, and it hit hard! My mother and I, the eldest child, would wait for my father to come home on Friday afternoons so we could take his pay and go food shopping right away. Inflation escalated overnight, and had we waited until Monday, we would have been able to buy only a third of what we had three days earlier. This went on for quite a while, as most of us remember.

One of my jobs was delivering newspapers to our neighbors. I could carry the papers under my arms; however, the money I collected for them had to be carried in a huge wicker basket strapped to my back. But even during those crazy times, our family never went hungry.

When I graduated from school in 1926, the inflation was over, but once again we felt the effects of the war: there were no jobs to be found or any apprenticeships to be acquired. I went job hunting for months with my father, looking for any position that might be available. I was not particular about what trade to choose. After several months I finally found a job in a glassworks as an apprentice glassblower. I had to agree to train for two years without pay. To my dismay, when the two years had passed and I was looking forward to my first paycheck, they hired new apprentices and I was laid off. The worst of it was that there was absolutely nothing I could do about it. Since I didn't have the means to start a glass workshop of my own I decided to leave my hometown and look for work elsewhere. I had heard about a glassworks in the nearby city of Jena that was looking for glassblowers in my specialized field. My parents were not exactly ecstatic about my decision, since I was barely sixteen years old. However, they decided to let me pursue my life away from home.

Shortly after breakfast on a cold November morning in 1927 I was on my way. My parents gave me some money for the train fare and a couple of marks as spending money to help me get through the first week. With a small cardboard box under my arm and my head filled with the greatest expectations, I left my hometown.

When I arrived in Jena, I walked straight to the glassworks on the outskirts of town, Schott & Genossen. To my distress, I was informed that there was no immediate opening for an artistic glassblower, but they did have an opening for a regular glassmaker apprentice. I would have to train for another two years, but afterward I would be able to make excellent money, I was told. Since I didn't want to go back home to burden my family or sit around idle with nothing to do, I had no choice but to stay and take the job. They assigned me a bed in one of the large sleeping halls. The company wanted to pay me only three marks a week, which wouldn't even have paid for my lunch at the cafeteria. I guess that they felt sorry for this skinny, pale-looking kid, since they did decide to pay me seven marks a week instead. Although that still wasn't enough, I did get by, supplementing my income by working as a laborer's mate on weekends. That gave me an extra five marks. With it I bought myself some wooden shoes, which I needed for working in the glassworks, and a new pair of slacks so I could at least change my clothes once in a while.

I got used to my new surroundings and the daily discipline and routine of hard work at the factory. I shared the sleeping hall with fifty young boys, most of whom were in the same predicament as I was. Each of us had a metal-framed bed with an uncomfortable straw mattress and a small cast iron cabinet that held our belongings. We did have the use of showers, toilets, a gymnasium, and the company library, which was stocked with more than fifty thousand volumes.

In the summertime, after working hours or on weekends, a few of us would get together and go exploring the Jena area. We roamed around the city and through the fields, where we could pick and eat seasonal fruits, such as apples, pears, and cherries. It was not against the law to pick fruits from the trees bordering the streets, so we took advantage of this and ate as many as we could, often with the most disastrous consequences.

After two years of apprenticeship, I was finally able to start working for wages with a glassmaker crew at the melting oven. My weekly salary of twenty marks was mostly spent on food. Food was very important to me. I was a growing young man and needed all the nourishment I could get to work at what was a demanding and laborious job. After I had saved a few marks, I wanted to buy myself a suit, but none of the local clothing stores was willing to extend me credit since I was still under age.

One evening as I strolled along one of the cobblestoned side streets, where children were playing on the sidewalks, I noticed a hand-drawn sign above a door: "Weissmann's Men's Clothes." There was no display window or any other visible sign of a traditional clothing store, but I decided to try my luck there. I entered and noticed right away that the owner was Jewish. Herr Weissmann came up to me and asked if he could be of assistance. When I explained to him that I wanted to buy a suit, he said that without my father's signature he couldn't extend me any credit. Trying to be friendly, he said that I could try on some suits if I wanted to.

I tried on two or three but took a liking to one in particular, a light brown English wool that cost about a hundred marks. It was a perfect fit and looked as if it had been tailored for me. Herr Weissmann was watching as I turned in front of the mirror. He smiled to himself and asked how much I could afford to pay down and what amounts I had in mind for installment payments. I promised always to be on time, and I kept my promise. From then on I bought all my clothes at his store, including shirts and socks. The service was always good, and I liked the fact that he trusted me. I reciprocated his kindness by bringing many good customers to his store.

Usually during my weekly visits to pay the installments we would sit and chat for a while. I learned that he had immigrated from Poland almost penniless. With the little money he had, he had gone from house to house as a vendor of household items, shoelaces, and shoe polish, which he carried around in a box strapped to his neck. He had jumped at the opportunity to buy his present business for a very small down payment. "I'm not rich and I probably never will be," he said, "but since I don't have any family I can live very comfortably on the income I have."

After a while my wages were increased, and this made it possible for me to rent a furnished attic room together with a fellow worker. In the building where we lived there were also a restaurant and a coffeeshop, where we ate most of our meals. Most of the boarders were university students, and at times as many as twenty-five were living there. A few were poor like us, but the majority came from well-to-do families.

Our landlady was a widow in her fifties, a round woman who obviously enjoyed her own cooking. She had a laugh as robust as her build and a temper as quick as her flashing blue eyes. Wisps of her tawny hair were always working their way out from under the scarf she wore when she worked in the kitchen, and she was forever tucking the strands back behind her ear. She took a special liking to me and encouraged me to sign up at the university. She offered to let me have free room and board, provided I would work for my food money as a waiter in her restaurant.

All this sounded very good, but in order even to consider passing the entrance exam at the University, I would have to complete several secondary school credits. Also, I didn't want to obligate myself to anyone and therefore declined her kind offer but took the job as waiter anyway. My working hours at the factory were from three A.M. until twelve noon. I usually arrived home around one o'clock, when I would have lunch at the restaurant with Herr Weissmann. We had our own little corner table close to the kitchen where we'd talk through the entire lunch hour. He was a man in his early sixties with very pronounced Semitic features, who spoke fluent Swedish as well as several Slavic languages. We never discussed politics or world affairs; rather, our conversations were about our own lives and those of people around us.

As the months went by the students who lived with me at the boardinghouse became more aware of the political changes sweeping Germany. Some supported Hitler, but the majority were dead set against the man and his politics. Our landlady, Frau Wenzel, was anything but a Nazi. She evicted any student who announced support for Hitler, swiftly and on short notice. "Hitler is fooling the people," she'd say. "He speaks of peace but means war! He just wants to take revenge against France and Russia to further his own economic goals. I've been through one war, and I'm not about to go through another. In the last one, my mother and I almost starved to death."

When the Nazi Brownshirts and the Communists started attacking each other openly in the streets, most people didn't seem to take the fighting seriously. However, other disturbances, such as strikes in the factories and mills, were more noticeable.

Schott & Genossen, where I was employed, was a corporation where most of the supervisors and even the management were Social Democrats. This made it extremely difficult for the National Socialist party to influence the corporation. Although I wasn't a Nazi or a Social Democrat, or even a political activist, I was chosen to represent the younger workers at our factory and became chairman of the Youth Council. My responsibilities consisted mainly of presenting workers' grievances to management. I was placed on the general works management committee.

Once, when one of the fellows working with me started greeting everyone overenthusiastically with the Nazi salute, someone knocked his front teeth out. Apparently, he had called another worker a "Jewish pig," and that had brought about the fight. Naturally, he came to see me to get compensation for his lost teeth out. I was obliged to report this incident to the works committee. After hearing the evidence, it decided to fire the man without any compensation as a troublemaker who had caused a disturbance.

Under normal circumstances, he would have been entitled to some kind of compensation depending on his tenure, but since he was accused of causing a disturbance at work they decided to fire him immediately. The young Nazi took his case to the labor court, and I was called as a witness. I told the facts as I knew them. As I left the courtroom, I was confronted by five or six SA men. One of them called out to me, "It will be your turn next." "My turn for what?" I asked. "Shut your trap," another one yelled, "or we'll knock out your teeth." At that same moment, some policemen appeared and ordered the Brownshirts to leave the premises. I was told by the police that they had harassed others besides me.

All this occurred before the Nazis' rise to power. On one occasion while I was working at the restaurant, a couple of bricks were thrown through the front window into the dining room. I'll never forget how outraged Frau Wenzel was. When we went outside to see who had done it, we saw six or seven Brownshirts running away. Of course, we called the police—their station was practically next door to us—but their response was that they could do nothing. Frau Wenzel swore that if ever an SA man entered her establishment she would single-handedly throw him out herself.

At that time I thought the government would eventually overpower the thugs. How wrong I was. When, with the help of the common parties, Hitler gained power in 1933, suddenly things at the factory changed. Quite a few of the devout Social Democrats turned out to be Nazi followers after all! Perhaps they were afraid of losing their jobs. Then one day the chairman of our works committee was arrested and dragged away under protest, together with three other committee members. I was among the first to receive a layoff notice. The reason given was lack of work. I could have protested since Youth Council members were protected from unlawful dismissal, but, remembering the fate of our chairman, I decided not to press charges. As time went by, I saw the cruelty and ghastly brutality of the Nazis. Every day people were picked up in their homes and in the streets and dragged away.

After hearing that I had been laid off, Frau Wenzel asked me to stay with her and even told me to keep the tips I received at the restaurant. Herr Weissmann also offered his support. He wanted to help me to start my own business, preferably leasing a small hotel or pension. We went out looking for possibilities but had no success.

Depression was spreading across the land like the Black Plague. In Jena alone, several factories had shut down and others like Schott & Genossen had cut their workforce. Dozens of small businesses had closed. Thousands of people were out of work. They could be seen on the streets, sometimes in groups of three or four standing on the corners, sometimes alone, sitting on a park bench or leaning against a building, restless men with worried expressions on their faces. Now I had joined them.

I slowly came to realize what a grip the Nazis would come to have on our lives and those of millions of other Germans. Many people thought Hitler's reign was just a phase that would disappear. It seemed to me that the only true rivals of the Nazis were the Communists, who were feared as much as the Nazis themselves. The catchphrase at the time was "Behold what's coming." What most people did not realize was that a high price would have to be paid for what lay ahead in the future. In the beginning, the Communist party was prohibited and any known member was arrested. Later on even the Social Democrats were hunted.

In Buchenwald, near Weimar, the Nazis set up a concentration/slave labor camp. Whoever arrived there was silenced, shot, or hanged. Only a few survived after being beaten and tortured, but none of the victims ever uttered a word or talked about their ghastly experiences, because they were sworn to secrecy. However, among family and friends, horrendous and unbelievable stories surfaced about life at Buchenwald. Whoever admitted to being an enemy of the Nazis was arrested and sent there.

Initially, actions against the Jewish population were handled very carefully. Although the Brownshirts were busy nailing up signs with catchphrases like "Don't Buy from Jews" or "The Jews Are Our Downfall," things were still under control. Of course, this changed later on when they started smashing windows and recording the names of and photographing people who patronized Jewish establishments.

Eventually, the Jew baiting got worse. In the eyes of the Nazis, the Jews were an incarnation of evil to be feared and hated. The system of terror that was established and upheld finally affected my friend Herr Weissmann. One day he told me he was going to emigrate to Vienna and open a business there. He asked me to come along. At the time it hadn't even occurred to me to leave Germany, for I considered myself to be a true and good German and wanted to remain one. An uncle of mine who had emigrated to the United States also wrote me to come and join him, but I declined for the same reason.

Had I known then what I know now, I certainly would have taken his offer, and I deeply regret I didn't.

One afternoon, suddenly and unexpectedly, a troop of SA men encircled Frau Wenzel's establishment and ransacked each and every room. She was accused of hiding Jews, which was not true. I recognized one of the Brownshirts as the man who had confronted me at the courthouse with "It will be your turn next." I took this as a warning and decided to leave Jena. I packed my suitcases, seven of them to be exact, and took the train to my parents' place. After arriving there I went to the labor exchange to ask for unemployment compensation. I was turned down since my father was employed as a relief worker earning twenty-two marks a week. On this meager amount he was also expected to feed me. In the meantime, someone advised me to join the volunteer labor service, where I would receive room and board.

Together with a former schoolmate who had joined the Brownshirts but was also out of work, I went to Weimar. At an unused airport, several old hangars had been converted into living quarters. The camp was run by the so-called Young German Order. Their flag in black, white, and red with an eagle adorning its center was displayed everywhere. This annoyed me a bit since Germany's flag was black, red, and gold.

We were given worn-out uniforms and shoes that didn't fit. My friend was ready to leave right then and there, but I convinced him to wait and see what would happen. During the evening a sergeant in military uniform gave a lecture on the labor service. He stressed the facts that the training would be tough but that in the end it would be worth it because once the Führer initiated compulsory military service it would be very easy for us to get into leadership positions. Well, my friend and I had anything else in mind but becoming soldiers. All we wanted was to get work.

The next morning, we had to line up in one of the halls. Even though it was late spring, it was still cold both outside and in, since none of the rooms had any heat. We were divided into working crews and assigned to do duty at Buchenwald concentration camp. I asked our leader what kind of work we would be doing there. "You'll find out when you get there" was his answer.

He had just left when the sergeant appeared again and gave us his orders. I had found out that he was actually the camp commander at Buchenwald. Apparently, he had overheard my question and called me and my friend forward. I asked again if this was a labor service, workforce, or military training, and I wanted to know what kind of work we would have to do at Buchenwald. The obvious happened: the sergeant almost bit my head off. In a voice full of fury he screamed, "Who do you think you are, asking idiotic questions like that?" I thought the question a reasonable one and also raised my voice when I asked, "Who says I don't have the right to ask a simple question?" "I do!" he snapped back. "And further- more, you have no rights here—only duties. Is that clear?"

It may have been clear to him, but not to me. "Forget about this labor ser- vice, then" was my answer. I had barely finished the sentence when he screamed at me like a madman, "Out with you no-good scoundrels! Someday you'll come crawling back on your knees begging us to take you in!"

"Oh, I don't think so!" I shot back. I need not tell you that we had to leave the camp within minutes. One of the fellows came over to me and said, "God, you really have guts to talk to the sergeant like that." Others packed us some food for the road. We barely had time to gather our belongings before we were thrown out.

So there we were, with just a few pennies in our pockets and a couple slices of rye bread and lard. To make our day even more exciting, it started to rain. We set off walking in the direction of Erfurt while we debated what to do next. Instead of going back home, we decided to go to Hamburg to find work on a ship. Actually getting to Hamburg was another story—we would have to go by foot and ask for handouts of food along the way.

Due to the heavy rain, we were forced to eat our bread earlier than we had planned, before it got completely soaked. We met a couple of traveling journeymen who were so hungry that we shared the bread with them. One of the men told my friend that he must not be seen in his SA trousers around the Thuringian Forest, for he would be killed on the spot.

After a five-hour hike we were hungry and drew straws to see who would go begging. We came to an inn, and it was my friend's turn to go in. Reluctantly he entered, only to appear again with just a cigarette in his mouth. "I'm sorry," he said, "I just couldn't do it. Instead I wasted my last thirty pfennigs on cigarettes."

"Well," I answered, "we'll just have to starve to death."

At the next house down the road it was my turn to try my luck. An old woman bundled in black from head to toe answered the door, complaining that I was the sixth person today to ask for handouts. Then she slammed the door in my face. We had no choice but to eat some unripe cherries from the trees bordering the road. That night we slept in an old barn.

The following morning luck was on our side. My uncle Walter passed by on his motorcycle, gave us fifty marks, and told us to go home.

At the next village, we asked the mayor for a free place to sleep. He handed us a pass and sent us to a nearby inn, where we expected to spend

the night. As it turned out, the innkeeper, who was paid from the municipal fund to put people like us up, sent us to his horse stable.

We never got to Hamburg. The rain wore us down. It rained almost
every day. When my shoes had several holes in the soles and my friend had
so many blisters on his feet he couldn't count them anymore, we bought
train tickets and rode back home.

I immediately went out looking for work, but I had no luck. I did have a
little bit of money stored away in a savings account, and once again I considered opening my own business. Out of curiosity I stopped by an import-
export business to inquire what items were asked for the most. The manager,
Herr Weinstein, who was very friendly, told me that they shipped a lot of
glassware to America, but that at the moment they had a large order for
nativity scenes. After I explained to him that I was about to open my own
business, he told me that he would buy a hundred mangers provided the
price was right. We agreed, and he gave me a sample to imitate and told me
to come back in a couple of days with the finished product.

Instead of buying the mangers ready-made, I bought the wood and built
them myself. We painted both them and the figurines, which I did have to
buy with money from my savings account. With so much artistic talent in
my family, it wasn't hard to come up with a beautiful finished product.
Herr Weinstein agreed. He was very happy with what I delivered and
placed another, much larger order.

Our twelve- to fifteen-hour workdays paid off. Everyone in the family,
even my youngest sister, Irmgard, helped in the production of the nativity
scenes. Irmgard's assignment was to glue the moss on top of the stable in
which the manger was placed. Word had gotten around of what fine work
we were doing, and within a couple of weeks orders were coming in from
several clients. Even though our price was very reasonable, we made a
good profit and I was able to pay back the money I had initially borrowed
from my savings. As our business expanded, we rented a large hall and
employed several people.

One day a Nazi official came to encourage us to join the Party. We
declined, giving lack of time as a reason.

It was about this time that I met the young girl who later became my
wife. She was employed as a salesgirl in a local bakery-café. One late
Sunday afternoon during our courting days we were on our way to a dance
in a small café outside the city. It was a pleasant walk since the café was
situated in a lovely forest.

On the road we passed two uniformed Brownshirts. Being engrossed in
our own conversation, we paid no attention to them. We had barely passed
them when they suddenly stood right in front of us. One of them barked,
"Why didn't you salute us?" "Why should I salute you?" I asked. "It's dark

and I can hardly see you, and besides that I don't even know you." The other fellow came up to me and made a gesture as if he wanted to hit me in the face. I quickly dodged him, but as I did his fist hit my girlfriend on her shoulder.

I took a firm grip on my walking stick and lifted it up to let him have it. Both men drew SA daggers. The other man, the one with the big mouth, snarled, "Come on, try to hit us!" My girlfriend pulled me back and kept me from hitting them. I had no alternative but to ignore them, especially since I had a woman with me. I was steaming.

The next day I went to see our village constable to report the assault. He gave me the name of a police officer in the city since he had jurisdiction only over the village. I then took my case to the city police and was told to go and file a complaint with the SA leader who worked at the local unemployment office. I arrived at his office late in the afternoon. The man didn't bother to get up. He sat behind his desk chewing on a pencil as I told him my story. When I finished he got up and said, "That was me and my assistant last night." "Well," I said, "then I would like to have a word with you—in private." "Whatever you have to say," came his answer, "you can say right here." However, his coworker got up and left the room. As soon as he was outside I demanded, "What is this, can't a person even be safe on the streets anymore?" He ignored what I said and demanded to know if I was a Party member or with the SA. I responded, "What does that have to do with it? I'm a citizen and under the protection of the law. I demand that you apologize here and now, and that includes your assistant." "I will never apologize," he said. "You did not salute the uniform. We work here the entire day for you guys while you're out going for walks. You'd better think over what you're asking me to do. And now I consider this case closed. I have work to do."

"Then," I said, "I'll see you in court." He gave a short laugh and said, "Do what you have to." With these words he left me standing there. I was furious and thought, now I do want to see how this will be handled in court and if there's still any justice left.

I hired the best lawyer in town, as I knew they would be found guilty and eventually would have to pay the costs. I paid the lawyer sixty marks, and he took the case. He commented that it was an insult, but he wanted to try to meet with my opponents first to rectify the situation.

As I left the building, I met Herr Weinstein, who asked me what I was doing at a lawyer's office. I told him my story. "I would have not gone to a lawyer," he warned. "These SA men are too influential." Obviously he had come to see a lawyer for a more important reason, but he wouldn't tell me what.

After about two weeks, I received a summons to see the lawyer in reference to a settlement. I went, but the accused didn't show up. Instead they had sent a letter, which the lawyer read to me. They accused me of being a traitor to the state because I showed no respect for the SA and what it stood for. Furthermore, I worked with and befriended only Jews and had absolutely no empathy for the National Socialist movement. "The letter has no relevance to your complaint, and if you like we can pursue this in court," said the lawyer. "The way I see it, you should win the case." I agreed with him.

My case finally came up. The two appeared in court out of uniform. I arrived with my lawyer. The judge was an older man. The two did not sit quite as confidently now; it was obvious they were nervous. The judge asked them why they had not gone to the meeting at the lawyer's office earlier. Both of them answered that they had pressing work to do and could not waste their time on such trivialities. The judge commented that they could have laid the problem to rest had they resolved their differences earlier; now it might become rather expensive.

"Are you ready to settle now?" he asked. "No," was the response. As the judge opened the case, one of the two asked, "How much will it be if we settle?"

"That depends entirely on the plaintiff, what he demands, how high the lawyer's fees are, and in addition there are the court fees," was the judge's answer.

The other man asked my lawyer how high his fees were and if they could pay in installments. The lawyer only said that that was not for discussion here. The judge then asked me what my demands were. I said, "I request a written apology to my girlfriend and myself, and additionally they should send a hundred marks to the Red Cross." The judge thought the request was a bit stiff but agreed. The judgment would rest on this. One of the fellows asked the judge how much the court fees would be, but the judge answered that this would be determined by the court's administrative offices. Both then agreed that they would settle but said that I should consider a verbal apology as they would not send me anything in writing. I was asked whether I'd agree to this, and after a brief discussion with my lawyer I accepted the settlement. Then, as far as I was concerned, the case was closed. Whether they ever paid and how much, I don't know. I do know that my lawyer returned my sixty-mark deposit by mail.

On another occasion, I was walking in the city with a school friend when we ran into a group of flag-waving Brownshirts. We didn't notice them as we were engrossed in a business discussion. All of a sudden four of them grabbed us, pulled us in front of the flag, and lifted our arms.

"This is how it's done. Remember that in the future!" They wrote down our names, but I never heard anything more about the incident. I imagine my friend straightened out the affair.

I went to see Herr Weinstein, who told me that our business association and plans would soon have to come to an end. He said the main branch of his business in New York wanted to close the stores here and he, as a Jew, would have nothing left. "Even though I'm an American citizen," he said, "I don't trust people around here anymore. They've already threatened me, which is why you saw me at the lawyer's office. I'm leaving for Paris to take over a branch there. It's too bad, Erich, you were a good supplier." This was in 1938!

That year my fiancée and I were married and built a house in the little village where we lived. Initially, we had plans to open another business, but my wife's uncle mentioned that the Siemens factory, which manufactured cables for the Wehrmacht, was still hiring. Without wasting any time, we rode our bicycles to the small town of Neustadt and inquired about the jobs. The director of personnel informed us that they hired only women. I told him flatly, "It's both of us or neither," and turned to leave. "Perhaps I can make an exception," he said. "You can start immediately." "We'll start on Monday," I answered. My wife was three months pregnant, and I really didn't want her to work. But for me it was important to have this type of job, since later on it could protect me from being drafted.

We both had relatively easy jobs inspecting the cables for visible defects. Although the work itself was easy, the smell of the tar on the cables affected me and I frequently suffered stomach upsets. Soon I was transferred to another, more responsible position. I sat in a small air-conditioned office with glass walls and was assigned to watch the instruments that showed, when the cable was immersed in water, whether it was waterproof or not. Eventually my wife had to stay home because of her pregnancy, which made it more difficult for us to meet the mortgage payments, but we managed.

In the late spring of 1939, our daughter was born and my mother-in-law came to live with us. My wife tended the garden and raised rabbits and chickens. I worked sixteen-hour days at the factory and received a good salary, roughly fifty marks after taxes, whereas the average worker earned only about thirty.

Because of my long working hours I was able to avoid becoming involved with the SA or the Nazi party. I wasn't the only one who wanted to stay out of the Party's grip in those days.

When the war started on September 1, the Nazis became more powerful and many people suddenly leaned toward their way of thinking. The early victories made the Nazis look even better than they deserved. No one dared to criticize them, and those who did ended up in concentration camps such as Dachau or Buchenwald.

I considered myself very fortunate not to be called to active duty, as my company declared me to be indispensable. We kept a low profile. But despite all these precautions, early in 1941 I received a summons from the SA to report, on a Sunday morning, to a local restaurant. No reasons were given. Initially, I was afraid that they had somehow found out that we were listening to foreign news broadcasts over our wireless radio set, or perhaps that there was some news from my hometown.

When I arrived, I saw that neither was the case, as some fifty to sixty other young men were already present. As it turned out, some of them were SA members and there were some who had already joined the Party. One of the SA men briefed us, talking mostly about defense tactics and how every German male up to the age of sixty should stand ready to serve and defend his country. The purpose of the SA was to make every man who had not been drafted into a useful and ready-for-action soldier. The main reason for this gathering was that everyone present could earn his SA sports badge. "Who wants to volunteer?" At first no one responded. One fellow said that he had fractured his leg the previous year and for that reason could not participate. As though they had been waiting for a "lame-duck excuse" such as this, the SA man in charge shouted, "If you can walk, you can serve."

As an example, they brought forward an older SA member who had been wounded during World War I, yet he had served in the SA faithfully for years and had never complained about his injuries. "Whoever does not want to work for his SA badge and thinks that he can shirk his duty will be drafted. No one is of such importance that he cannot be replaced," the leader said. With this they circulated a piece of paper entitled "Notification to Take the SA Sports Badge." A few SA members had already signed, and no one else dared to say anything now.

Probably everyone thought, as I did, that it was better to exercise a bit than die at the Russian front. The majority of the men present were not interested in Hitler or his war.

At the end of January 1942 I received my draft notice. I reported to the infantry in Coburg, where I trained for the next two weeks. Then we were sent to Domazlice in Bohemia for an additional two weeks of training. Most of the drilling consisted of walking, rifle practice, and singing marching songs. A regiment was formed, and we were shipped out in cattle cars.

During the night the train stopped in Karlsruhe at a train station immersed in darkness. We were supposed to get out and get coffee and food, according to a yelling woman who opened our boxcar door. Still half asleep, we reached for our canteens and dishes and jumped out of the car one by one. We found ourselves standing at the station and assumed the woman would supply us with food and coffee car by car. Suddenly, the train started to move. A station attendant assured us that the train was just moving to another track.

We stood there half naked as the red taillights of the train disappeared into the night. A short time later, another official wearing a red
cap came up to us and asked what we were still doing there. One of our
men answered that we were waiting for the train to change tracks.
"What?" exclaimed the attendant. "That train's gone, and I can assure
you it's not coming back." Now, of course, he was upset; apparently he
had not seen us standing there and he had let the train go. "Didn't any
of you dingbats hear the departing signal?" he screamed. We answered
that we had been asleep and except for the woman's yelling hadn't heard
anything. Now he wanted to blame the woman for what had happened.
But she quickly justified herself by saying that her only job was to supply
the men with food and drink, which she had done, car by car. She said
she had heard a whistle blow but had assumed it was meant for the
other train.

So there we stood, forty men, unshaven for three days and only partially
dressed. Some didn't have any shoes on; others didn't have their jackets or
their hats, and we had left our packs and rifles on the train. The train official had no idea where the train was headed. There was a corporal among
us who took us to the stationmaster, who didn't know what to do either.
All he could say was that nothing like this had ever happened before and
that we were probably all AWOL and we should be locked up.

Meanwhile, the official had sounded an alarm, and within a few minutes
a number of armed soldiers arrived. We spent the night under guard. In the
morning they were able to find out that our train had gone toward
Saarbrücken and only then had our commanders realized that we were
missing. Still only half dressed, we were put into a luxurious French train
car, first class, that was then hooked onto another train, and off we went
toward Saarbrücken. The car doors were locked and the key handed over
to the corporal. No one could get in or out. The only food we had was
what the woman had given us in Karlsruhe. The trip took an entire day,
and we arrived in Saarbrücken the following morning. During our trip we
had collected food stamps, which some of the men had with them, and
when the train stopped we asked the corporal to let us go and buy some
cold cuts and butter to go with the bread and coffee the woman had served
us. Two of the forty men had shoes on, but no jackets. We dressed them
properly and sent them shopping. At least we had some food now; without
the stamps we wouldn't have gotten anything.

Finally we were met at the station and transported on an open truck to
barracks at the other end of the city. Whoever saw us probably thought we
were a bunch of prisoners; we certainly looked the part.

Eventually we arrived in Orléans and saw our original train sitting on a
siding. When our transport leader saw us, he cheered. He was glad to see

us because he could already visualize himself in prison. Our belongings were still in the car, but our food rations were gone.

The trip continued in the direction of Paris, but we all got off in a small town nearby. There, at a troop training center, we were to be polished up to be shipped out again—to Russia.

It took us two weeks, traveling day and night, to cross through Germany into Russia. Several times we were shot at by English airplanes, and we had quite a few casualties.

The overcrowded train took us to Poltava, where we detrained. Our first orders were to assist in the battle of Kharkov. I was assigned as first machine gunner, First Platoon, First Company, First Battalion, 673rd Regiment, 376th Division, in the Sixth Army. Then I was sent to the front line.

Obviously, our command orders were changed because we missed the battle of Kharkov. We didn't get to see too much of Poltava since the railroad station was located on the outskirts of the city. Anyway, we were always taken around the larger towns or cities. Why this was the case, I don't know for sure. Apparently they didn't want us to come into contact with the Russians. All the necessary equipment to run a division, such as tanks, artillery, horses, wagons, and a field kitchen, were located in Poltava. The infantrymen were the first to set off in a southeasterly direction.

Our company commander, a first lieutenant, was an inexperienced, arrogant snob who rode on a black stallion with a monocle over his left eye. He had little, if any, knowledge of war leadership. The noncoms were also very young men straight out of school with no experience in the field. Under normal circumstances a noncom was supposed to head up the troop, but since there was no replacement available for him, I had to take the lead as first marksman in my troop. Once in a while, our company commander would ride up beside me and tell me to walk faster. I had always watched to make sure that our troop didn't fall behind, but when I followed his orders the troop was stretched out too far because the horse-drawn vehicles couldn't keep up. As long as there wasn't any enemy in sight this was all right, but it showed me that the man had no idea of how to lead marching troops. Theory is quite different. During training in the barracks we had never had to walk or march sixty kilometers at a stretch.

During the day, for the first two weeks, we saw neither Russian soldiers nor their planes. But at night the sky would be filled with planes. We moved sometimes south, sometimes north, but always steadily east. When we arrived in the Ukraine we couldn't help but notice the black, fertile soil. We passed through small villages where most of the people were friendly, but we were not allowed to drink from any of their wells or fountains, since they were supposedly poisoned. Since our field kitchen almost always lagged behind, thirst became an ever-present problem. Later on, our company commander placed two or more guards at each well to ensure that no one would take a drink. However, he made sure that his orderlies always carried at least four bottles of boiled tea around for him. Even though at that time we still had plenty of food in our field kitchen, many men robbed the peasants of their geese, chickens, and ducks. It didn't take very long for the initial friendliness of the people to turn into a fierce and understandable hatred.

The rainy season hit us hard. The soil, including the roads, turned into a bottomless mire where we wallowed around like pigs. At times the mud clutched us so tenaciously that we sank hip deep into the sludge. Our horse-drawn vehicles and ammunition wagons got stuck. We were in a very perilous situation, and our only hope was to make it to the next settlement.

Whenever we passed through a village—about every forty to fifty kilometers—we were able to take shelter and at least dry off. But it was becoming more and more difficult. Our troop was pulled farther and farther apart. The field kitchen lagged so far behind that it disappeared. Our company leader's handsome black stallion had to be shot because it broke a leg. During the fall he also lost his monocle. The loss of both his favorite horse and his monocle became unbearable for him. Now, that he was forced to walk like the rest of us, he asked me on several occasions to please slow down and not pull the troop too far apart.

At this point we made our first contact with the enemy—not on the front lines, but behind us. I believe the attackers were partisans, although we could never see them. Soon the miserable rains stopped and the weather cleared up and we advanced at a much steadier and faster pace. Our advance came to a halt at a larger village, where we were to reunite with our battalion.

A field camp was set up, but it took three days for the battalion to reassemble. But out of the momentary relief arose a new disaster. Our once magnificent Belgian-bred horses were nothing but skin and bones now, and most of them had contracted a mysterious disease that made them nod their heads uncontrollably. It was a pitiful sight to see the animals die one by one. With no horses left to pull our ammunition wagons, we were ordered to abduct some of the villagers' short-legged, half-wild horses. Even though we harnessed four to six horses to each wagon, they couldn't handle the load. Later, we reloaded everything onto smaller Russian wagons, and for a brief time we advanced at a steady pace.

The next region we passed through was covered with small hills of chalky soil that turned into a slippery white mess under our feet, making it extremely difficult to advance. We slid all over the place, and our uniforms were covered with the white stuff. Sliding down the hills, we were also easy targets for the Russians. By the time evening came, we had suffered thirteen dead and eleven wounded. There wasn't any way for us to avoid the hills. It took the battalion three days and nights to cross them. We were constantly forced to lie down in the wet white mess. Now the Russians were using flares and projectors to watch us. During the day, every once in a while a grenade would explode into a hillside. At last we came to a valley where a river flowed. Luckily, the water was not very deep and we were able to wade through it. The water reached up to our hips, and at least we could wash the white soil from our boots and pants while wading through the river.

At this point, the war really started for us. Now the enemy hit us from all sides with grenades, artillery, rockets, and low-flying airplanes.

I was walking farther up front with my group, so we were able to throw ourselves into the road shoulder for cover. They were aiming their bombs and grenades farther back on the wagons, which could not be hidden so quickly. At the next village we were met by a thunder of grenades, rifle shots, and machine guns. We could not attack, for the defenders would have shot us down like ducks. We had to employ artillery and dive-bombers to quell the Russians. Then there was a deadly silence, not a Russian to be seen. This was one of the delaying tactics they used. We were attacked again on the far side of the village. My company was trapped in a field without any cover. Our first lieutenant did not request artillery or airplane support but gave the command to attack. A few men got up to obey his command and were shot down immediately.

The officer threw himself down next to me and gave the order to open fire. "I can't do that," I said. "I only have a few shots left, and we'll all get killed. Besides, I don't see the other gunner anywhere."

The first lieutenant became outraged and yelled, "Damn you, you can't refuse to obey my orders!" As he spoke, he stood up to take over my machine gun. A bullet hit him in the neck, and he collapsed. Dying, he looked up at me as if to say "How right you were."

All this happened within a couple of seconds. I now had to assume that the Russians were aiming their fire at me. I yelled out for the other gunners to bring me some ammunition. One of them dashed up from behind me and practically threw the ammunition against my back. All of a sudden he screamed, "I'm hit!" and fell to the ground. Now I yelled for the third gunner to come and assist me so I could aim, but no one came. I cursed out loud. To be frank, I was scared to death that I would be the next target. Suddenly, a lieutenant from another group came out of nowhere and threw himself down next to me. He said, "Look, there's one sitting up in that tree; he's going to kill all of us." He took the machine gun and swung it over his legs onto his shoulder, and I took aim and opened fire in the direction of the tree.

I must have hit the Russian, since the next thing I heard was a crashing sound and the shooting stopped. What a relief! The lieutenant patted me on the shoulder and asked me my name. The other machine gunner appeared. He held his right arm up, and I saw that his hand was bleeding. It looked as if a finger was missing. He came up to me and hissed that it was my fault he had been shot at. Quickly I answered that I had needed the ammunition to save us all and that he should be grateful for not being one of the fatalities.

The sight in the fields surrounding us was horrendous—bodies of soldiers sprawled everywhere, soaked in their own blood. The ones who were still alive screamed for help, but our new troop commander insisted that we advance or we would be charged with desertion. What a moral disgrace!

After walking for several minutes, we entered a small village just past the tree I had shot at; a huge branch lay on the ground. Close by was a rather large hut. A Russian soldier appeared with his hands in the air, holding a rifle with a white scarf tied around it. One of the noncom officers from another group shot the Russian down with his machine gun without blinking an eye. The hut was actually a dugout that harbored about thirty armed Russians. After seeing the fate of their fellow soldier, they didn't want to come out, so our commander called in some engineers, who blasted the bunker into the air. There were thirty or forty dead, so that day the casualties on both sides were the same.

After we had a day of rest, a man rode up on a motorcycle, and I was informed by our company commander that I had to go with him before the regiment command post. He said he didn't know why.

After riding about an hour, we came to a large farmhouse. At the entrance stood an officer, a noncom officer, and two enlisted men. One of the officers must have noticed the puzzled expression on my face, because he said, "Don't worry, you're going to get a decoration."

As I entered I saw several high-ranking officers sitting around a table holding a council of war. I overheard our division commander, Major General Alexander Elder von Daniels, saying, "Gentlemen, if we're not able to beat the Russians on this side of the Don, we're going to lose this war." The regimental commander, Colonel Rupprecht, arose and walked over to welcome me. He took me in front of the conference table and said, "You are a brave soldier, and through your heroic action you saved the lives of many of your comrades; therefore, I present you with the Eisernes Kreuz [Iron Cross]." He shook my hand with intense sincerity and pinned the medal onto my uniform. "It's a high honor for me to pin this on you, especially since you're the first soldier in the division to receive one."

The other officers now came up to shake my hand. When Major General von Daniels did so, the ceremony was repeated. Upon our return to company headquarters, our troop commander, the sergeant, and other officers had no choice but to congratulate me when they noticed the medal pinned to my jacket. The sergeant was the first to break the silence when he asked me why I had received this honor. Truly, I was not able to give him an answer. I just repeated what Major General von Daniels had told me, that I was a brave soldier who had saved many lives. The only incident I could recall was shooting that Russian out of the tree.

That same day everyone in our company received a bottle of schnapps and twenty-five cigarettes apiece. I decided not to drink in order to keep a clear head. That must have been foresight, since the next day we were engaged in a big battle without warning. Orders came for us to attack a wooded area. At first all we heard were a couple of shots here and there, but otherwise there was no resistance; we didn't see any enemies. Suddenly, we were attacked mercilessly with heavy artillery—our own. Twelve of our men were shredded to pieces, and more than twenty were wounded. Confusion set in, no one knew what was going on. A few of the soldiers were still under the influence of alcohol from the night before and couldn't function well. Due to the deadly grenades, shredded pieces of human limbs were hanging from the trees and the bushes dripped with blood. Bile crept up our throats and we threw up, for none of us had ever seen anything so horrendous.

To make things worse, the bushes came alive with Russian tanks. Most of our men fled, but a few started shooting at the tanks with their rifles, not realizing that they were digging their own graves, because the Russians reciprocated by emptying all their guns at us.

I screamed, "Get into the bushes, you idiots, and lie down!" All this occurred in less than three minutes. The tanks swung to the right and disappeared into the woods, crushing quite a few of the wounded as they passed. Our troop commander came out from behind a bush and told us that our artillery had seen the tanks before we did, and that this was the reason they had aimed so close. For the next few moments the scene was one of panic. No one knew what to do. Luckily, my group was still together. Our new corporal, who turned out to be even worse than the last one, came over to join us. We got orders to advance one kilometer into the woods and take up a hedgehog position. We had no enemy contacts and formed a circular defense position within earshot of one another. The two machine gunners and I lay down on a hill covered with field grass. The Russians had been there before us.

There was silence now. Only the soft whistling of the wind and the singing of birds could be heard. The three of us took turns sleeping since we were emotionally and physically drained from all the excitement that day.

It wasn't until late in the afternoon that the rest of our troop appeared. They were now all overly cautious. The slightest cracking of a branch or rustling of a bush would set off gunfire. We advanced farther into the forest and, after walking for about three hours, arrived at a clearing. I was ordered to go with my two gunners to set up a post on a hill on the other side of the valley before us. The valley had a shallow river flowing through it that we had to cross. The entire terrain was marshland. Our second gunner went back to the field kitchen to get some food.

Once dusk had set in, we were attacked by tormenting hordes of tiny, almost invisible gnats that managed to get through our mosquito nets and bite our faces and hands. Although we never really noticed their bites, within a few minutes our faces and especially our eyelids were swollen beyond recognition. The following morning, we looked at one another in disbelief; it looked as if our entire company had contracted the mumps.

Regardless, with our deformed faces we started marching south along the river. Most of the villages we passed were on the other side of the river. I observed that the settlements were always a way up the valley slope, apparently to avoid flooding. The valley narrowed, and we had to cross a shabby-looking wooden bridge. Then we advanced straight east for the entire night. The following morning we had left the wooded area behind and came to the half steppes. There were no roads or any paths through the fields anywhere.

During the day it was unbearably hot, and at night the freezing cold made our joints stiff. This constant change from a saunalike environment to a winterlike freeze took its toll on us. But we had to go on. We passed through a few scattered settlements where the people didn't know that there was a war going on and that we were Germans. They spoke their own language, which didn't even resemble Russian. We had to advance fifty or sixty kilometers a day in the steaming heat. Slowly the steppe turned into rugged terrain with deep, wide gorges that had to be crossed. It looked as if these gorges had been either riverbeds or ditches at one time.

Now it was impossible for our vehicles and our field kitchen to follow; they just couldn't get over the gorges. The farther we advanced into the steppe, the worse our situation became, especially with regard to food. The nomads clad in animal skins and the people living in settlements didn't have any food themselves. They lived mostly on honey, goat or sheep milk, and the meat of those animals. Bread as we know it was unknown to them. They all chewed sunflower or millet seeds continuously, which gave them a special oily body odor. We could smell them before we saw them. At one point we entered a settlement of primitively constructed clay and straw huts where we found only women and children.

Being in the lead of our troop was to our advantage, since we usually got something to eat. These people had not much food themselves, so they could only give us what little they had.

We kept on marching for three days, with nothing to eat or drink. It was quite a task to haul around seventy-five pounds of equipment on our backs in the unbearable heat. Our field kitchen had ceased to exist. Our last meal had been a watery soup mixed with sand and topsoil.

We arrived at one village where we located a Russian food supply dump; we thought all our troubles were over, at least for the time being. There were crates filled with slab bacon, sugar, hard bread, noodles, and even bars of soap.

All this was at our disposal now, but none of us was able to get down a single bite. We hadn't had any water to drink for several days, and even here there was no water to be found. We were allowed to camp for only a couple of hours before it was time to advance. Of course, we stuffed our canteens, pockets, and whatever other containers we could find with food and supplies. Not too far from this village I located a pond. Under normal circumstances, nobody in his right mind would have taken a drink from its water, which was covered with slimy algae and insects. When I saw the water all I could think was drink, drink, drink! And so I did. Half insane with happiness, I filled two canteens to the top, lay down on my back, bent my head back, and opened my mouth while I let the awful brew flow down my throat without even swallowing.

The rest of the men came running and didn't even bother to use their canteens; they threw themselves down onto the ground and slurped up the water like dogs. Some of them jumped in and immersed themselves while drinking. Rapidly the green-looking pond turned into a brown mud puddle.

It took us a while before we were able to get some food down. We started out with the bacon pieces and advanced on to the bread, which was more difficult to eat since it was hard as a rock. However it didn't take long for the contaminated water to take its effect. We all came down with diarrhea. Every two to three minutes we had to stop at the wayside to relieve ourselves. Some of the men didn't bother to put their trousers back on; they just swung them over their shoulders and let nature take its course while they marched on.

To make the situation worse, we were suddenly attacked by low-flying airplanes. We now had to worry about the screaming of the wounded. Two men were shot. Although our platoon leader had not drunk any of the water, he jumped around like a madman. We didn't have any medical orderlies in our outfit, but there was a doctor who had only a few bandages left. The poor man wailed out of sheer frustration that he couldn't help. We were afraid the planes would return, but they didn't.

Our platoon leader stressed that we had to go on and reach our assigned destination. The doctor remained behind with the many wounded. Although we started marching again, we were still not able to reach our goal. Suddenly Russians were everywhere, attacking us from all sides.

So there we were, scared to death, sick as dogs, with excruciating stomach pains and diarrhea. Some of the men collapsed while walking and had to be supported by two other men. Luckily, night came fast. We camped in a hedgehog formation since we expected to be attacked during the night. As far as the eye could see, the sky was illuminated by flare lights. For us this was a sign that the Russians had built up a front. In the course of the night planes flew over us, dropping bags full of small bombs. We lay there on the ground clenching our teeth together, we were so afraid of being hit. We were so tired and worn out that even our guards were too weak to keep watch. One of the men was awakened by a nightmare and started shooting. Of course, the rest assumed that we were being attacked by the enemy and fired their guns in all directions. The bullets whistled through the night, and it was a miracle no one was killed. After this incident, totally exhausted, we were overcome by sleep.

The following morning, we started marching again, a funeral procession. Our original destination had been changed, and we received new marching orders to advance south. We were told we would have to march only sixteen kilometers, but as it turned out we had to march through half the night and must have covered about sixty kilometers instead. Even our platoon leader was outraged. That night we camped close to a riverbed, and all of us collapsed into a deep sleep. Had the enemy attacked us that night, there wouldn't have been any resistance on our part.

The next morning a couple of the men were unable to get up. They had jaundice. The first lieutenant screamed at them, but this didn't help because they couldn't move, they were much too weak even to lift their heads. They had to be left behind. There was no doctor, no shelter, no foreseeable help for them.

The remaining troop advanced east. In the course of the day we met two motorized radio dispatchers who helped us set up better communications. One of the drivers left us a large canister filled with drinking water and two loaves of bread. But what are two loaves of bread among eighty men? After a couple of hours we were told we could rest for two days. We were lucky, as we found a small hamlet to set up camp in where even drinking water was available. The village population consisted of a few old women. There wasn't anything edible to be found. A few tomato plants with still-green fruits, one or two apple trees with unripe fruits, and a couple of white cabbage heads were all there was. The sky was cloudy, and it looked as if it was about to rain. Everyone now tried to find a house to take shelter in. My two machine gunners and I were looking forward to spending the night under a roof. We entered a one-room house where a substantial amount of space was taken up by a huge oven that extended over an entire wall. The top surface of this oven was flat, and several people could sleep on it.

One of the men in my outfit spoke Czechoslovakian, which is somewhat related to Russian, and asked the sole occupant of the hut—a sick old woman—what was the matter with her. She answered that she was suffering from bad headaches and hadn't been able to eat for days. The interpreter thought that if she hadn't eaten, there might be some food left for us. He told her, "We have a good doctor here"—pointing at me—"who will cure you fast." After he translated I caught on and moved over to the bed and placed my hand on her forehead, looking concerned. I reached into my pockets for some quinine tablets we had been given to fight off malaria, dissolved ten of them in some tea, and gave it to her to drink. After about fifteen minutes she got up from the bed and joyously announced that her headache was gone. Now some other women came up to me and asked what kind of miracle medicine I had given her. Instead of giving them an answer, I gestured that we were hungry. Through the interpreter I let them know that I would give them some of this wonder drug provided they would feed us.

It wasn't long before one of the women appeared with a huge iron kettle filled with cooked meat. Where she had hidden this was a mystery to us, since we had searched the entire area. After we had eaten I gave the other women five tablets each and advised them to take this medicine only when their headaches were severe.

When twilight set in, the women left us to ourselves. But we had hardly finished washing when orders came to break camp. There went my dream of sleeping in a real bed. This was insanity. First we had been told to rest for two days, and now we had to break off again, unrested and ill and in the middle of the night. Even our platoon commander was upset, I noticed. Our first lieutenant didn't report to duty, and after searching all the houses and the surrounding area in vain, we had to leave without him. We marched straight south for the rest of the night. There were no roads, only rugged terrain with one gorge after another to cross. The night was bitter cold, but in a way we were happy to be on the move. Yet we were nothing more than a group of staggering, starving men, in no condition to fight for their country.

When morning dawned we saw some tanks that turned out to be German, although not from our division. They were heading in the direction we had just come from. We were informed that we were too late and that there was no more action going on around here. This made us happy, and visions of having a well-deserved rest and sleep ran through our minds.

But lo and behold, about a thousand meters to the south of us all hell suddenly broke loose. About twenty Russian tanks attacked a company that didn't belong to our division. Our orders didn't call for attacking, so we just kept quiet. That was the first intelligent decision our commander made. Finally, a couple of our scout planes appeared and the Russian tanks retreated toward the east. The shooting stopped. Our communications dispatcher wasn't able to make contact because there was something wrong with the radio. Our destination was still a few kilometers to the south.

When we arrived at the battlefield, a lieutenant came up to me. "What do you want now? There's nothing left here but a graveyard full of dismembered bodies. You should have arrived earlier, and our tanks should have come to assist us instead of pulling off to the north. Didn't you pass them?" he asked. Once more our air scouts had failed completely. He continued, "Our orders were to act as an advance platoon to detain the Russian tanks until our tanks could offer relief. But I'm the only one left alive out of the entire platoon. The others are either dead, captured, or walking around in a stupor somewhere. I haven't seen any of my men."

Our radio dispatcher still wasn't able to set up communications. The lieutenant joined our outfit. After a three-hour walk we finally arrived at our assigned objective, a bridge over a river. The riverbanks were covered with underbrush and small trees and bushes, so it was easy for us to camouflage ourselves. Our meat rations had spoiled, and we had to drink water from the river just as the locals did. Even our platoon commander didn't complain about this anymore. We managed to establish radio contact again, and our new orders were to remain stationary until the rest of the battalion arrived. I set up my machine gun between two bushes for air defense. Then I removed all my clothing and jumped into the river, as all the others did. Apart from the splashing of water, all was quiet and serene. On the other side of the shore were a couple of farmsteads. Through my binoculars I saw goats and sheep grazing undisturbed in the green meadows.

My two machine gunners asked permission from our commander to go and find some food for us. He agreed. I followed them through my binoculars as they climbed up the steep embankment on the other side. After a couple of minutes, as I saw them returning, sliding down the embankment, we heard the engines of an approaching airplane. It was a Russian bomber that had spotted our men and was now headed for the bridge. Our two men jumped back up the embankment to take cover as I covered them with my machine gun, but it was too late. Two or three bombs were already falling. As fast as the plane had come, it disappeared. Luckily, our men had survived and came running across the bridge with their faces and clothing blackened with smoke and dirt, but the two containers of goat's milk they had managed to get hold of had spilled during the encounter.

The next two days, which we spent waiting for our battalion to arrive, would have been almost enjoyable, but without food in the stomach they were an ordeal. I ate watercress from the river. Some of the others tied their mosquito nets together and caught some tiny fish, which they baked over an open fire. When our battalion finally got there, we were eager for food, but all they had to offer was moldy bread. We cut out the spoiled parts and ate what could be saved. Even our platoon commander had to eat it. I overheard him complaining to the lieutenant that a company without food and decent drinking water cannot fight a war.

The first company divided to cross the bridge and protect the battalion. They assigned us two antiaircraft guns, the two radio dispatchers, and the lieutenant from the other outfit. He took over the command of my group. Our assignment turned out to be lucky after all, because we arrived at an area that hadn't been touched by the war. People still had plenty of food and livestock and didn't mind sharing them with us. We felt again how good it was to drink a glass of milk, eat a fresh egg, and taste freshly baked bread.

We passed through a neat village where we saw a large two-story frame house. We entered and found the owner to be a pharmacist who spoke German fluently. All the shelves in his store were empty, and so was the supply room. He told us that since the previous year he hadn't received any medical supplies. He also explained that the village forefathers were Germans who had settled this area several generations ago. The old man continued telling us that life had changed drastically around here since Joseph Stalin had taken over the country. People had lost interest in tilling the land and worked only as much as their family really needed. A couple of the peasants had been shipped off to Siberia, he said, but even these drastic measures didn't seem to bother the people.

The lieutenant remarked to me that we had to be careful; people like this talk nice and friendly to your face and then stab you in the back. This old man doesn't exactly look like a back-stabber, I said. He brought us some fresh straw, and we bedded down on the first floor of the house. The following morning we went to look for the old man, but he wasn't anywhere to be found. We searched all the houses and found that the entire male population had disappeared overnight. Only a couple of old women were left. All the food and supplies were gone, too. When we confronted the women, they shook their heads and acted as though they didn't know anything. Before we left they brought us a couple of eggs and a canister filled with milk. That same day we broke camp and didn't arrive at the next village until late that evening. Although it was already dark outside, we did notice an old man sitting on a bench in front of his house. He was knitting something in the light of a lantern. The rest of the village was immersed in darkness, and no one was visible, not even the animals.

The old man didn't speak any German, but he did understand our Czech interpreter, who asked him where everybody had gone. Initially he tried to ignore us but decided to answer when the interpreter gave him a slight shove. He told us that all the men, women, and children had left during the night but he didn't know where they had gone. We searched all the houses and stables and found the information to be correct. The food and supplies were also gone. The old man had two eggs hidden in a cabinet, but I told my gunners to leave them for him.

Our commander decided we should camp here and spend the night. My third gunner and I took first watch. Night had fallen, and it was completely dark outside. The village looked like a ghost town. We walked over to a house situated on the outskirts, where we felt we had a better overview of the area.

As we opened the door to the house, two women jumped up and quickly disappeared through a door leading to the stables. My buddy lit his cigarette lighter so we could see, and we found a candle sitting on the table and lit it. Now we had a better view of the interior. In a corner were two leather suitcases and two neatly folded parachutes. We brought one of the suitcases to the table and pried it open, since we thought it might contain food. Instead, we found medical instruments and supplies and in the other suitcase elegant woman's silk undergarments and quite a bit of Russian money. It was our duty to report this immediately, but we felt our comrades needed some sleep and so did we.

After an hour our relief came. Before going to sleep, I thought it best to go and check out the stable. Inside, there was another, larger suitcase filled with ammunition. Leaning in a corner were several guns and pistols. Our relief guard felt we should report this since there might be partisans close by. I went to awaken the lieutenant, who said he had felt something was not right ever since we had set foot in this place. He quickly gave the information to our commander, who gave orders to awaken everyone and prepare for a counterattack. We stayed awake the rest of the night, waiting to be attacked, but nothing happened. The next morning, half asleep, the commander and lieutenant examined all the suitcases and had the ammunition and the stacks of rubles thrown into a nearby well.

We broke camp again and marched on for two days without incident. Once again, at a bridge, we had to wait for our battalion to secure the crossing. There were a couple other companies present when we arrived.

On the following day the battalion was once more complete and gathered on a hill not far from the bridge. Our company was still sixty-two men strong. Another outfit—with heavy artillery, two tank destroyers, and an ammunition vehicle that looked like a small tank—was assigned to us.

In the middle of the night, we broke camp and started advancing toward the east at about fifty to seventy kilometers a day. We saw no people, animals, or birds. We had arrived at the wide-open steppe.

At this point, a tank crew gave us a can of gasoline, which the driver of our ammunition vehicle immediately emptied into his tank. It was already too late when he noticed that the can contained water instead of gasoline. What a catastrophe! It took us all day to clean and rebuild the engine before the car would even start. Luckily we had two more cans of gasoline, otherwise we would have had to carry all the ammunition on our backs. Apart from wasting an entire day working on the motor, our first lieutenant lost his compass. Our orders had been to advance east up to the Don River. The sky was cloudy, and in the open steppe it is extremely difficult to tell direction. Once in a great while we would pass by a surveying point, usually mounted on a wooden pole with a cross on its top. This made a lot of sense to the local people, who were somewhat familiar with the area, but not to us, since they were not marked on our maps. But we could determine direction by the poles, whose weather-beaten side always faced west. So we kept advancing until after a couple of days we came across another outfit of German soldiers, who told us where we were. We were in the vicinity of the Don River–Volga canal, which had not been our assigned objective. Our orders had been to advance to the small Don River bend.

Making a correction, we marched steadily north and finally reached our battalion and the regiment. We feasted on bread hard as rocks, slab bacon, and tea, and then our entire company advanced northeast for two days toward the original place of assignment.

The first platoon, equipped with three heavy machine guns, was assigned to occupy a hill from which the town and the river area could easily be observed. On the way there we had to cross a shallow swamp. On the other side we rested, and I tried to get some drinking water from the ground by digging a narrow but deep hole with my spoon and waiting for the water to filter through the sand and dirt. It worked well, and I was able to fill one of my canteens. The other soldiers decided to come back later to fill their canteens. On the main hill stood a surveying cross where we were supposed to dig ditches to take cover, but since none of us had brought any spades or shovels, it was useless even to try. About a hundred meters closer to the river was another hill. I walked over to check it out and found a position already prepared for cover, one made out of wood and cement. I returned and asked the corporal if my gunners and I could set up position there. He didn't see why not. So my two gunners and I, a medic, and two other soldiers from my squad took up a position on this hill overlooking a wide, peaceful valley. One of the gunners, a young fellow from Nürnberg, went back to the hole I had dug to get some more drinking water. Our lieutenant gave orders to chop down the cross. I really don't know why he gave that command, it made absolutely no sense to me. And, as it turned out, it betrayed our location to the Russians.

Twilight came, bringing with it the tormenting insects that nibbled at us mercilessly. We had discarded our mosquito netting, so we had nothing to protect ourselves from them. As it grew dark, I saw several crouched-over soldiers approaching, materializing from behind a large pile of straw in the direction of the big hill. Our lieutenant called us to join them. I recognized our doctor, whom we had left behind with the wounded, and our former first lieutenant. The remaining men were four high-ranking officers, including our division commander, General von Daniels. He recognized me and asked how I was. Standing next to him, I noticed he was a rather short person.

"Comrades," he said, "you have an extremely difficult task ahead of you. We have just been informed that the Russians will attempt to cross the Don tonight. Your immediate assignment is to open fire at everything that moves, especially the machine gunners. You will be relieved around four A.M. so you can catch some sleep." With these words the officers turned and left quickly, leaving only the doctor behind.

Our machine gunners returned with two empty canteens and a third one only half filled. At least we had something to drink, though it tasted awful. The night was quiet and short. Around two A.M., as dawn broke—in the summer in that part of the country it gets light about then—a heavy grenade hit where the cross had stood and several others followed close behind. We jumped into our ditches as fast as we could and thought, this is it! We could hear or see no sign of the enemy.

Our Nürnberger gunner called out from the straw pile that he was hit, but the medic didn't move from his ditch. I got angry and jumped up and half crawled over to the straw. Only the night before the members of our squad had sworn to one another that if one of us got injured we would help, no matter what the circumstances. When I arrived at the pile, the fellow was lying on the ground with his behind exposed and bleeding. He said he had been going to the bathroom when he was hit. He couldn't move, and he was still trembling with fear as I half carried, half dragged him over to our position. Several meters from our ditch, the medic came crawling out of his hole to assist me. The gunner was lucky after all; a grenade splinter had barely scratched him across his backside.

I asked the medic if he thought we should sneak over to the hill to find out why it was so deadly quiet there. If they had evacuated the hill without notifying us, we'd be responsible for holding back the Russians ourselves, single-handedly. We snaked over on our bellies only to be confronted by a horrendous sight: bodies of what once had been men and parts of machine guns, totally dismantled and lying about. It was the most appalling scene. Heads, shredded limbs, arms, hands, and feet were strewn everywhere in pools of blood. Both the medic and I vomited. We noticed one man still moving and rushed over to him, only to find a human being without a face; his head was still attached to his body, but his face was completely torn off. Since he was still alive, we decided to drag his body to the straw pile, where we found the doctor and our radio dispatcher. We barely made it before the man died.

The doctor said if they hadn't removed the surveyor cross on the slope, none of this would have happened. I certainly had to agree. We now saw that there were several other wounded who had been able to get away, lying behind the straw heap. A young, husky-looking fellow from my squad sat up holding his chest. I eased over to him and asked him where he had been hit. He was able to pull off his shirt to expose a tiny, perfectly round hole in his chest. "I'm afraid it's not enough of an injury to be shipped home," he said. Suddenly, having barely spoken the sentence, he turned pale and keeled over against the straw. Blood gushed out of the corner of his mouth, soaking the straw and the ground beneath him. Then he raised his arms above his head and died.

The doctor said matter-of-factly, almost lethargically, "Internal bleeding, there's not much to be done." After checking him over, the doctor turned toward me with a bewildered and angry look in his eyes. "You know, Erich," he hissed between his teeth, "the youth of our country is bleeding to death here in this godforsaken rat hole, and with it is going the future of our fatherland." Raising his voice, he hammered away, "I'm an officer, but I could kick myself for not opposing these ludicrous orders of Hitler's generals. They seem to have only one goal in mind, and that is to kill each and every one of us. Apparently, the army is the sacrificial lamb. The only thing left for us is to shoot ourselves because none of us, and I mean not one single person, is going to get out of this hellhole alive."

The man had talked himself into such a rage that I thought for a moment he had lost his mind. I had never heard an officer talk with such hatred. Of course, he was right. It seems that only the younger generation can be enthused by war, and consequently they also become the victims. A war cannot be won by old men.

Once again the valley had become peaceful and the light fog that had settled over the river disappeared and revealed the smoothly flowing waters again. The river had an almost timeless feel to it; there were no boats, no bridges, no Russians to be seen. Shortly after two in the morning, things started up again. Some soldiers arrived with bicycles on their backs—our relief platoon, it seemed. I screamed at them to be careful, that we were under fire, but somehow this didn't faze them, they kept walking toward us, about twenty men with a corporal and sergeant in the lead. The sergeant came up to me and asked where our position was set up. I pointed toward the hill. I also told him that our own organized position here had saved our lives. He then told me that they were our relief assigned to hold off the enemy and that his group was only an advance detachment. More were on their way with heavy artillery to be set up on the larger hill.

We gathered our belongings and equipment and moved over to the straw pile, where the doctor, the medic, and the radio dispatcher plus two other men from our platoon were stationed. Among them were a half-dozen severely wounded soldiers and several dead. The radio dispatcher informed us that there were only dead on the main hill and that the wounded were being picked up to remain here with the medic while we were to advance west. "Aren't we supposed to meet up with our battalion down in the valley?" I asked. "They were relieved last night and left early this morning," he said.

Completely exhausted, with nothing to eat or drink, we kept walking through this desolate area for hours on end, our company in the lead as always. We rested for about two hours out of sheer exhaustion. The moment we hit the ground like felled trees, we fell asleep. Before advancing again we were given some tea and Russian bread. A sergeant had taken over the rest of the platoon as we kept marching west. After about three hours, we turned again, this time toward the south. My squad marched five hundred meters ahead of everyone else.

An old, bearded man in a shepherd's outfit approached us, asking for a light for his cigarette. We didn't have any, so we pointed toward the back, where the rest of the men were walking.

After another kilometer, we spotted a couple of mines on the road. We waited for the rest of our troop to catch up so we could warn them about the mines. A couple of the officers and our first lieutenant came up to the front. After deliberating for a while, they came to the conclusion that the old shepherd must have planted the mines since there were no other Russian troops in the immediate vicinity. They sent a motorcyclist to go and fetch the old man and bring him back for questioning. The man obviously didn't understand what the officer asked him, nor did he seem to know what the objects were when the lieutenant pointed in the direction of the mines. The Russian had just bent forward to pick up one of the mines when one of the officers kicked him from behind so he fell to the ground. They thought the old man was going to set it off. The man just lay there on the ground without moving. Then the officer who had questioned him pulled out his pistol and shot him through the back of the head. To justify his action, he told us the old bastard was probably a partisan pig and he had had no choice but to kill him.

My squad had to move up front to set up a protection post. We walked deliberately, at a slow pace, since we had found several other mines. Some of them were still exposed, and the spades with which they had been dug in were still lying around on the winding footpath. As we advanced south, the area became more alive; at least we passed a village now and then. The wheat had ripened, and the peasants were busy harvesting. We were able to get some real food to eat—eggs, chickens, and ducks. All of the larger livestock, cows, goats, and pigs, must have been hidden in caves, since the people had plenty of milk. Once, outside one of these villages, we came into contact with some Romanian soldiers—our allies. Since their uniforms were very similar to what the Russians wore, we almost opened fire on them. None of us had been informed that they were operating in the area. They certainly were well equipped with food and supplies. They shared delicious corn bread, pork lard, and wine with us.

The Romanians had come from the west with instructions to advance east. We stayed there the entire night, resting. Our battalion had completely reassembled. Through the constant firing of Russian signal rockets, we were able to see the front clearly. Russian bombers were flying above us, dropping their bombs, throughout most of the night. It was obvious they had spotted us the previous day.

The following morning, we received orders to advance eastward again. Once more we marched through the endless steppe. We passed demolished Russian tanks that had been shot to pieces. From the look of the fields, it must have been some battle that took place. Our command didn't seem to be too certain about which direction to take because we took a zigzag course first toward the north, then toward the east, then once again northward.

Suddenly and unexpectedly, we were attacked by the Russians in full force. They came toward us in a broad front, their infantry taking cover behind their tanks and yelling "Hurrah, hurrah!" as they fired at us. As fast as they had appeared, they retreated, leaving our battalion with thirty-three dead and twenty-one wounded. The Russians had lost three men, and they took their wounded with them. Then low-flying planes appeared and bombarded us with machine-gun fire. We had no more casualties, perhaps because before they attacked we had decided to get off the road. However, the fear remained with us during the entire day, although there were no further attacks.

Our battalion assembled again that night, ready for advance and combat. My company flanked the battalion to the north. After we walked just a few kilometers there was another mass attack. Russians charged at us from everywhere. We threw ourselves to the ground as fast as we could and counterattacked. Suddenly there was silence. An eerie silence. Our first lieutenant yelled out, "Get up and get ready for assault." No one obeyed him, so he stood up waving his pistol about. A Russian bullet penetrated his hip. He screamed for help but no one volunteered, since he himself had given orders not to assist the wounded during combat. Then the Romanians came from the flank and counterattacked the enemy, and the Russians had no choice but to surrender. We took forty prisoners and one dead first lieutenant. Most of the soldiers were Mongolians, whom we turned over to the Romanians. I took along only one of the prisoners, a schoolteacher from Odessa who happened to speak some German. He carried my machine gun and cursed Stalin all the way, insisting he had lost the war for the Russians.

Once again we advanced to the east, only to be given orders to halt. Our battalion was spread out with my company flanking it in the east. We were told to dig ditches and ready ourselves for another massive attack by seven Russian armored divisions in the early-morning hours. Our company leader was now a second lieutenant. We set up an antiaircraft gun on a small hill. The gunner told me that he had only nine rounds of ammunition left and that they certainly were not suitable for attacking heavy tanks. We dug our holes, but not very deeply, since we only had one spade to go around. The Russian prisoner helped me dig mine and camouflaged it with thick grass from the steppe. I had noticed that the Russian had worked up a thirst because yellow foam started building up in his mouth. He asked me if he could go find some water. Initially, I thought he just wanted to escape, but since all of us were thirsty, I gave him permission. Where he would find water around here was a puzzle to me.

He insisted that he had smelled water and would be back shortly. Three hours passed—I had already given up on him—when he reappeared, smiling, with a small wooden barrel over his shoulder. Next to him walked another Russian who was carrying a bunch of onions and some Russian bread. "I found this man wandering around," he said, "and since he had no place to go, I brought him along." "All right," I said, "he can stay, but we'll consider him a deserter. Now let's hear where you found this water!" He answered that he was a clairvoyant and could actually smell water. "I found the barrel in an abandoned tank."

Suddenly he was an authority. Everyone wanted to ask him questions. My only interest was if we would survive tomorrow's battle. "Only a very few will make it through the day," he said, looking at me strangely. "You, Erich, will be among the lucky ones." I didn't pay too much attention to what he was saying since I didn't take him seriously.

The Russian poured the water from the barrel into two containers and brought it to a boil over a fire made with bunched-up steppe grass. After we drank the dreadful stuff and ate our bread with onions we went to sleep.

Well before dawn I awoke to the rumbling of distant engines. I got up to take a look and saw a large number of enemy tanks on the horizon advancing in our direction. Several of the other men had also heard the noise and got up, screaming "The tanks are coming!"

I woke all the men in my squad and told them to take up positions in their ditches. "Let's not shoot unless we have no other choice, because if they see us we're goners." I removed my pistol and placed it next to me. "Whoever stands up or wants to escape, I'll shoot down, for all our lives would be endangered by such an act." I peered out and saw that there were hundreds of tanks approaching in several rows. A shot was accidentally fired from the antiaircraft gun up on the hill, and within seconds shells tore the gunner and his weapon to shreds. That's what would happen to us, I thought.

Then the tanks appeared to the right and left of us. Anyone getting up to shoot was crushed to death like an insect beneath the heavy wheel tracks.

The Russian schoolteacher lay next to me, covering himself with the tall steppe grass. The other Russian had disappeared. Although the tanks had passed for over half an hour, not one man had gotten up out of his ditch. We were afraid that infantry would be behind the tanks. The schoolteacher was the first to get up. "They're gone now," he said. I slowly emerged from my hole, and the rest of my squad came crawling out one by one. We had all survived.

We were barely on our feet when our second lieutenant came running down the hill from his own hole. "Goddamn it!" he screamed. "How do you like that, these bastards expect us to fight off several armored divisions with a couple of lousy guns! We can't fight a war like this, it's insane."

Still out of breath, he barked, "Let's assemble everyone, hurry!" Only thirteen men out of our entire company were still alive. The rest had been crushed to death or shot to bits.

Finally, around nine A.M., we were able to continue. The battalion had shrunk to forty-five men. Aside from the many casualties we had suffered, the Russians had captured quite a few of our men. They linked up the prisoners with hooked rods, heaved them on top of their tanks, and carried them away.

The second lieutenant was forced to take over the company. He debated frantically what to do next. "We have to try to catch up with our regiment. Parts of the regiment should be to either the south or the west of us. Let's follow the Russian tanks toward the south."

Again the steppe was covered with these deep gorges, so we walked along in one of them, heading south. The lieutenant ordered three of us to walk on top of the ridge for reconnaissance. After walking like this for hours we came to a road. A destroyed tank and an overturned ammunition truck lay in the ditch. Several meters away there were bodies scattered all over the place. A couple of soldiers who were still alive and had taken refuge behind the truck yelled, "Watch out, take cover, the Russians are nearby!" I grabbed the machine gun away from the Russian schoolteacher and set it up behind the destroyed tank. The rest of the men took cover behind the truck. They chased the schoolteacher away, and he came running over to my position and lay down next to me.

As soon as he hit the ground the firing started. The tank cupola caught fire, and flames shot into the air. I yelled, "Get the fire out, I'll cover you. If the flames reach the tarpaulin, we'll all be blown up."

One of the men climbed on top of the tank and tried to beat out the fire with his jacket. As he jumped back down it flared up again. At the same moment, as I set my machine gun a bit higher on the destroyer, I felt a blow. I was hit on my left hand. It was as if someone had chopped off my hand with an ax. I called out that I was hit, but no one came; the others jumped up from behind the tank and ran in panic to a ditch to take cover. I frantically searched for a bandage in my first-aid kit. The Russian schoolteacher came sliding over on his stomach and bandaged me up. My hand was torn to pieces, with black gunpowder all over it. My index finger was missing, and my middle finger was turned completely around.

Surprisingly, I felt no pain. I had been hit by a gun shell that had exploded on impact. What should I do next, I wondered, take a chance and run over to the ditch? Surely I'd be hit if I did, but if I stayed, the rapidly spreading fire would eventually explode. The schoolteacher grabbed me by the arm and pointed toward a ravine about a hundred meters north of us. "We go, we go," he kept on saying. We crawled on our stomachs. Each jerk forward took a tremendous amount of effort, but I made it. I'd had to leave my machine gun and my waistbelt and pistol behind. The schoolteacher had removed the cartridges from the pistol and the cocking slide from the machine gun to make them inoperable.

By the time I fell into the ditch, my entire body was trembling and I broke out in a cold sweat. I remained in a state of delirium for about an hour before I could collect myself and think again. I looked over at the schoolteacher, who was sitting next to me, staring at me wide-eyed. "Who's the prisoner now?" I asked with clenched teeth. "You or me?"

"If I hand you over, nothing bad will happen to you, because you have the bird on your chest and not on your arm." The Russian was referring to the insignia the SS men carried on their sleeves. Since I was not a member of the SS, I would be treated like a man, he meant. At the moment I really didn't much care what would happen to me. We kept trotting along the ravine in a northerly direction. It was around three in the afternoon. My bandages were soaked with blood. The pain became worse, and I got weaker with each step I took. I had no choice but to rest every few minutes.

The schoolteacher noticed a troop of Russian soldiers coming toward us from behind, about twenty men altogether. I thought to myself, this is it. As they approached, however, I saw that none of them was armed. They just walked by, completely ignoring us, a sad-looking, pitiful bunch of wounded men, all trying hard just to keep on going. Apparently, they had been taken prisoners at a Russian first-aid camp, and since they had been able to walk, the Germans had taken them along. However, the two guards assigned to them had disappeared one night, and therefore they had decided to walk in a northerly direction to try and meet up with Russian troops. The schoolteacher suggested that we had a better chance to stay alive if we walked with them, so we did.

Trotting along, in a kind of stupor, I tried to imagine what would happen to me. How would these Russians treat me, their enemy? I was in despair, feeling abandoned by my own men. Had we not sworn to one another that we would help if one of us got wounded? I guess what it boils down to is every man is for himself. Yet this Russian, who had been my prisoner, had helped me. While all these negative thoughts circled around my mind, a jeep with a young German officer at the wheel came thumping up the track and to a full stop in front of me. "What on earth are you doing walking with these people? These are prisoners—and where are the guards?" he demanded. After I briefed him on what had happened he was outraged, especially since the guards were apparently from his outfit. He told me to get into the jeep and come with him. As we drove off, he explained that he was an observation officer for an armored unit. After a short drive we caught up with his unit and found a first-aid station. But no one wanted to accept me since they had their hands full with their own wounded. The truth was, they didn't have enough supplies to bandage their own men.

When it was suggested that I try to reach an infantry first-aid station that was supposedly very close by, I thought to myself, what kind of comrades are these who expect a wounded soldier to go looking for another station? The officer came up to me. "These poor guys don't know what they're doing anymore. The wounded are screaming, and they can't help them, they don't even have any paper bandages left." Looking around, I noticed that the majority of the injured had burn marks all over them. Only a few were lucky enough to be bandaged. Once again the officer came to my assistance. He said he would drive me and two others he had picked up to the nearest infantry first-aid station. With the help of a wireless car radio set he was able to find the place within an hour.

The camp consisted of a large tent where about forty to fifty wounded were bedded down on straw. A truck with a stable lantern hanging from its roof served as an operating theater. The tent was only sparsely lighted with kerosene lamps. The severely injured were under a roof; outside were the less severely wounded. I lay down next to a man who had been shot through the lung. Despite his injury, he was smoking a cigarette. "The doctor gave me permission," he whispered. Around midnight two first aiders came and took me to the truck. They laid me on a field bed, and two very young doctors in white overalls that were more red than white examined me. One of them told me that my middle finger had to be removed before gangrene set in. They gave me ether as an anesthetic. When I awoke, I was back in the tent. I tried to move but couldn't. Spasms shook my entire body. I tried to speak, but my lower jaw wouldn't work. I thought perhaps I had contracted tetanus. The fellow lying next to me noticed my condition and told me that during the night, when the first aiders had brought me back to the tent, one of them had slipped and they had accidentally dropped me to the floor. He added, "I'm surprised you didn't break your back."

One of the first aiders came now and gave me an injection. My body relaxed, and the spasms disappeared. When I got up after a few hours to relieve myself outside, I saw a large ditch filled with dead bodies. One of the dead was the man with the perforated lung who had smoked his last cigarette the night before. Apparently, they all had died during the night and there hadn't been time to cover the bodies with dirt. A first aider stood next to me and remarked, "Well, at least those fellows are at peace. Who knows what's in store for us now that we're completely encircled by the enemy? I don't think any of us will get out of this nightmare alive."

The next evening, an ambulance arrived to take some of the severely wounded to a field hospital. Usually, four men were transported at a time. I knew I wasn't considered severely wounded, but I noticed there was a little room left between the stretchers. I asked one of the drivers if they could take me along, but his answer was no. The other driver recognized my accent and came to the back of the car to speak with me. He asked me where I was from and I told him, "South Thuringia." He was so happy to have found someone from his home region that he told me to get onto the truck and said to the other driver that he would take full responsibility.

We drove in a westerly direction into the night. Three of the wounded screamed in agony as the truck bounced over the bumpy terrain. The fourth man was either unconscious or dead, for he didn't move or utter a sound. After several hours, we arrived at our destination, a field hospital consisting of three or four farmhouses whose floors were covered with straw. Hundreds of wounded lay about with only two or three medics to take care of them. The stench in the rooms was unbearable, and millions of flies and crawling insects made the place appear even less sanitary than it was. I'm truly surprised the plague didn't break out in those places. I followed the example of the others and bedded down outside, covering myself with straw.

The next afternoon a medic hurriedly wrapped another paper bandage on top of the old one and gave me a tiny white pill for the pain. Our food ration that day consisted of stale bread and tea. Fine sand in the tea water stuck to the inside of my mouth, but at this point I really didn't care what kind of water I was drinking. I sat down by the road behind the farmhouses; all was quiet now except for the moans of the sick. A jeep drove by on the road, passed me, turned around, and came to a stop in front of me. I assumed the man needed some information. As I got up I straightened my hat and walked over to the jeep. I noticed that the man was a high-ranking officer in a uniform with violet collar patches and stripes running down his trousers. He greeted me and asked where I had gotten wounded. He remarked that I must have endured a lot being an infantryman and added that I was a good soldier for saluting in this time of chaos. Just then, I noticed the banners on the front of the jeep. He noticed the Iron Cross ribbon on my chest and asked what regiment I belonged to and if I had all my papers. I told him that my regiment was the 673rd and my pay book was hanging around my neck. He copied down my name and my field post number. I was just about to ask why he wanted all this information when he said, "Get in, I'll drive you to an airport. Maybe you can get out of here." I couldn't believe my luck! What had made me sit by just that road?

After about an hour's drive we came to an airfield where several large planes were sitting. Piled next to them were boxes and crates of food. The first two pilots the officer asked refused to take me along in addition to their regular load. The third pilot said he would take me, provided the officer gave him a written authorization taking full responsibility. He suggest-

ed we try another plane farther up the runway that had some engine problems that should be cleared up by now.

The officer, who was a high-ranking chaplain, drove me about three
kilometers up the road. A plane was sitting there, surrounded by boxes and
crates, but unfortunately for me, it was filled to the last seat, according to
the pilot. He added that he had been just about to leave when he saw the
jeep coming toward him. The chaplain asked if all the passengers were
wounded men. The pilot said all except one, who claimed to be a courier.

He then pointed toward a man in a steel helmet sitting close to the window. The officer called to the man, who ignored us. Then the chaplain
gave him a direct order, and he came down from the plane. As he was
showing his identification papers, the engines started and the pilot gestured for me to come on board. He helped me get onto the wing and
quickly closed the door behind me.

Looking out the window, I saw the two men arguing. Now the chaplain
motioned to the pilot as if he wanted me to get back out, but the pilot
ignored him and soon our plane rolled down the runway, left the ground, and
turned toward the west. Looking down, I saw the two men standing there
among the boxes and crates, still arguing. I couldn't believe my good luck.

I looked around. Three of the men were sitting up, but the rest were
bedded down on the floor. Next to me sat a soldier who had an injury
similar to mine. He was a first lieutenant but was not wearing an officer's
uniform or the proper insignia. He told me that his uniform was buried
someplace down below. He gestured toward the outside. "The reason the
pilot is flying so low is that we're right at the front." Looking out the window myself, I could see the Russian soldiers digging themselves in. They
fired at us and one bullet penetrated, striking the fellow across from me
in the right arm. In a few minutes all was quiet again.

My eyes followed the contours of the land below. I saw peasants harvesting their crops. Some of them took off their head scarves and waved to us.
The first lieutenant continued, "Did you know that the entire Don River
bend is enclosed by the enemy? None of those men left behind will ever
get out alive. You were lucky you got the general's permission to come
along, because our plane was one of the last to land there and get back out.
I'm positive the general got himself into trouble, because the courier whose
place you took had important information to be delivered directly to the
Führer's headquarters. A major and two corporals had brought the courier
to the airport."

The plane flew to Artemovsk, where we disembarked and were transported to a school that had been converted into a hospital. There our bandages were changed and we were given some food.

The next morning all the wounded who could be moved, including myself, were taken to the nearest railroad depot and loaded onto a freight train. In cattle cars padded with straw and hay, we rode for twelve days and nights through Russia toward the west. Although we stopped frequently and were given enough food and water, the jostling of the train and the constant moaning of the wounded got on everyone's nerves.

In Lvov we disembarked and slept in makeshift houses near the railroad station. The medics had run out of supplies and told us that in a few days we would be in Germany, where we would receive professional medical care. My injured hand itched continuously, and the odor from the wound was horrendous. Maggots crawled out from beneath the crusted bandage. When I told this to the medic, he said, "Don't worry about the maggots, they eat the rotten flesh and help keep your wound clean." Somehow I had never thought of maggots as having sanitary qualities. But he wrapped another paper bandage on top of the old one and left me behind to be shaved and have my hair cut by a Polish woman.

The following day, as scheduled, we boarded a passenger train for Germany and eventually arrived at Meissen, where we were sent to a reception camp. There I was bathed by an attendant and powdered with a lice disinfectant. I was X-rayed and informed that my hand still harbored parts of the shredded shell and hundreds of tiny metal splinters that would have to be removed surgically.

The next day I was operated on. The surgeon gave me a splinter as a souvenir. On September 4, 1942, during a brief ceremony, I was awarded the Wounded Badge, Second Class. An attendant came around and asked me where I would like to be hospitalized. Without hesitation I said, "Coburg, my hometown."

I had barely gotten back home when I had to be operated on one more time since my hand had developed a nasty-looking inflammation. After the operation I was moved to a large dance hall in our local Hofbräuhaus. There I finally got to see my wife and daughter again. How good it felt to be back home and look at familiar faces! By mid-October of that year, as soon as I was allowed out, I went to visit old friends and former coworkers at the Siemens factory in Neustadt. I hoped to be rehired in a supervisory position similar to the one I had had before I was drafted.

When one of my friends greeted me with the German salute, I told him that I had had enough of all this nonsense and he need not greet me that way. I then remarked that they should consider themselves extremely lucky to be able to experience the war in their homeland and not at the front, where one simply hoped to stay alive for one more hour. "At least here you have food and a roof over your head," I said.

The man who had saluted me interrupted, "We heard Göring's speech just yesterday where he stated that all the soldiers on the fronts are well provided for."

"And you idiots believe that?" I retorted. "Göring can say what he wants, but I know from my own experience that there were days and even entire weeks when we didn't get any food to eat. Someone should smack him in the trap for telling such lies."

The foreman walked in to join us and told me to go to the Personnel Office to pick up a free pack of cigarettes that each soldier was entitled to receive. After ten minutes I arrived to pick up the promised cigarettes. As I entered the room, I noticed three men standing together talking. They gave me a sinister look. I greeted them anyway and asked for the cigarettes. One of the men stepped up to me and said, "What kind of nonsense are you spreading among the workers? First you don't return the German salute, and to make things worse you insist that Göring is a liar."

"Everything I said is the truth," I replied. "And if anyone doesn't believe me, I dare him to go out on the front and fight for the Fatherland as all my dead comrades and I did."

Another man came forward. "Very well, we won't make anything of this, but the next time keep your mouth shut and your opinions to yourself."

I couldn't help thinking what fine coworkers I had, who informed on me when I came to visit and express my happiness at having survived the war. Instead of showing comradeship or friendship, they were eager to put a rope around my neck. Aren't honesty and the truth appreciated anymore?

I went back to the workshop to inquire who the heel was who had informed on me. "Every second man around here has turned informer," whispered one of the machine operators. "It's really best just to do your work. Forget about expressing any thoughts or opinions. They could cost you your freedom or even your life. Many of them have become informers to save themselves from being drafted."

I left the factory downhearted, bitter, and frustrated and from then on was more careful as to what I said and did.

During October of that year, the Nazi party planned to place a memorial plaque in front of the Hofbräuhaus (where I was hospitalized) in honor of their victorious march on Coburg in October 1922, which Hitler detailed so elaborately in his autobiography, *Mein Kampf.* Party members came on a special train at the invitation of the city's right-wing organizations to participate in the celebration of "German People's Day." Upon arrival eight hundred or more SA members unveiled flags and banners and brought out their own marching bands. Meanwhile the people had found out that the Nazis had been invited, and a revolt started.

In commemoration of this event two decades earlier, the town had rounded up as many Nazis as it could find. Labor Front leader Dr. Robert Ley was to inaugurate the ceremony. An SA band played loud marching music just as had been done in 1922. The memorial plaque, covered by a swastika banner, was waiting to be unveiled. Dr. Ley whipped off the banner, and there underneath was a poster with the slogans "Hitler Is a Mass Murderer—Long Live Freedom—Down with War" glued to the plaque.

Dr. Ley tried desperately—but in vain—to tear down the poster. Two SA men held one of the banners in front of it while Dr. Ley continued with the ceremony. However, most of the people present had already read the slogans. Flyers and similar posters had been posted all over the city. Naturally, the Nazis were fuming that their day had been ruined. The day's events were the chief topic of conversation in our hospital for weeks. The local police searched frantically day and night for the villain, but to no avail.

During the second or third week after this incident, I was called into the hospital administrator's office and asked to write some inscriptions to be used as identification tags over the beds. I was surprised that they had asked me to do this work but didn't think it too unusual at the time. While I performed my duty, one of the clerks whispered over my shoulder, "Were you the one?" "Was I the one for what?" I asked. "Did you draw the slogans?" "What?" I exclaimed. "You must be joking!"

"Listen," he continued, as if he knew the world's most treasured secret, "I'm telling you this in strictest confidence. A sergeant by the name of Weiss from Bayreuth, who is also a self-proclaimed clairvoyant, swears he saw a man in a vision. He was of your age and build with a wounded left hand and a couple of missing fingers who was hospitalized in an infirmary in Coburg and also lived near the city. After a thorough investigation it was decided that you were the only one who fit the description."

After listening to this astonishing tale, I told the man, "Don't worry, it wasn't me, they can't accuse me of anything."

However, the next morning I was told by my ward neighbor that the head of the medical staff and a corporal had stopped by to search both my bed and my night table. The same day, my wife, excited and very frightened, visited and told me that the Gestapo had gone to our home and ransacked the entire property without even showing a search warrant. They were looking for some documents, my wife had been told. Their search had included tearing open the septic tank and the toilets and removing the ashes from the oven and stoves. My wife was petrified; she didn't know what to think of this invasion of our privacy. I explained to her that the police were looking for the man who had written the slogans on the poster and in their desperate attempt to find the guilty person, they were looking everywhere.

I asked to see the chief of staff so I could lodge a complaint. He advised me not to take any official action. A week later, I was summoned to appear before an investigating judge at the judicial palace in Nürnberg. I had to wait for him for more than an hour before he entered the courtroom. He first asked me personal information and then went on to question me about the poster incident in Coburg.

I told him only what I knew from hearsay and that I had not even been present at the ceremony. "Now tell me about the other incident at the cable factory," he continued in an accusing tone. "Didn't you make some slanderous remarks about Reichsmarschall Göring and mock the German salute?"

"As far as Göring is concerned," I began, "I merely stated that he wasn't telling the truth, provided he actually did say that the men on the front were well provided for. I know for a fact that this is not the truth, because there were lots of days when we didn't have any food. And furthermore, I did not mock the German salute. I merely stated that I didn't care to perform it anymore."

"Let's make a transcript of this conversation, and then we will investigate further; somebody isn't telling the truth," said the judge. He repeated all his questions, and I answered once again while a court clerk recorded everything that was said.

A day later I was arrested. My appeal was denied by the chief of staff, who felt that I was in good enough condition to be moved and able to stand trial.

"That's it!" I said and gave a sigh. "Now you all know what brought me here."

Looking around the room, I saw that everybody was tired, including myself.

Before our lights were turned off, good old Phillip made his rounds with his medical supply box around his neck. "Who needs to see the doctor tomorrow?" he asked. Fritz and I were the only ones to raise our hands. Fritz asked for a painkiller. Gerhard's loud snoring made it obvious that he was already sound asleep. The lights went out, and all was quiet.

CHAPTER 13

FIRST DEPARTURES

After breakfast on the morning of December 29, first Fritz and then I were called in to see the doctor. The older man I had seen before unwrapped my bandages and took me into the examination room, where the physician looked at my hand. "You still have quite a few splinters in there that have to work themselves out," he said. "It's best that we keep up the warm baths."

The old man bathed my arm in a warm solution, rubbed some more Perubalsam ointment into the wound, and then bandaged me up again. During the procedure, he mentioned that the doctor had told him I belonged in a hospital. "This is supposed to be an infirmary, isn't it?" I asked. "Yes," he responded, "if you could call it that. I overheard the two psychiatrists saying that this place is to be closed down soon; that's why no new inmates are being sent here." I thanked him and said I'd like to be able to call him by his name. "I told you before, I cannot reveal my real name," he whispered. "Just call me Otto for the time being. Someday, when this place no longer exists, I'll tell you." "Very well," I said. "I'll call you Otto, if you'll call me Erich."

As Otto thanked me, I saw tears well up in his eyes. He patted me on the shoulder and said, "Until next time, my friend," as Phillip brought in another inmate. Phillip escorted me back to the cell, where Alex suggested that we put off our discussion until the afternoon. "No," Fritz objected, "we should continue as soon as everything has quieted down. I have a feeling we won't be together much longer."

Richard agreed with Fritz. "We can start with Willi and go in the same order as we did with our life stories. Willi, you were the first."

"You can start with me for all I care," said an embarrassed Willi. "No one can help me anyway, and I certainly can't do anything about the fact that I deserted."

"That's true," said Fritz. "But someone sent you here with the intention of having you declared of unsound mind. So far your actions have only helped the authorities believe there really is something wrong with you."

"Maybe that could even save your life," Alex added. "Even though we know you're as normal as the rest of us. But we do want to discuss whether your actions were right or wrong."

"What you did was against the law," said Richard. "In every country in the world, desertion is a punishable offense, not necessarily by death but certainly by a stiff sentence."

I said, "Let's assume that the laws put into effect during wartime do not apply to us since we didn't want war to begin with. Hitler started the war without asking or listening to his people. His political philosophy is not democratic but dictatorial. He cannot be removed easily, for he considers himself untouchable, as do most of his followers. He doesn't have to worry about being elected by the people, even though he was put onto his throne with the help of the conservative parties, as Fritz's uncle explained so well. The elections that followed were not free; only a few people were brave enough to ask to vote in a private booth. Most people voted in the open and in front of SA members so they could be seen voting for the Party. Besides, the election results were falsified. I know this for a fact, because even though my parents and three of my friends voted 'No,' when the election results were announced, our district reported one hundred percent 'Yes' votes. So much for accuracy.

"Willi, unfortunately none of this can help you," I continued. "It's best if you continue playing the disturbed young man. There has to be somebody out there who has an interest in keeping you alive; and if you do get killed, then consider that you died for yourself and not for Hitler and his mass murderers. Chances are you would have died somewhere on the Russian front; most sensitive young men like yourself didn't make it. Don't think of yourself as a bad person. You were unfortunate enough to be around people who didn't give a damn about their fellowman, and besides, lacking experience, you thought everyone was like that. I know this is not much of a consolation for you, but by now you must realize that some people do care; I hope we have all conveyed this feeling to you. The way I see it, you're neither a criminal nor a suicidal maniac, but a victim of our imbalanced society and your surroundings. Perhaps if you hadn't met that fellow Ralf, your life would have taken a different direction."

"That's true," Willi answered. "I've often thought of what motivated my actions, but I've come to the conclusion that I alone am responsible. I should have kept my eyes open and been more aware of the political changes around me. Also, I should have socialized more with people of my own age. I was under the impression that people should approach me, and when no one offered their friendship, I developed complexes, for example with girls. In a way, my grandfather is to be blamed because he never allowed me to play with other children. Ralf didn't ruin my life; he enlightened me, and had it not been for my own stupidity and carelessness at the border crossing, I would now be a free man living in Sweden or some other neutral country. If I had another opportunity to escape, I wouldn't hesitate even though I might be shot."

"Alex, what do you think?" I asked, keeping the discussion going.

"The question of who is to be blamed is difficult to answer," Alex responded. "For example, had Willi acted because he hated war, it would be easier to make a decision. But his desertion probably resulted from the Czechoslovakian's influence. Previously, he might have done it on his own because he disliked people. I'll be honest with you: without entering the privacy of a voting booth, I too voted 'Yes,' just like most of those in my area who in fact were opposed to war."

Richard interrupted, "I said earlier in reference to desertion that it is punishable in all countries, and since this fact affects me directly, I must admit that if I had not been so naïve and stupid and allowed myself to be led into Hitler's traps, I wouldn't be sitting here."

"Richard," I said, "just comment on Willi—you're not to be judged yet."

"All right," Richard continued. "What I want to say is that Willi is not Hitler's only victim. Those who are his followers, willingly or unwillingly, are also victims. Therefore, I myself am at fault. How I wish the war was over today and we all could be free men! I'll say one thing with conviction, and that is, if I survive this nightmare, I'm going to become more aware of the political life around me and never again be influenced by one person."

"Let's drop Willi's case and go on to Richard's," I said.

Alex started by asking, "What do you think your friends in Switzerland would say about your opinions now, Richard?"

Richard's answer came quickly. "They'd say that if I hadn't been such a fanatic sympathizer of Hitler and had followed their advice and that of the newspapers, I never would have returned to Germany. I know they wouldn't laugh at me but would be concerned about my situation. I also assume that my father-in-law doesn't think any differently of Hitler. Because Hitler made such a good showing against the Communists, my father-in-law assumed that he had acted democratically. Being used to Swiss democratic elections, he believed that Hitler had been voted in democratically. If anyone made a negative remark about Hitler, he immediately took it as defamation of character. It never crossed his mind that there might be any truth to the accusations. I'm truly embarrassed for having been so stupid and gullible. In my eyes, the true heroes of our group are Franzl and Fritz, even though their situations are altogether different."

Fritz interjected, "A hero, I'm not; I just did what everyone should have done. Richard, you were incorrectly informed about the Communists, not only by Hitler's propaganda but also by the Swiss. You believed everything you were told about them."

"But, Fritz," said Richard, "I have to tell you that when I think of Russia and the way the people live there, there's nothing to admire."

"You still don't understand," Fritz insisted. "First one has to understand the history of the Russians, which was taught completely incorrectly to all of us."

"Wait a minute," Alex interrupted. "Let's not argue among ourselves. What we should be doing is trying to discover the faults that lie in each of us."

"Fault or no fault, there's nothing to fight over about my situation," said Richard. "I know I'm guilty because of my own stupidity; I should have known I couldn't swim across the Rhine in the middle of the day and not get caught."

Franzl, who had only listened so far, said, "Richard, you acted out of a conviction that did not come from within you, but from others who persuaded you, and you accepted what they said as the truth. Before coming to Germany you should have asked your mother if what was written in the Swiss papers had any truth to it, or perhaps you should have come for a visit to find out how things really were. But you were a fanatic, and so you went in only one direction. Now you're blaming the Nazis and Hitler. I am convinced that you're ignoring my own convictions exactly as the Nazis did. It's the same with Fritz: you judge him according to Russian conditions, ignoring the fact that here in Germany the background for his ideas and convictions is completely different. If you have to die, don't blame yourself, as you are not committing suicide. Try to do as I do: pray to the Lord and include in your prayers those you love and are near to you, and you will see that the idea of death becomes easier to accept."

Richard looked at Franzl. "I know you're being honest with me, and I thank you for that. I firmly believe that the true Christian kingdom, as you represent it, would be a benefit to mankind. War would certainly not be on the agenda. Ideally, a nation that believes in Christianity should use it as the foundation of its government."

Fritz couldn't wait to comment, "Aren't we supposed to have these types of governments already, since most of the Western world claims to abide by

Christian laws? Tell me, how can priests and preachers sanctify weapons and other tools of war when they know for a fact that they will be used to kill their brothers? With these hypocritical people one cannot form a government. Of course, if everyone acted as Franzl does, life would be Paradise and mankind could live together in harmony. Unfortunately, people like him are a minority and disappear from society as soon as they're found out. I do not, of course, want to say that an ideal government is an impossibility, but before one can exist the people will have to be enlightened about the true Christian way. This, of course, is impossible not only under Hitler's regime but also under the so-called democratic governments."

Noises in the corridor interrupted us. Willi rushed to get the food bowls and put them into place. He had just completed his task when the door flew open and the potato carrier came into the room. This time we were also served some tomato sauce and a cutlet made not of meat but of a pressed-together mass that tasted very much like fish. Everyone had a hearty appetite, and we ate our lunch quickly without talking.

After we had finished eating Fritz started the discussion again. "I'm surprised we're still getting so much to eat. In the concentration camps the inmates, especially the Jews, are starving to death or dying from poisoning. I heard this from an SS man who was traveling with us. He told me he'd be glad to be relieved of his duty at the camp and be sent to the front, where he could show his courage, strength, and bravery. Someone had told him to go and volunteer for the front. He had wanted to go but had been told that his duty at the camp overseeing people's deaths was just as manly and important to the Fatherland."

Alex said, "We don't want to deviate from our main theme, so we're now going to examine Fritz more closely. Fritz, you call yourself a devout socialist. You're convinced of this ideology, and you're willing to die for it. Just like Willi, you were indoctrinated. Had you not met this Professor Sommermann, I don't think you would be in the predicament you are in now. Many young people let themselves be led by an individual or a cause they admire or by someone who impresses them in a positive way. Fritz, I'm not comparing you with people like that because I know you're convinced that your ideals and convictions are true and sound. As you've pointed out, you've read Marx and Engels. I can only tell you that my parents and I have experienced a Communist revolution. I also know for a fact that if my mother had not had her jewelry to sell, we would all have starved to death. With the Communists everything had to be done immediately. They robbed from the affluent, and when nothing was left they didn't know what to do next. My father always said that the Russians were going to go downhill. But then Stalin took over and more or less made slaves of them, just as the tsars before him had done. As Richard said, he has seen with his own eyes how the Russians live and wouldn't want a life like that. Even knowing Russian history does not help in these situations. As Erich said, the rich, who gained their wealth by exploiting the poor, are still living. In France and Switzerland the Russian expatriates are enjoying a good life with the money they stole from the Russian people during prerevolutionary times.

"As far as I'm concerned," he concluded, "there will always be rich and poor."

Fritz became agitated. "But at least in Russia there are no more filthy rich people like those robbers and leeches. The fact that the Russians are in such terrible straits is certainly not the fault of the Communists. It can only be blamed on those who took all the gold and riches out of Russia. Of course, every revolution has its swindlers, cheats, and criminals. Those types always surface during hard times. But the majority of the Russians had to start again from scratch, which was not an easy task in a country that had no heavy industry and was surrounded by hostile countries. If Stalin had not armed the people and forewarned them, Hitler could just have strolled into Russia and taken over. It seems that people cannot be ruled without pressure. The only question left is, who should apply the pressure? My opinion is that Stalin is a great and powerful ruler. His advisers and backup men are workers and farmers. In capitalist countries you don't find workers acting as advisers. Hitler, for example, has factory owners and other big entrepreneurs as advisers. He doesn't say so, but that's the way it is."

"Fritz," I said, "you might be right about Hitler, but I don't think that in Russia there are people like yourself acting as advisers. You're ready to die for your convictions, but is it really worth it? In my opinion—no. Nonetheless, I do admire both you and Franzl for your convictions."

Fritz interrupted again. "Not every war is unjust; for example, I'm all for civil wars. I'm against wars of conquest, and this war is a prime example of one. Many before Hitler have tried it and have found it to be their downfall. The ones who will suffer as the result of Hitler's power struggle will be the people of Germany. Hitler himself has said that if this war is not victorious, the German nation will go down with him. But I don't think I can discuss things like this with you, because you don't want to understand me." Fritz rose from his bed, swung his cane in the air, and shouted, "We who are about to die greet you!"

"Sit down, Fritz, don't get so worked up," said Franzl. "We do understand you, and we know how you feel. Think of your mother, who always prayed to Jesus Christ in both good and bad times. Think also of your dear Gitta, with whom you will be reunited in heaven. First you must believe in the

Lord, and then all your political strivings will be resolved. Only He knows if the Socialists or Communists are right or wrong. Also, you have not been sentenced to death yet, and I don't think they'll stoop as low as to execute an injured man."

"How I wish you were right," Fritz said as he limped to his bed and sat down. "But I think you're a dreamer. Hitler has murdered his best friends when they criticized his politics. What makes you think the Nazis will take a mere injury into consideration if they want to get rid of me? Take Erich: because of a few words of criticism, and despite his injury and medals, he was locked up and they want to execute him according to Paragraph Five, 'Undermining of the Military.' These murderers are shameless."

Alex said, "That paragraph of the War Crimes Special Penal Law is nothing but an artificial clause, like many of the Nazi laws. It states that anyone suspected of undermining the Wehrmacht or who openly challenges or declines to do his duty in the German or any allied armies, or otherwise hinders the German or allied people in any way, is to be sentenced to death. This means that if a housewife, for example, goes to a store and says, 'If we didn't have this lousy war, we could have better food,' one could say that she was undermining the Wehrmacht and therefore might be sentenced to death. This paragraph could send thousands of Germans, even members of the Nazi party itself, to the scaffold. The other martial laws are similar. If you were accused under one of the laws and the evidence was not sufficient to sentence you, the judge could still sentence you by using another paragraph that would fit the situation. Erich, your case could be considered a misdemeanor, but it will depend entirely upon the judge who handles your case. If he is an unscrupulous Hitler supporter, he will not take your injury or your medals of honor into consideration."

Franzl said, "Erich, you had the courage to keep your promise to your comrades on the front, even though they did not help you when you were injured. Don't forget that the Lord observed your actions. You promised that the homeland would hear about what was going on at the eastern front, and when you told the truth the homeland set a trap for you and put your life into jeopardy. That must have been a great disappointment to you."

"Franzl," I said, "thinking about this kind of thing can drive you over the edge. I guess there will always be both constructive and destructive people. It depends on who has the upper hand. The destructive forces have the upper hand today. But better times are bound to follow. I'm convinced that Hitler is going to lose this war, so to me it's just a matter of waiting it out. Should the Russians win, they'll impose their social laws on us. If the Western allies win, they too will try to impose their laws. I think Germany will be occupied for quite some time. We'll have to pay, more so than after

World War I, for the destruction we've caused. Germany will not be able to think of war again for a long, long time. During this peacetime we should reevaluate the destructive people in our society. We could turn Germans into a people who would again be accepted all over the world."

Fritz said excitedly, "This will never happen on a voluntary basis. Never! The destructive forces around us will fight the idea with all their might. They will get the victorious allies who occupy Germany to fight among themselves."

"You may be right, Fritz," I said. "Maybe we should first eliminate Hitler so that foreign troops do not come into Germany, then build up our own version of communism, as taught by Marx and Engels. However, I believe that to be impossible, because Hitler cannot be disposed of so easily. Most likely, the Western world and the Germans themselves would not be in agreement on this. I myself am all for a democracy as provided by the Weimar Constitution, but not for one that permits criminals like Hitler to take power."

We were so engrossed in our discussion that we didn't notice that Willi had gone to the window and looked out through the tiny hole in the glass. "It snowed about a foot, and we didn't even notice!" he called out excitedly.

As we were about to continue with our discussion, Phillip came back to take Gerhard to see the doctor. We thought this rather strange, since the doctors were normally present only during the early part of the day. After about fifteen minutes, Gerhard returned. His face was pale and glistening, and he smelled strongly of garlic. Alex asked him what had happened. Pointing to his left arm, he answered, "They gave me an injection, and it still hurts."

Alex led Gerhard to his bed and helped him lie down. Shaking his head, Fritz looked at Gerhard. "This is just great. Those son of a bitches do whatever they please. Gerhard is being used as a guinea pig. His injections have never smelled this strongly of garlic before. Who knows what they have in store for us?"

"There's still some time before we have to go to sleep," Fritz said. "Let's talk about Erich's situation."

Fritz faced me directly, as if he were an attorney giving an opening statement to a jury. "Your fate was that, of all places and of all dates, you had to be hospitalized in Coburg on October 20, the anniversary of the Nazi party's attack on that town. I've read *Mein Kampf* carefully and am familiar with what happened. I am convinced that the conservative parties that organized the 'German People's Day' rally needed Hitler to make the celebration in this rather small city seem important. I can imagine how outraged those scoundrels were when the 'slanderous' poster was unveiled. Now, I don't know if you, Erich, were the one who wrote the slogans—

according to you, you had nothing to do with it—but remember that a scapegoat is always needed, and you were obviously it. You happened to be in the hospital, and a clairvoyant gave a description of a man who looked like you. I'm certain the Gestapo was behind it all. They needed to find a villain quickly. That's why your house was searched. And then there were the remarks you made in the factory against Göring. Your only good luck was that you were in the military, otherwise they probably would have tortured you until you confessed. The court, however, has to have some kind of evidence other than that of a clairvoyant to convict you. Therefore, your fate is now in the hands of the judge who presides over your case."

"Yes," I said, "that's what I have to wait for now."

Gerhard moaned quietly. Franzl remarked, "Just look at him, he looks as though he was made of wax. Maybe he wants to go to sleep. Why don't we leave our discussion until tomorrow morning?"

Gerhard was in no condition to undress himself, so Franzl helped him. Suddenly a shudder ran through Gerhard's body and he broke out in a cold sweat. Just as we were about to bang on the door to summon Phillip and tell him, Gerhard stopped trembling and fell asleep. We remained very quiet so as not to awaken him. A few minutes later, the lights were turned off. Without supper another day had come to an end.

We awoke the next morning to be met with a harsh truth. We had all gotten up, but Gerhard remained motionless in his bed. Willi tried to wake him, calling, "Gerhard, wake up, buddy." But Gerhard didn't move. Rigor mortis had set in, and his body was cold and stiff. "My God, he's dead," gasped Willi, moving a step back from the bed, his face white.

Alex too lost all the color in his face. "What should we do?" he asked, clearing his throat. For a few minutes we looked silently at one another, helpless and unable to find words.

"May the Lord give him everlasting peace," came Franzl's soft voice, breaking the silence. His hands gripped each other, and his head bent in prayer. "Our Father, who art in Heaven . . ." Franzl continued his prayer under his breath, for Fritz banged his fist against the wall, roaring, "Goddamn it, these murderers have found their first target in our cell! Now I know for sure they gave him a lethal injection yesterday. There are no words to describe these sons-of-a-bitch butchers, I hope they rot in hell! Man, we have to do something!"

Fritz was out of control. Still shaken, Alex walked stiffly over to Fritz and laid both his hands on Fritz's shoulders to calm the trembling man.

"I understand your outrage, Fritz, but please, calm down and stop yelling," said Alex. "You're going to get us all into trouble."

"All right," said Fritz after he had regained his composure. "You're right, and you're now the most senior here. You have to report this immediately. But first let's look for the letters from Gerhard's sister; perhaps we can use them someday."

Alex agreed and hesitantly took the letters from Gerhard's pocket. His hands were trembling as though he were committing a crime. Fritz noticed and hissed, "For God's sake, Alex, you're not doing anything wrong; we're saving these letters for his sister. Those murdering pigs would probably destroy them. Now go and bang on the goddamn door." Alex quickly hid the letters behind the metal sheet and then banged his fist hard against the door.

Within minutes, the door was flung open and an officer we didn't know entered. Alex stood at attention, gave the necessary information, and added, "Silkenaski lies dead in his bed."

The officer looked at the corpse as though it were an everyday occurrence and said without emotion, "Yes, I can see that he has croaked. I'll have him removed immediately." Quickly he turned and left the cell, slamming the door behind him.

The word "croaked" echoed in our minds, and I know each of us would have liked to choke that cold-blooded officer.

Ten minutes later two stretcher bearers came for Gerhard's remains. They threw a gray horse blanket over him and without a word disappeared as fast as they had entered.

Shortly thereafter, the top sergeant appeared with Phillip. Alex had to repeat his findings. The top sergeant inquired, "Who saw it first, and at what time?"

Willi got up according to regulations and reported, "I did, sir, a half hour ago."

Alex swallowed hard as he added, "We noticed last night how very pale Silkenaski looked when he returned from the doctors. He moaned, complained of a pain in his arm, and went to bed. Otherwise we didn't notice anything until just a little while ago."

"Where are Silkenaski's belongings?" the top sergeant demanded. Alex pointed to the night table. The sergeant instructed Phillip to gather all of Gerhard's personal items and remove the bedsheets.

Phillip waited until after the officer had left. Then, looking around the room, he asked: "What on earth happened? Gerhard was alive and well yesterday."

"He came back from the doctor late in the afternoon looking like a wax figure," Fritz told him. "He said he had received an injection that hurt badly. He was so weak that we had to help him get undressed and put him to bed. Now he's dead."

"Well, there wasn't much that could be done for him, since he definitely was insane," Phillip said.

"Insane, like hell!" Fritz snapped. "He didn't behave crazy while he was with us."

"The guy is dead now and can't do any more spying," Phillip retorted. "The doctors will most likely notify his family, who live in east Prussia somewhere." Irritated, Phillip stalked out of the room.

We sat around dumbfounded. Fritz broke the silence. "If he was crazy, the doctors made him that way by torturing him. I'm not so sure about Gerhard's accident—I don't think it really was an accident. The officials didn't have to be so secretive about it. But we'll probably never learn the truth. The letters are going to stay behind the metal sheet. If any of us gets out of here alive, he'll have to take the letters with him."

"Unfortunately, Gerhard's murderers will go free," Franzl said. "Everything is behind him now, but it's still in front of us." Willi and Richard sat on the bench next to the radiator, still shaken by what had happened.

Fritz's eyes became accusing as he turned to Franzl. "Tell me, Franzl, where's this God of yours at times like this? Why does He let injustices like this take place? All of us have to die, but I'm convinced that after our physical death there is no so-called afterlife. Wasn't it invented by people only so that the 'hell on Earth' we are experiencing now can be more easily endured? Franzl, I don't want to take away your hopes of an eternal life, but in a situation like ours everyone has to stick to his own beliefs. How can your God, He who is the Lord and ruler over Heaven and Earth, let millions of young people be butchered?"

"Fritz," Alex interrupted harshly, "I don't think this is the time to discuss this. Drop it!"

"This is the time, right now, when Gerhard's been murdered," Fritz shot back.

Richard mumbled from the corner of the room, "We don't really know if it was murder."

"That's a true statement if ever I heard one," snapped Fritz. "No one, I assure you, but no one, will ever know the truth. That's for sure. You people still don't want to face the facts. Maybe you still think the Nazis are rational people. Believe me, they're the most ruthless murderers and criminals; their only objective is to stay in power.

"Let's take Gerhard as an example," Fritz went on. "According to his sister's letters, they own a sizable Junker estate that's worth a lot of money to the Nazis. The next thing that'll happen, now that Gerhard is dead, is that some Nazi big shot will set himself up to administer the estate. Just as when Göring and other Party bosses did the same thing, the

Nazis will claim they acquired the property legitimately." Fritz pointed at Alex, at Franzl, and then at me as he continued, "That's true for the three of you as well. Willi and I don't count, because we don't own any personal property, and Richard's property in Switzerland is untouchable for now. For now, I say, because if the Nazis win this war, Switzerland will not remain unmolested. The Nazis have gigantic sums deposited in numbered Swiss bank accounts for future security, just in case their criminal plans don't work out. Many other countries must also harbor Nazi riches, since it must be relatively easy to find governments willing to go along with this."

I had not seen anyone as angry as Fritz for a long time. His face was flushed as he raised his voice: "Before the Nazis came to power, an immense propaganda campaign was put into action to make Hitler's rise seem inevitable. All the capitalist nations seemed to be in agreement. Communism was hated by all. But despite all obstacles, communism will gain recognition not only in Russia or Germany but eventually worldwide. Only then will we live in a peaceful and just society."

Alex shook his head in disapproval. "Fritz, I cannot agree with you. And even if communism were the solution, you said yourself that there won't be anybody left after the Third Reich to perpetrate your ideas. You know as well as I do that the Germans are not easily persuaded by outside powers. Even your group's leader wanted to overthrow Hitler so he could create his own version of a Communist regime completely severed from Russia. Other ideas must come into being that will be feasible and acceptable to both the East and the West."

"That's exactly what I think," I interrupted. "A democracy where the people are the leaders is the ideal government. A system where equality is guaranteed to all human beings, men and women alike. I hope the victors of the war will be honest with us and help us to reach that goal. Let me tell you about an incident that touched my family.

"My uncle Bill, who lives in America, assured me that a Hitler could never have come to power there. During his last visit to Germany in 1936, he said this and was practically thrown out of his native land as an undesirable alien. He had to leave Germany within forty-eight hours after his own brother-in-law, an SS official, denounced him. My uncle was deeply hurt by his forced departure, for he felt strongly for Germany, although not for Hitler or the Nazis. He had invited my family and me to join him in America, but, like Richard, I felt too strongly for my country and still believed in the honesty of its citizens. Today, I would gladly live in America instead of remaining in this never-ending chaos."

Willi joked, "Why don't you send your uncle a telegram to come and get you out?

"All this talk about politics and good or evil empires is no consolation for me," he continued. "Nor for any of us. We're here in this hellhole, and that's the only true fact." His round young face looked up at Alex. "If only I had enjoyed a good and exciting life like you, Alex, I would be a happy man. But as it is, I haven't experienced anything worth mentioning, not even love." Turning to Franzl, Willi asked, "Don't you have anything to add?"

"Keep talking," Franzl answered quietly. "I'm listening. It's just that I'm still occupied with Gerhard's death. I can't help but think about his sister. Poor Gerhard, he was such a harmless fellow. He must have disliked war and weapons as much as I, otherwise he wouldn't have been a medic despite his noble background. I assume that Gerhard and his family were anti-Nazi, and possibly for that reason they accused him of spying. His sister's letters are written in a very tactful manner without showing anger, although she had ample reason to be suspicious."

"Gerhard is gone, and no one can bring him back," I said. "Should one of us survive, perhaps an investigation of why he was killed can be undertaken."

Lunch came. It consisted of a watery soup with a couple of pieces of carrots and a few green leaves swimming on the top. It looked and tasted like dishwater. Willi ate a piece of his hoarded stale bread and placed the remaining slice back into his night table drawer.

We had barely finished our meal when the door was thrown open and a guard announced that it was "time for weighing." This usually happened only once every four weeks. Phillip and Otto, who were in charge of this, were waiting for us in the hallway with the scale set up. Phillip had told us once that if the inmates lost too much weight the food would improve. One after the other we stepped onto the scale and, as always, found that we had each lost a couple of pounds. So far, however, the food had remained the same, weight loss or no, with the exception of Christmas dinner, which had tasted almost decent.

When we were back in our room, Franzl went over to the radiator, from which he retrieved a cigarette. "Here," he said to Fritz, "this is the last one."

"Thanks, Franzl," said Fritz as he lit the cigarette. Then he gasped after inhaling too deeply. "This is the only consolation I have now." Between puffs he said, "God, Franzl, you are really a man who cares deeply about others. It's a shame you've decided to give your life for this God of yours. If I were you I'd immediately call for the top sergeant and tell him you've decided to join the Wehrmacht. Perhaps you'll never have to shoot anyone, and your life would be spared. They would have to give you a lesser sentence, and you could see your wife, children, and mother again. Take their feelings into consideration. Surely you can serve your God and your faith in some other way, with a less drastic end result?"

Franzl listened pensively but answered in a steady voice, "You might be right, but you, dear Fritz, will never understand me. All your words sound tempting and seductive, but they concern only earthly matters. I have conditioned myself and have already left the mortal life behind me. I belong to my God and obey His will, and someday, when Jehovah shows himself to you, you'll understand me, but only then."

"Let Franzl keep his faith. He seems to know exactly what he wants," I said to Fritz.

"If I had an opportunity like Franzl," Fritz said, "I'd make use of it without hesitating. I'm convinced that a man's life can only be fulfilled here on earth, where he is born and dies, and not in some imaginary glorified heaven with God."

"Fritz," I said, "Franzl is the only one among us who seems to be at peace with himself and who doesn't succumb to despair. For him the ultimate happiness is to be with his God; he's willing to sacrifice his earthly life, and his faith is firm. Franzl is the only one among us who, as an individual, made it clear to the Nazis that he is against violence and war and will not have any part of it. The only question remaining is, is he really achieving something for his fellowman? Technically speaking, no. In a way, we're all lone wolves, Fritz, perhaps, being the only exception since he was a member of a group of resistance fighters trying to overthrow the political system."

"I wish I could take off," Richard sighed, "never to return. I'd rather hang myself than let these scoundrels kill me."

"With you they have to take into consideration that you came from another country of your own free will to serve in the German army," I said. "For desertion you could get sentenced to hard labor in a penitentiary. There must be a reason you were brought here, to a prison infirmary, without any injury or mental illness. The same is true for Alex. Willi's case is different, since he's here for his mental instability."

Fritz interrupted, "If only my Gitta would be declared mentally unstable, her life may be spared. If they kill her, I have no reason for living. For me, the only consolation is that these murderers will eventually be destroyed."

Willi quietly got up from the bench and walked over to his night table, removing the remainder of the slice of bread he had saved. "I'm so hungry," he complained. "And this"—he held up the tiny slice of bread—"is my last piece."

When Willi had finished eating, he said, "What if we all hanged ourselves tonight? Wouldn't that be a demonstration?"

Richard interjected, "Not a bad idea, but who would care?"

Franzl shook his head in disagreement. "How can you guys talk like that? It would be a mortal sin! Remember, Willi, it wasn't you who gave you life, it was the Lord, and only he has the authority to take it away."

"A demonstration of that sort," I pointed out, "wouldn't really serve any purpose. Look what happened to Gerhard. Just like him, we would be taken to the dissecting room and no one besides the participating attendants would ever find out how we died or under what circumstances. We certainly wouldn't be the first or the last to take our lives because of these criminals in power now. Let's just forget about it."

Fritz brought up his idea of escaping, but Alex cut him off. "We've talked about your berserk plan before, and it just won't work. How are you going to escape?"

"We'll dig a hole through the wall and remove the bricks, then let ourselves down with tied-together bedsheets," Fritz said patiently.

"Then what?" Alex asked with raised eyebrows. "How do you figure on getting over the outside wall? It's four meters high. Your plan stinks. Forget it!"

Franzl said, "Stop discussing unrealistic ideas."

"Well, Fritz," continued Alex, "one thing is certain: should the Russians win this war, you and your resistance groups will be glorified and your names will be engraved in granite with golden letters. But that will not be the case for us lone wolves, as we won't be counted or recognized. Probably all our legal files—if there are any—will be destroyed, and no one will ever know what happened to us or what we stood for. When I think about it, I prefer it that way, because in my case they'll name only cowardice, homosexuality, draft dodging, and military subversion, not resistance. I am not in fact a resistance fighter; I simply abhor war and its consequences. It destroys what man has built, and that's wrong. I also don't want to kill anyone. I believe in living and letting live. I'm proud that I was brought up in a capitalist environment. My parents worked hard at their business, and since only the rich were able to afford our merchandise we certainly didn't take anything away from the less fortunate. We lived comfortably but not in unreasonable luxury." Looking up at Willi, Alex continued, "I could never have endured the barracks life; I probably would have died. Of course, if I could be chauffeured around like Göring or some of these other Nazi officials, I wouldn't mind playing soldier. The formalities and the speeches I could handle too. A coward I'm not, nor am I a homosexual. That Major Kramer wanted to make a homosexual out of me but didn't succeed. I pretended to go along to get out of serving in the Wehrmacht, but I never took part in any of their orgies."

Changing the subject, Alex turned and said to me, "I have a lawyer, Dr. Schwarz, who might be able to help you, provided he'll take your case. I know you have no money now, but perhaps your wife can come up with the two-hundred-mark down payment on his fee. He's one of the best trial lawyers in Berlin. If he does take your case, your wife will at least know you're alive even though she won't know where, because I don't think he'd be allowed to give her this information."

"You really think it's worth a try?" I asked.

"Definitely," Alex said. "In your case, a good lawyer can do a lot. I'll ask him when I see him. He was the one who had me brought here—otherwise I probably would have been shot by now."

I told Alex to go ahead and gave him my wife's address.

Fritz said, "Yes, Erich, do what Alex suggests." He sighed. "Man, if only I could have another cigarette."

"All right," I said. "Here's a half cigarette." He took it eagerly and started smoking immediately. "If we had as many cigarettes as we have matches now, I would be in seventh heaven. We can all thank Alex for this. Material wealth does have its good points." When Fritz had finished his cigarette, the atmosphere once again dropped to zero. Willi asked, "Isn't it time for supper yet? I'm starving."

The voice of the guard could be heard out in the hall announcing latrine time. He opened one door after another and let us walk to the toilets unsupervised. It was a guard we had never seen before. After about five minutes he returned and chased us back to our cell.

Shortly thereafter, Phillip appeared at the door with his medical supply box around his neck. "What can I do for you gentlemen tonight?" he asked.

"A painkiller for me, for sure," said Fritz. "And how about a pack of cigarettes on the side?"

"Römer," Phillip complained, "how often have I told you to keep your mouth on a leash?"

"So sorry, sir," Fritz minced, placing his right hand on his chest and bowing. "I forgot where I was." Serious again, he asked Phillip to put his name down to see the doctor tomorrow. I asked Phillip to put my name down as well. Before Phillip left, Alex asked him who the new guard was. "He's not new," Phillip answered. "He usually works on the first floor but had to help out up here today."

We had barely finished our meal when the sirens came on, and within seconds all the lights were extinguished. The enemy planes above sent shivers through our bodies, while the floor beneath us shuddered from the constant firing of the antiaircraft guns. We were all frightened, but Willi was the only one whose shaking voice could be heard. "God, I hope they don't drop a bomb on us." No one answered. After two nerve-wracking hours, the crashing of the bombs actually helped us to fall asleep. None of us heard the all-clear signal.

The next day was Silvester Abend—New Year's Eve—and we toasted one another with a weak brew of tea instead of chilled champagne. Our depressed, somber mood replaced the happy anticipation one normally feels at an approaching new year. As on the days before, bombing provided us with fireworks.

The next couple of days were uneventful. However, on Monday, the fourth of January, a corporal appeared in the doorway and asked for Keminski. Alex immediately stood at attention and was told that his attorney was there to see him. He had barely finished the sentence than the door opened again. Phillip told Willi to come with him to the psychiatrist. "Before you leave, comb your hair," he commanded. After Alex and Willi had left, Richard remarked, "There's certainly a lot of action today."

Phillip returned for me a few minutes later. When I arrived at the clinic, Otto asked me about Gerhard's death. "There's not much to say," I responded. "He returned as always from the clinic, only this time he had a strong garlic odor about him and he looked like a wax figure. He showed us where he had been injected, and it looked as though they'd given him a pretty big dose."

Otto agreed that he had also smelled an unusual odor when Gerhard walked past him after coming out of the doctor's office. "The doctors have confiscated his files, but I did find an empty ampoule with the identification number scraped off, and there was this strong, lingering smell of garlic. I remember," he continued in a whisper, "that during the First World War you could smell the same odor after a poison gas attack. I don't want to make any accusations, but I suspect someone helped the count to see the other side sooner than he had anticipated. But not a word about this to anyone." Otto stared at me for a brief moment. "Like many others here, I'm labeled mentally imbalanced. What I'm telling you now is in the strictest confidence. I was a colonel and wing commander in the Luftwaffe and received direct orders from the Führer himself to bomb a German city in the Black Forest mountains. The reason I didn't obey this order, I'll tell you the next time we meet. I'll also tell you my real name and the city involved. We've talked enough for now; someone will get suspicious if we spend too much time together."

Phillip walked in at that moment, accompanied by a prisoner with a bandaged head. He left him there with Otto and took me back to my cell.

Shortly before lunch, Alex was brought back by the corporal. "Did you have a chance to talk to the lawyer about me?" I asked.

"Yes, I did, and he'll take your case." Alex sighed. "My own situation looks very serious. He read me all the paragraphs that will be used to convict me, and my head is still spinning. Since most of my codefendants are military personnel, the case will be tried before the highest court-martial. I was sent here to be examined to determine whether I am of sound mind to stand trial. I tell you, all my hopes have disintegrated now."

"Wait a minute," Franzl said. "You can't give up hope just like that. Mankind would be lost without faith and hope. Many a man has held on to a straw and hasn't drowned because of his faith. I'm telling you this, Alex, in case you want to turn to God, as I have."

I didn't know if Alex heard what Franzl was saying. He sat at the table, head bent forward with both his hands covering his face, and didn't move until Willi was brought back from the psychiatrist.

It was obvious that Willi was in a very bad mood. "What did they do to you today?" asked Alex.

"Just the same stupid questions, and I had to be extremely careful to answer them like I did the last time. The doctor double-checked against my previous answers. All this seems like a Greek comedy to me, one that could quickly turn into a tragedy with me as the victim. However, I have a slim hope that he believes me. The real question is still, will the judge and the court feel the same way? That's the gamble."

A commotion in the hallway indicated that it was mealtime again. Richard removed the food bowls from under the bed and placed them on the table. After Alex gave his usual report, the corporal said that there were only six prisoners present. Alex had accidentally included Gerhard in the count. The food server remarked, "So, you guys wanted to cheat again." He threw twelve tiny potatoes into the bowl and spooned out six servings of what looked like spinach.

"Damn!" came Fritz's voice. "Who wants to eat this crap?" He pushed the plate away from him, but Franzl shoved it back and said, "Eat, you have to keep your strength up." Fritz looked at Franzl and shook his head but without another word began to eat.

The rest of the afternoon and evening we spent brooding and worrying over our unpredictable future. At night the bombs kept dropping, and we expected to be hit any minute. The next day we had to skip breakfast, lunch, and dinner completely.

It was not until the following afternoon, around two P.M., that an all-clear signal allowed us finally to get something to eat.

Phillip came for Fritz and Richard to take them to the doctor. Alex clasped his hands firmly behind his back and started walking around the room restlessly. "If only I could hear from my attorney," he said with a sigh.

"You just saw him yesterday," I said.

"I know," came Alex's voice again. "I'm worried about being called in to see the shrinks, and I forgot to discuss it with my lawyer." Alex barely had spoken than Phillip appeared again to pick him up. "Your lawyer wants to see you again," he said to a relieved Alex.

Less than an hour later Alex walked in briskly, pulled up a chair, and sat down. Brusquely he placed his suitcase on the table and motioned to me to sit down. "Erich," he said, "Dr. Schwarz has taken your case. He's planning to write a letter to your wife, so she'll soon know what has happened to you. Believe me, he's one of the best lawyers you can have. He told me that he has petitioned for my case to be considered separately from the Kramer case, which is to be heard at the Volksgerichtshof. Your case will very likely be held before a court-martial in the Turmstrasse military courthouse. Dr. Schwarz will meet with you prior to the hearing date to get your authorization to defend you and the necessary statement about your case."

I went to see Otto twice that day, but he had used up all of his miracle ointment and a warm hand bath was the only remedy for my hand, which again showed signs of infection. There were still many tiny splinters embedded under the skin trying to work their way out. This kept my hand inflamed with a constant throbbing pain. I was told that the doctors here did not perform operations, but something would have to be done soon or I would lose my hand. During my next visit to the clinic, Otto asked me whether a trial date had been set for me. I told him no, but that I had acquired a good attorney.

When I mentioned Dr. Schwarz's name, Otto was astonished and asked me how I had ever found such a renowned and fearless lawyer. I didn't answer. Phillip came to take me back to the cell.

Willi stood by the window and gestured to me as soon as I entered. "Erich, come here, look out the window, now you can see for yourself." I looked through the tiny hole and saw a furniture truck being loaded with oblong black boxes. "The caskets filled with the remains of old people, just as Fritz said." We heard the door being unlocked and quickly stepped away from the window.

It was Fritz and Richard. As soon as the door was locked behind them, Richard went to his bed and sat down. One look at him told us he didn't want to talk. Fritz complained about the treatment he had received and, as always, cursed the doctors.

* * *

Two days later Alex was called in for a psychiatric evaluation. He was very apprehensive that he might be injected as Gerhard had been, and he left reluctantly.

It was another bad day for us. The entire afternoon passed before Alex returned, pale and tired-looking.

"Did they give you an injection?" was my first question.

"No, thank God they didn't," he assured us. "But I'm mentally and physically tired, and besides I haven't eaten all day."

"We left you some bread and tea," I said, pushing the food toward him on the table. Alex started eating and finished the slice of bread in just a few seconds. Then he wiped his fingers on his pants, which I had never seen him do before. He really must have been hungry.

Willi and I sat waiting to hear about his experience. Alex disappointed us with "I've talked all day long and have a terrible headache on top of it. I'll tell you about my session tomorrow."

Richard was sitting on his bed staring into the room, oblivious to his surroundings.

Willi sighed. "God. I do hope there will be a tomorrow." The air-raid sirens sounded once again, and we lay helplessly in our beds while the bombs crashed around us. The furniture and walls vibrated from the impact of the bombs, the entire sky seemed to be aflame and illuminated our room. In the building silence prevailed, an eerie silence that invited terror. Alex was the only one who had fallen asleep, snoring like an old man taking a nap. It must have been out of sheer mental exhaustion that he was able to sleep through the turmoil.

On Wednesday, the thirteenth of January, I was given permission to see my lawyer. I was led past the top sergeant's office to an interrogation room where a young man, apparently one of Dr. Schwarz's assistants, invited me to sit down. He handed me a few documents, asked me to read them, and said that they were already prepared for my signature. He then informed me that he had to take a statement since Dr. Schwarz was to defend me personally at the trial. He interrupted me only once as he noted everything I said down in shorthand. I asked him if Dr. Schwarz had to see me prior to the trial date, and he said he didn't think so. When I questioned him what sentence I could expect, he told me anything from a prison term to the death penalty. I don't know what I had expected him to say, but "death penalty" was certainly not something I wanted to hear.

That night the bombing continued without letup. We could hear the engines of entire squadrons of planes flying above us. Hardly had we heard the all-clear signal than the sirens screamed again and the bombing resumed. But, as always, exhaustion overcame us and put us into a semi-sleep.

On January 16 our routine was shattered. Around seven in the morning a corporal appeared and called for Fritz. He ordered him to put on his jacket and hat. We stood around wondering why he needed a hat for an interrogation—unless he was to be taken off the premises? After they had left, Franzl theorized that he was being taken to another Gestapo interview, but even those usually didn't start until nine A.M. And why the hat?

We ate our evening meal, and there was still no sign of Fritz. We all became concerned. Each of us had his own ideas and visions of what could have happened to him. Night came and went. Then another day and another night. Since Fritz's earthly belongings were still in the room, we felt he couldn't have been taken to another prison.

When Phillip, who we hadn't seen for a few days, came by to pick me up to take me to the clinic, he was surprised not to see Fritz. Even Otto, who bandaged me, didn't know anything.

When I returned to the cell, Willi was the first to ask me what I had learned about Fritz. "Nothing more than we already know," I told him.

At around six P.M. the door opened and in limped a completely broken and shattered Fritz. We couldn't believe our eyes. In those two days he had aged visibly. His parchment-colored face was even paler than usual, and his glassy eyes stared aimlessly as he collapsed onto his bed.

Before anyone could say anything, he started screaming in an unrecognizable voice, "Those murderers! Those goddamned murderers have sentenced me and all my friends to death, without right of appeal!"

Had we not expected this verdict all along? And yet this sudden, brutal reality choked us so that none of us could react or utter a sound. Not even Franzl could find a word of comfort. Fritz began to sob and cry uncontrollably as I had never seen a man cry before.

Franzl was sitting at the table with his head bowed and his hands folded in prayer. He was the first to regain his composure and spoke loudly, clearly, and deliberately: "Lord, heavenly Father, give us strength to bear the hour of our death as your son Jesus did. Amen."

With a jerky motion Fritz wiped the tears from his face and spoke, now softly but with hatred. "I can endure all this, but think of my poor dear Gitta and our unborn child. The woman is over six months pregnant, and they are going to kill her! That devil of a judge told us at the trial that he was going to execute not only us, but also each and every one of the people who had been in contact with us. 'I want to assure you,' he said, 'that you are not going to die as martyrs as you would like but will be executed because you are nothing more than common criminals.' Those were his final words before ending the trial."

Fritz had calmed himself. "Now I'm worrying about you guys in here. No one is ever to find out what we have talked about, or it could cost you all your lives just by having listened to me. If it should ever come to an interrogation, we have to agree that we only talked about irrelevant and insignificant things, like food or family. All of the others who appeared in front of the judge with me had been in solitary confinement. I'm not really able to tell you more tonight, I'm completely drained of all my energy, but I'll tell you the rest tomorrow."

The lights were turned off, but none of us was able to sleep. "My parents live at Harzerstrasse number 23, in case any of you is in need of help someday," said Fritz. He began to sob again and whispered, "If only I could die tonight, if only I could die. . . ." No one answered him.

By midnight I was drifting off to sleep when the lights were suddenly turned on, our door was forced open, and a top sergeant, a corporal, and two enlisted men intruded. The top sergeant barked, "Get out of your beds—this is a raid!" Clad only in our underwear, we jumped from our beds. Alex wanted to give his official report, but the sergeant motioned to him to be silent. "Everyone behind the table at once!" he commanded. Fritz couldn't get up fast enough and was told to remain seated. Then the two enlisted men went to work, tearing apart the mattresses, scattering the wood shavings from the mattresses all over the floor, raising a cloud that became so dense we could hardly see one another. Everyone started coughing, including the sergeants. The top sergeant removed four cigarettes from Willi's night table. "Whose are these?" he demanded.

"They're mine," answered Willi quickly.

"Are there any more around here?"

"Yes," said Alex, "in my night table."

The sergeant walked over and found the cigarettes and a chocolate bar. He held it up. "Look what I've found." Turning toward Alex, he grinned. "I trust you're in charge here? I want you to report to me tomorrow morning for further questioning, understand?" Turning toward Willi, he asked, "By the way, do you have a smoking permit?"

"No sir, I don't," came Willi's voice from somewhere behind the dust cloud still filling the room. They continued checking for other possible hiding places, turning over the table and chairs. But they didn't body search us. Apparently the dust was too much for them, and with a final order to clean up the mess they left our cell, slamming the door shut with a clang that vibrated in our ears.

Everyone went to work to restuff the mattresses. We sweated, coughed, and cursed and had just about finished the last mattress when the lights were turned off. However, no one came to check if we had cleaned up. Once again, the room was dark. We felt our ways to our beds. Sleep didn't come that night. We tried to figure out why we hadn't been asked where the cigarettes and chocolates had come from. It seemed almost as if they had known, but how? "Herms is behind this," guessed Willi.

"I don't think so," disagreed Alex. "No, they were looking for something else, a large item, otherwise they would have body searched us. I just hope Phillip doesn't get into any trouble. God, what am I going to say to them tomorrow?" He sighed. "There's only one possibility left; I'll tell them Fritz's fiancée had them smuggled in."

"Are you insane?" protested Fritz. "That's all I need, another charge against me."

"Come on, Fritz," said Alex, "you've been sentenced to death, a few cigarettes won't change the verdict. If we tell on Phillip, that makes us traitors, and besides, we'll lose the only contact we have left with the outside world."

After a long moment of silence Fritz said solemnly, "You're absolutely right. I almost forgot that I am to die and that you guys still have a chance for survival. Go ahead and say I had them smuggled in, but please leave my poor Gitta out of it."

Alex suggested that Fritz tell us about his trial since none of us was able even to think about sleep. In the distance we heard a church bell chime one in the morning. Because it was a very dark night and there was no light shining through the window, we couldn't see one another, but we could hear Fritz's voice as he began.

"After I was picked up here I was taken to the top sergeant's office, where I was informed that my trial proceedings were to take place at the Volksgerichtshof that day. After this short explanation, I was handcuffed and accompanied by two corporals to the courthouse, where I was locked in a cell. My cell mates were Heinrich—whom I hardly recognized, he had aged so much—and two other fellows who were sitting there awaiting their fate. When Heinrich saw me, he came over and shook my hand. 'Fritz, that's you, isn't it?' he asked. 'Your Gitta is here, too; she'll be happy to see you. Mathilde and several other comrades you know are also present. Some of them you won't recognize because solitary confinement and the daily Gestapo interrogations have taken their toll on both body and soul.' Gesturing toward the other two men, he said, 'This is Waldemar and Harry.' Taking a closer look, I remembered seeing them occasionally at Dr. Ritz's meetings. Waldemar remarked that he barely recognized me because I had lost so much weight. Heinrich took hold of my left arm and pulled me toward a chair to sit down. He began to speak rather fast without stopping, as if he wanted to get as much information to me as he possibly could. 'Fritz, I hope you've come to the realization that your life will end soon. Hundreds of our comrades have already lost their lives. Professor Sommermann, the lieutenant colonel, my father-in-law, and your dear uncle have all been executed by hanging. Professor Werner is still being held. These judges are not human; they're ferocious beasts disguised as humans. You'll find out for yourself.'

"I told Heinrich that I was at Buch and not in solitary confinement. 'But Buch is an insane asylum!' Heinrich interjected. 'How did you wind up there?' I had to tell him I didn't know myself, but perhaps my injury had had something to do with it.

"Heinrich went on, 'Our comrades were all imprisoned in different places around Berlin. I was at Tegel. Eric, the inventor, and his girlfriend, Monika, blew themselves up together, with boat, boathouse, inventions, and all. I heard that Dr. Ritz and Olga took poison, and the lieutenant colonel who worked with Göring was put into a cell with a pistol on his night table. But he didn't use the pistol. Instead, he insisted on standing trial. From what I heard, he said he wanted to die like all his comrades. He must have presented quite a speech in court; if he had lived, it would have made him famous. Unfortunately, like the others, he was sentenced to death.

"We interrupted our conversation when two guards appeared in the doorway and took all four of us upstairs into a large courtroom already filled with people.

"Then I saw my Gitta. My heart raced. She jumped up and ran over to meet me, falling into my arms. Tears were running down her cheeks as she sobbed, 'Darling, my darling Fritz.' For a few moments we were oblivious of where we were or why we were there. I held her tightly in my arms, and we kissed each other as we had never kissed before. Nothing mattered. Forgotten were the war, the trial, my injury, the murder of our friends; there were only Gitta and me. Later on I realized that the guards had granted us that brief moment.

"As I held Gitta, I became aware of her pregnancy and asked, 'Will they let you bear the child?' She sighed. 'I don't know. You know, my love, we're not dealing with human beings here, we're dealing with animals.'

"Despite her imprisonment and her swollen body, she was still the most gorgeous woman I had ever seen. Looking at her, the thought of her being executed by those beasts brought tears to my eyes, tears of hatred and contempt but mostly of frustration, for there was absolutely nothing I could do to prevent this tragedy. Gitta must have read my thoughts, as she so often had before. Her hands came up to gently caress my face, and her warm dark blue eyes projected the deep love she felt for me and I for her. 'Fritz,' she whispered, 'I know it hurts, but these criminals are filled with terror, and it's because of this fear that they're killing everyone who threatens or endangers them. There really isn't any hope for us. We have to come to terms with our fate, no matter what it is. You know I'll always love you, and I just wish we could end our life together. My consolation has to be that we died for a cause that we believed in and for the betterment of mankind. We're the brave and courageous ones, not those cowards up on the bench. Fritz, darling, you're the only person I have ever truly and completely loved.' She embraced me again and placed her head on my shoulder. Stroking her lovely flowing hair, I whispered into her ear, 'I know, I know, I love you too.'"

Fritz's voice broke and he had to stop. "I can't continue. I'll tell you the rest tomorrow and—" He wasn't able to finish.

I was lying in my bed with my right arm tucked under my head, feeling a painful, choking sadness in my throat for these two young people who would have had so much to live for had it not been for the Nazis and their idiotic war games!

Slowly I dozed off into a light sleep, only to be awakened by a penetrating scream for help. It was Alex's voice, calling, "Help, someone help me, I'm falling!"

I jumped up from my bed, bumping my head in the process, and with my hands felt my way toward Alex. He was trembling convulsively and soaked with sweat. "Alex, Alex, wake up!" I shook him awake and convinced him that he was in his bed having a nightmare. I couldn't make out his face but knew he had understood. He pressed my arm and said, "Thanks, Erich."

Morning came. We washed and walked in the courtyard without having been given breakfast. We thought this a bit strange, but then, what was not strange in these times? During our courtyard walk, we noticed how the number of inmates had shrunk. Our thoughts now centered mainly around where we would be taken next.

Only Fritz didn't participate in the courtyard walk. He sat at the table with both hands clasped around his head. When we returned from our walk, he was still sitting in the same position. Franzl walked over to him and gently placed his hands on his shoulders, but Fritz shrugged him off. Franzl, however, would not give up. "Fritz, I was awake half the night, praying for you and Gitta."

"Yesterday the woman I love and I were sentenced to be decapitated. Do you know how terrible and horrifying it is for me to let them kill Gitta and our unborn child? Those pigs!" Fritz's hands were back on the table, clenched into fists, as he continued.

"'No mercy for this Jewess,' were the words that beast who calls himself a judge screamed. He then turned to me and asked, 'Is this Jewess your fiancée?'

"When I said, 'She is,' his answer came swiftly. 'Alone on that account you are guilty. Your defense of not having actively participated with these radicals is unacceptable. And your injury is not sufficient reason for mitigation of sentence. Other accusations have been brought against you. While serving on the Russian front as communications operator you were in contact with the enemy.' When I protested, I was told to shut up."

Fritz was interrupted. The door was unlocked, and in came a corporal. "Römer," he addressed Fritz, "you are to come with me to see the top sergeant."

Alex had lost all the color in his face; apparently, he had thought the corporal had come for him.

Fritz had no choice. He stood up and without a word limped out into the hallway behind the corporal. The door slammed shut.

About fifteen minutes passed before the door opened again and Phillip appeared. Turning to Alex, he asked, "Where are Römer's belongings? I have orders to take them to him; he's in solitary confinement now. The top sergeant discovered, after going through Fritz's files, that he should have been in solitary confinement ever since he was brought to Buch." Phillip now turned so he could see all of us and asked if we had told on him during last night's raid.

"No," answered Alex for all of us. "We decided to say that Fritz had the cigarettes smuggled in. By the way, what exactly were they looking for?"

"A weapon. A pistol, I think," answered Phillip. "One of the guards at the courthouse was missing a gun. They assumed one of the convicts had taken it. The sergeant won't bother you today, Alex. He's too upset about Fritz being in this cell. But thanks, guys, for not snitching on me. I appreciate it." Taking Fritz's bundle of clothes, he left our cell.

"Poor Fritz," said Alex with a sigh. "I guess that was the last we'll see of him. I just wonder how much time he has before they execute him. Now, Franzl, you can start praying hard that no one finds out that Fritz was in here with us all this time. I'm sure the sergeant isn't going to advertise his mistake."

Alex stared at us wide-eyed as he continued with an overtone of anxiety and desperation in his voice. "Remember," he cautioned, "it was Fritz himself who told us not to talk about him to anyone, or it could cost us our lives. Therefore, we have to make an agreement that, should it come to an interrogation, all of us will say that Fritz was an outsider who kept to himself and trusted no one."

We all nodded in agreement because we understood Alex's rationale, but in our hearts we felt as if we were betraying a man who had become our friend.

CHAPTER 14

HEAVY LOSSES

That same morning, January 19, shortly after Fritz had been taken away, two corporals and the top sergeant entered our cell. They ordered a stunned Franzl to get his things together and come along. Franzl did as he was ordered as if in a trance. He was so shocked he couldn't even say good-bye to us. When he was almost at the door, he half turned and looked at us with sad, warm eyes that spoke the words his lips could not.

These two blows in the space of only a few minutes put us into a state of high anxiety. Although we were silenced by the shock, the question of who would be the next victim was on everybody's mind.

I remembered Otto's statement that the prison infirmary was to be disbanded soon. I tried to break the silence: "I wonder who our next cell mate will be?" Nobody replied. We sat around like children who had been abandoned by their parents. Alex clasped his hands behind his back and started walking restlessly around the room.

Richard apparently had Fritz on his mind. "If Fritz is kept in solitary," said Richard, "he'll go insane. God, do I feel sorry for him. Why on earth did he have to get mixed up with those Communists, who are just as bad as the Nazis?"

I exploded. "What a stupid thing to say! Look here, Richard, you said you yourself were a Hitler fanatic and follower, and you still can't understand why you followed him. Remember, the masses are like a herd of sheep who look for a ram to follow. Each one believes he's following the right leader. Richard, our fates will not be much different from Fritz's. All of us here abhor war and Hitler's politics. But all of us are lone wolves who can't change things much. That wasn't the case with Fritz. He was one of the many small lights who could eventually have created a flame that would have destroyed Hitler and his Nazi regime."

Willi was about to say something when the door opened and Phillip walked in, looking solemn. Without speaking, he walked to Fritz's bed and then Franzl's to strip off the linens. Before Phillip left Alex asked him what had happened to Franzl. "Tomorrow morning he'll be transported to Brandenburg, where he is to be executed. He wasn't the first Jehovah's Witness they sent here; there were three others before him who were also beheaded. Römer will probably be next. He's screaming and raving around his cell like a lunatic." Phillip paused. "By the way, Alex, the top sergeant is willing to forget the incident with the cigarettes and chocolate since Fritz confessed to having them smuggled in."

"How long do you think Fritz has?" asked Alex.

"Oh, maybe a couple of days, maybe a couple of weeks—it's hard to say. I only know he'll be taken to Plötzensee. The execution usually takes place on the day of arrival. We still have thirty candidates for execution left in here, and all of them are being examined for their mental condition. Three truckloads of inmates were taken away this morning before sunup."

"What will happen to this place once everybody is gone?" asked Alex.

"It's going to be what it was before, a hospital for mental patients," he replied. "There's going to be a lot of action in the next few days."

"Phillip," I said, "if you should see Fritz, tell him that everyone in cell seven remembers him and that if any of us should survive, we'll do what he asked and visit his parents. Please do us that favor."

Phillip nodded his head slightly and left.

Willi walked over to the window and looked out. "We're no better off than those poor souls over there, but their only crime was old age." He turned and leaned against the wall with his hands behind his back. "Fritz was a good guy, he always found the right words to say. If one of us survives, he should go and visit his parents to tell them what a fine, brave son they had."

"Perhaps Fritz still has a chance," interjected Richard. "After all, he was a damn good soldier and almost lost his leg in the war."

"Didn't you listen at all to what Fritz told us about the judge?" I asked. "For his sort of person, there is no mercy. And no one is going to contradict a Nazi judge."

"I listened." Richard shook his head. "I just can't believe how much the Germans have changed. There has to be somebody out there who sees or cares about what's going on. Why aren't they doing anything about it?"

"We've talked about this before," I said tiredly.

Willi was still leaning against the wall but jumped when he heard the key being turned in the door.

I thought it was the breakfast server, but instead a corporal entered our cell, accompanied by Phillip, to summon Richard. He was told he would be transferred to Tegel. With trembling hands, Richard packed his few pieces of clothing. Then, with tears welling up in his eyes, he turned toward us and said in a halting voice, "So long, friends. I'll never forget you, come what may."

Once again another bit of hope was dwindling away. Alex said, "I'd really like to know why they ever brought Richard in here. Maybe they wanted to have him declared insane, or they needed a hiding place for him."

We lived now in terrifying suspense. Every time we heard a noise, we would jump. Anxiety played havoc with our nerves and stomachs. I noticed how depressed Alex had become. Not one word he spoke was of a positive nature. Probably he was afraid of the outcome of his visit with the psychiatrists.

"If they kill Franzl, my hopes for survival will vanish," he kept saying.

Willi, who had moped around for the last hour, walked up to Alex and said, "Look here, you still have some hope and a life outside to look forward to. But take a look at me. What have I got? Nothing. There isn't a single person out there who thinks about me or waits for me, so why should I want to live? But you, Alex, you have money, a family, a profession, and up to now you've always been optimistic. Don't give up now."

It was shortly after breakfast when a corporal and two enlisted men came to take me to the military courthouse. Somehow, I had not expected this to happen so soon. My heart pounded as if I had been running in a marathon. I was taken to the top sergeant's office, where I was given a belt and instructions on how to behave. Strangely, during the ride to court, my fear and apprehension changed to listlessness and apathy.

The car rolled through the streets of the shattered city. Smashed bricks, shards of glass, pieces of torn-up furniture, and dead bodies were scattered all over. The whole city seemed to be on fire. Entire blocks of houses and office buildings had burned to the ground. The smell of smoke was everywhere. Here and there a single wall miraculously remained standing. Distraught people shuffled along the streets, clutching their suitcases or pulling hand wagons loaded with pieces of furniture, mattresses, or whatever else they had been able to salvage. But the swastika flags—which once had flown high—weren't visible anywhere.

When I got off in front of the huge building where my fate was to be decided, my legs began to tremble. I was led into a room already occupied by two soldiers and their guards. The two privates who were accompanying me and I sat down. The corporal left briefly to notify the court clerk of my presence, returned shortly, and said the hearing had been scheduled for 10:40 A.M.; in two hours. Those two hours were torture for me; never in my life had time passed at a slower, more nerve-wracking pace.

The first soldier was taken into the courtroom around 10:30, and the other was called in shortly thereafter. As I waited my turn, two handcuffed men were brought in by armed guards. Both were hardly able to walk upright and looked as if they had just arisen from the dead.

As I was called into the courtroom, one of the men who had been waiting with me earlier came stumbling through the doorway, this time handcuffed, not only distraught but severely shaken. What will I look and feel like, I thought, when I leave this room?

Upon entering the large, sparsely furnished room, I saw a single soldier sitting up front at the podium. He was occupied with reading some papers and didn't even bother to look up. The two privates took a seat behind me on the benches. There was no chair for me to sit on. I stood there for about fifteen minutes before the soldier up front called out, "Court is in session."

In marched a major, a first lieutenant, a corporal, and two enlisted men. Since I had never been in front of a court-martial, I was surprised to see only three officers; somehow I had envisioned that there would be at least five or six officers present.

The first officer, who was the prosecutor, a tall man with a slender build and a receding hairline, took a seat to the left of the podium, next to the clerk. Another officer, a first lieutenant, who was the judge, and a corporal sat down in the middle of the bench with the two privates at their side. As they seated themselves, I began to wonder where my lawyer was. After leafing through a pile of documents in front of him, the judge called, "Case will be heard against Private Erich Friedrich, on trial for subversion of the military power, according to Paragraph Five of the War Crimes Special Penal Law, established August 17, 1938."

"Are you the defendant?" he asked me.

"Yes, Your Honor, I am."

I was told to come forward and present myself to the bench, which I did.

"Do you have an attorney representing you?" the officer asked.

"Yes, Your Honor," I said. "Dr. Schwarz is my lawyer."

"If Dr. Schwarz is your attorney, why isn't he present?" the judge asked. I had to tell him I didn't know.

"Was the attorney notified of the trial date?" the judge asked the clerk. The clerk frantically leafed through the files in front of him, but apparently he couldn't find anything that would answer the judge's question.

The judge looked at the clerk and then at me, shaking his head disapprovingly. "Through an oversight, your attorney was not notified; you therefore have the right to ask for a mistrial. Do you wish to do so?" the judge asked. At the moment I had no idea what he meant by mistrial, and on an impulse I asked the judge if I could defend myself. He looked at me, somewhat puzzled, but agreed. The session continued. The prosecutor arose and read out the charges against me.

His accusations included that I had refused to make the German salute and had made remarks to the effect that "I've had it up to here with the system." In addition, I had openly offended Reichsmarschall Göring and called him a liar. I had made the remark that my comrades and I "didn't get shit to eat for days at the Russian front." After hearing Reichsmarschall Göring's statement that all soldiers were well fed and cared for, I had said that someone should smack him in the trap for telling such lies. The facts thereby satisfied Paragraph 5: the remarks had been made publicly in front of coworkers with the purpose of encouraging refusal to serve in the war. Paragraph 1 of the specified statute should therefore be applied.

The judge then asked me if I understood the charges as read. I said I did.

"What do you have to say for yourself?"

"What can I say?" I began. "It's true I made the alleged remarks, but under no circumstances did I ever have the intention of subverting the Wehrmacht. How can I be accused of such an atrocity when I can say of myself that I have been a good and brave soldier and like many others had to endure hardships that go beyond what can be told in words?"

The judge interrupted, "This might well have been the case. But others who have endured as much as you did don't go around openly attacking the establishment."

"That's true, Your Honor," I replied. "But while on the front my war buddies and I swore an oath that if any of us came out alive, we would make it known what had been asked of us!"

"Looking at the other charges against you," the judge continued, "why did you make such a slanderous accusation about Reichsmarschall Hermann Göring?"

"I didn't mean to offend anyone."

"Then kindly explain to me what your remark 'Someone should smack him in the trap' is supposed to mean. It certainly sounds offensive to me."

"In Bavaria, expressions like that are very common. One doesn't really intend to offend anyone."

"Then give me an example in High German, so I can compare them," he said.

"If I do, Your Honor, another charge may very well be filed against me."

"No, for your defense you can say anything you wish," he answered.

"Very well. An appropriate expression in High German might possibly be 'Hermann Göring can scratch my ass.'"

As if bitten by a tarantula, the prosecutor jumped up from his seat. "There you are!" he bellowed. "The defendant shows no respect whatsoever for the first officer of the German Reich. Had he offended the Führer in such a manner, even his gallantry in the field would not save his neck."

The judge then asked why I had refused to make the German salute. I answered that I hadn't been aware that I, as a soldier, had to do so, and for that I should not be accused of being an enemy of the state.

"No one is accusing you of being an enemy of the state," the judge said matter-of-factly. He then called in the witnesses.

Still standing, I turned and saw two of my coworkers from the cable factory. Both were members of the SS and nothing but draft dodgers. Looking into their faces, I had the feeling that they themselves felt like traitors, since their answers to the questions they were asked came out haltingly and subdued, even though at the factory they were known as big-mouthed show-offs. One of the two tried to incriminate me even more by saying he had heard that I had said "Göring's mouth should putrefy." I couldn't recall ever having made such a statement.

After the testimony was given, the judge asked the prosecutor if he had any questions. He said no. He then turned to me and asked the same. I said I had none but just wanted to state that the two witnesses were liars and known as braggarts.

The judge then read out two statements from people in my hometown. One was the mayor and the other the local Nazi party group leader. Among other insignificant information it stated that I was known for making negative and critical remarks about the Nazi party. Secondly, after Vice Führer Rudolf Hess's flight to England I was said to have remarked to a neighbor "One scoundrel has left the country, perhaps with some luck the other nuts will follow."

When the judge had finished, the corporal read aloud a recommendation from my troop presented by a private first class. It acknowledged that I was a disciplined, courageous soldier and had received the Iron Cross as first private in the division. Furthermore, my record as a soldier was impeccable, and I had participated in more than fifteen attacks and was a candidate for the assault badge.

After this the judge asked me to tell how, when, and where I had been injured.

When I had finished my story, the prosecutor started anew. "The defendant is without doubt guilty of all charges brought against him. He himself acknowledged and testified to the fact that he made these outrageous and slanderous accusations. Even though his remarks about Vice Führer Hess are not part of the indictment, it does show us some of the negative and what could turn out to be very dangerous characteristics of the accused. Taking into consideration the gallantry he displayed in the field, I will refrain from asking for the death penalty and the seizing of his personal property. I therefore propose a sentence of five years' penal servitude or imprisonment. I leave it up to the discretion of the court."

"Do you have anything to add to your defense?" the judge asked me.

"If I may, I beg the court to consider a milder sentence since even a short detention would teach me a lesson," I said.

The three officers arose and left the room with the prosecutor trailing closely behind.

Within ten minutes they returned and seated themselves. My heart pounded in my chest and I swallowed hard as the judge spoke these words: "In the name of the Führer and the German people the following verdict is pronounced: you are hereby sentenced to one and a half years' imprisonment. The hearing is adjourned."

The entire procedure had taken no more than thirty minutes.

I was relieved, even though I did have a prison sentence to look forward to. Then came a delayed reaction. An attack of fatigue took hold of me, and I almost collapsed. On the way back to Buch, my mind was a complete blank.

When I arrived at the cell, Alex and Willi were seated at the table having lunch. Both of them stopped eating and turned their heads toward me, even the ever-hungry Willi. Quickly I announced: "One and a half years in prison!" Willi jumped up so fast that the chair he was sitting on fell backward against the wall. He ran up to me and embraced me as if I were the greatest love of his life. "My God, Erich, I'm so happy for you!"

Alex pushed Willi aside and shook my hand. "I knew it all along, you'll be the only one who'll make it."

Willi ventured that he felt his trial would also take place in the Turmstrasse. "My case, however, will have to go in front of the Volksgerichtshof," said Alex, "from which no appeal is possible. I already feel myself to be a condemned man."

"If only Fritz, Franzl, and Richard were here to share your good news," Willi said, still smiling.

"Well, as soon as I can I'll go visit Fritz's family," I promised him.

When Phillip came that evening with his tray, he had already heard about my verdict. "Congratulations, Erich, you should consider yourself lucky. Two others tried before you received the death penalty for desertion." Turning to Willi, he said, "They'll lose their heads within the next couple of days, and so will you." Then he noticed that Willi was biting his lips, and he handed him two sleeping pills. "You look as though you might need these."

That night the air-raid sirens assaulted our ears again. The bombs that fell were heavier and closer. Chunks of plaster fell from the ceiling and walls, and the entire building vibrated. Doors rattled as if they wanted to jump off their hinges.

Willi whispered, "That's probably Gerhard's spirit, giving us a sign from the other world."

Alex got angry. "Don't make stupid jokes! Our situation is serious enough as it is."

The bombardment went on all night. God, I thought, what will be left of this beautiful city after the war is over? With these thoughts I succumbed to sleep.

As I walked into the clinic the next morning, Otto was extremely happy to see me. "You've made it, thank God." He patted me on my shoulder.

"Do you have any idea where I'll be taken to?" I asked.

"I'd guess an army prison. There are quite a few right here in Berlin, and although they're known to be strict, at least the Gestapo hounds can't touch you there. Your chances of surviving the war are good, taking into consideration that the enemy knows the locations of these prisons and probably won't bomb them."

Otto paused. Then he walked over to the door, opened it, and peeked outside. Quickly he closed the door, came back, and sat on the edge of the table. "Just checking to make sure no one's listening," he said. "I want to tell you a few more details about myself, as I promised you earlier. Do you recall when I mentioned that I had received orders to bomb a German city? Well, the city was Freiburg in the Breisgau area. Our airplanes were to be camouflaged as French fighter planes so the French would be blamed for the attack. Do not reveal this information to anyone, at least not for the time being, since it's a top state secret."

We heard footsteps approaching in the hall, and Otto quickly added, "My name, rank, and some other relevant information I'll tell you another time."

The footsteps came to a halt in front of the door. It was Phillip coming for me. Otto told me he would see me on Friday. Out in the hall, we passed three soldiers carrying small bundles under their arms, each one looking more forlorn than the next. The two armed guards accompanying them marched behind with rifles swung over their shoulders. "These poor souls are on their way to Plötzensee," whispered Phillip.

Back in the cell, the day passed uneventfully. Around ten the following morning, two soldiers came for Willi. Like Franzl, Willi became speechless. One of the privates ordered him to gather his belongings, which he did quietly. "You're to be taken to Tegel for examination," said one private.

Willi looked at Alex and then at me. "If I've left anything behind that belongs to me, it's yours to keep," he said.

"No conversation!" barked the soldier.

"Can't I even say so long to my comrades?" asked Willi.

"All right," came the answer. "But instead of so long, you might as well say good-bye, since you won't be seeing them anymore."

Willi started to tremble as he walked slowly over to Alex and embraced him. Alex held him close and patted him on the back without being able to utter a word. When Willi turned toward me, the private snapped, "That's enough of this sentimental hogwash. Let's go." He took hold of Willi's arm and pulled him toward the door. The other soldier grabbed the bundle from the table. Willi turned and yelled, "So long, you guys. If Franzl's right, we'll see each other again in the other world—a better world." His words faded away.

Alex and I stood in silence, tears filling our eyes. I'm sure our thoughts were the same, and with our silence we expressed our grief.

Alex sat down first, still surprised and shaken by Willi's embrace. He sighed. "He was a sensitive, warm person after all."

"What are we going to do with Gerhard's letters?" I asked. "We have to decide soon."

"You take them with you. Perhaps you'll have a chance to visit his sister in Lyck, even though it's far away."

After lunch Alex searched Willi's bed and I went to work on the night table. I found two slices of stale bread neatly stacked one on top of the other. In reaching for them I hesitated. It seemed as though they were waiting for Willi's return and could be eaten only by him. Alex was watching me. "We'll eat the bread for dinner."

Phillip appeared the next morning to pick up Willi's bed linens. I told Phillip that I needed to see the medic today. "I'll get you later," he said. I was surprised when a private came for me instead. Expecting to see Otto at the clinic, I was disappointed to see Phillip instead.

"Where's Otto?" I asked.

"He's been taken to a concentration camp in Sachsenhausen," Phillip answered. "I'm taking over his work for the time being. Since almost all of the inmates are gone now, there wasn't enough for him to do." Phillip was getting the washbowl ready and started to unwrap my bandages.

"Otto was a fine gentleman," he continued while soaking my hand. "That wasn't his real name, you know. He was a top-secret case brought here under the name of Andres Will. Where he came from and why he was brought here is anyone's guess. He hardly talked to anyone, almost shunned people. When he was first brought here, we assumed he was a mental case because he never said anything to anybody. After a while we noticed how very polite and sophisticated he was. He must have been a high-ranking officer, that's all I can say."

I kept silent, sadly reflecting that I would never find out Otto's true name now that he was gone.

On my return to cell 7, I asked Alex if he had ever heard of the Sachsenhausen camp. Alex said it was near Oranienburg, north of Berlin.

My bandages had been wrapped too tightly. Alex took them off and rewrapped them.

Alex hardly spoke now. He sat at the table or lay on his bed. When footsteps were heard, he would jump up and sit at the table. As soon as they subsided, he would go back to his bed. There was nothing left for us to say.

Again during the night there were violent aerial attacks. Berlin was aflame. We looked through the tiny hole in the window, watching the sky light up.

On the morning of the twenty-second of January, a private came to take me to the top sergeant's office. I was informed that I was to be transferred to a military hospital in Kreuzberg. I had to sign a statement to the effect that whatever I had heard and seen at Buch was to be considered classified information and not to be revealed to anyone. I read the two pages and signed it gladly, my hand trembling with happiness. The top sergeant then explained that my sentence would be suspended until my hand was completely healed.

He told me that at the military hospital no one but the chief of surgery would know where I was to go. Under no circumstances was I to leave the city of Berlin. He then placed another paper in front of me which I had to sign as acknowledgment that I had been properly informed of all the regulations I was to live by until my imprisonment.

I asked if I could go and gather my belongings, thinking mostly of Gerhard's letters and saying good-bye to Alex, but my request was denied. "The private can pick up your things," said the sergeant. "And to ensure you won't get lost out there, I'm sending a sergeant with you to the hospital. Berlin is a mess and in turmoil."

A soldier brought my belt and hat, and Phillip came with my personal items. I asked him to let Alex know where I was going. He promised me he would.

I left the building. As the car drove through the main gate, I wanted to look back, but superstition kept me from doing so.

CHAPTER 15

PROVISIONAL FREEDOM

When I arrived at the infirmary, a former schoolhouse in Kreuzberg, I followed a young nurse to my assigned bed in a large hall crammed with the beds of wounded soldiers. I had arrived during lunchtime and was immediately given something to eat. After I ate I was allowed to take a shower and change clothes. Decent food and a real shower! I felt lucky and reborn, since I had not showered in months.

The physicians making their rounds were certainly busy. Even the corridors and closets were lined with beds or cots. One of the doctors said they would take an X ray of my hand and, depending on what it showed, an appropriate treatment would be determined.

The atmosphere in this large hall was not particularly congenial, but for the moment I was content. No one paid attention to what anyone else did. As we ate dinner, Willi came into my memory. How he would have enjoyed this meal of buttered bread, lunch meat, and black sugared tea with an apple for dessert! I thought of my wife. First thing in the morning, I would write her a letter.

The following morning, after having looked at the X rays, the doctor told me a specialist would perform the necessary surgery on my hand. "The splinters close to your wound will be removed, and so will your middle finger. Otherwise you'll lose the ability to grip with your hand." I was happy to hear this news.

I soon noticed that the Nazi influence was predominant here. Everyone was greeted with "Heil Hitler!" Only a few dared use the common "Good morning." Remembering Fritz's experience in the military hospital, I was extremely careful of what I said and did.

My neighbor was from Berlin and managed to get me some paper so I could write a letter to my wife. The field post letter was prestamped, so I needed no money—which was just as well since I didn't have any. I wanted to write so many things, about all my experiences at Buch and how much I had missed her; but instead I wrote that I was stationed in Kreuzberg and she could come visit me as soon as I felt better. I told her about my operation and that I was well. I didn't write much, as I assumed the mail would be censored. Four days later, I received a letter from her. She was ecstatic with the news but said she would have to see for herself that I was all right when she came to Berlin. How good it will feel to have someone to trust, I thought. A warm, wonderful feeling came over me.

I was permitted to leave my bed five days after the operation. The changing of the bandage was very painful, but as long as I knew my wound was healing, I could bear the discomfort. Before asking my wife to come visit me, I decided to get more familiar with the surrounding area. My permit allowed me to move about freely, as long as I was back at the hospital by ten P.M. Berlin certainly was a large city. I started out by walking around the Kreuzberg/Tempelhof area and eventually worked my way by streetcar toward the inner city. As a wounded soldier I did not have to pay for public transportation, and to avoid making the German salute I kept both my arms in a sling. I saluted officers by throwing back my head with my chin up in the air. This was the proper way of saluting if neither of the arms could be used.

Surprisingly, since I'd arrived at Kreuzberg there had been no air raids.

I therefore wrote to my wife that it was safe for her to come visit me now. Her answer came quickly. She said she would arrive by train the following Saturday at 5:30 P.M. at the Anhalter station. I practiced getting there and back on the different streetcars to ensure that I would be able to find my way even during the evening hours, when Berlin was blacked out. I found a room at a boardinghouse in Tempelhof where my wife could stay.

But two days before her arrival the worst air attack yet took place. Hundreds of enemy planes filled the sky. The antiaircraft guns fired away night and day. The skies over Berlin became a burning inferno. The results were even more catastrophic than before: entire streets and once tree-shaded boulevards were erased. Large buildings and houses burned to the ground.

While none of the bombs hit the hospital, they smashed dangerously close by. Those hospital patients who were not bedridden had to go down into the cellar until the raids were over. I stood near a small window, watching the beautiful city being engulfed in flames.

On Friday and Saturday of that week, there were no attacks. On Saturday, in the early afternoon, I started out for the Anhalter station. I wanted to make certain I would be there on time to greet my wife. While I was waiting at the station, I looked for a bomb shelter just in case we needed one, and I found one right across the street.

Back at the station, an announcement was made that the train from Nürnberg/Lichtenfels had been canceled. My heart dropped to my feet. Had the train been bombed? Worried about my wife, I was told there would be no other scheduled train from Nürnberg. Debating what to do next, I walked about the station aimlessly. But as I was ready to walk out the front door, I heard another announcement: "The special train from Nürnberg/Lichtenfels to Berlin is arriving on Platform Four." I wasn't sure I had understood correctly, so I asked a stationmaster what kind of train was arriving and was told that it was a military transport from Nürnberg. I shoved my way through the crowd down to the platform and watched soldier after soldier disembark.

Suddenly, amid the sea of uniforms, my wife stepped off the train! My heart raced as I called out to her. Dropping her suitcase on the cement floor, she came running into my arms. We stood there holding each other for a long time before she noticed that her suitcase was not by her side. We rushed down the platform, and lo and behold, her suitcase was still there. She explained that after the scheduled train had been canceled she had boarded a military train, thinking it might still get her to Berlin. The train had been jammed with people, and she had had to stand for five hours.

During her entire stay—five full delightful days—not one bomb fell on Berlin. We joked that my petition to the English to lay off their attacks had been approved.

Now I told her in detail about my experiences in Buch, the trial, and its outcome. She already knew about the court decision since Dr. Schwarz had sent her the information and refunded the two hundred marks. I didn't know myself at which military prison I would be serving my term, but I felt sure I would be allowed to write to her.

The days and nights passed by far too quickly, and before we knew it, that lovely time came to an end. Her departure was difficult for both of us, but it had to be. She left early on Thursday.

The next item on my agenda was to locate Fritz's parents, as I had promised. This was not easy. I had to be extremely careful not to leave the city limits. Between the bombed-out buildings and all the rubble and debris scattered about in the streets, it was difficult to find the right house number. One afternoon, after spending two hours searching, I stood in front of Harzerstrasse 23. It was one of the few apartment buildings still standing in a ruin of burned-out structures. I went to the front entrance and looked for the name "Römer" but it was not listed on any of the name-plates. I decided to push the first button and ask whoever opened the door. A lady answered and I told her I was looking for a war buddy's family. She said no one by that name lived there.

"Wait a minute." She hesitated, then asked me to follow her. I walked down a narrow corridor behind her. Suddenly she stopped, putting her hand on my arm. "My God, I guess you couldn't have known," she whispered. "I heard Fritz was convicted and is to be executed for high treason and espionage. Such a fine, handsome boy," she continued, shaking her head. "No one here understands any of this. Last week the Gestapo came to get his mother and sister, and they haven't been seen since. A truck was here a couple of days ago to pick up their furniture and belongings; they cleaned out the entire apartment. One of the drivers told me confidentially that they had been taken to a concentration camp someplace here in Berlin. The Römers were such quiet and friendly people and always neighborly. I don't think they were involved politically, but then nowadays one never knows what's going on. Please don't tell anyone what I've told you." I promised her I wouldn't. At least she had been kind enough and trusted me enough to tell me that much.

Walking slowly down the front steps, I thought, my dear Fritz, I wasn't able to fulfill your last wish after all; but how well you knew these Nazis, that you realized they'd eventually destroy anyone who was in contact with you and your group.

Swallowing hard to hold back the tears that threatened to flood my eyes, I boarded a streetcar and rode to the Alexanderplatz. There I disembarked and headed for the Leipziger Strasse to locate Alex's fur business. I couldn't believe the ghastly sight of this once elegant and stately business district. Only fragments of buildings remained standing; most were burned to the ground. The trees that had once adorned the avenues smoked as they disintegrated into ashes. I asked an old man staggering across the street if he knew where the Keminski business had been.

"You're standing in front of the store," he said, blowing his nose hard into an oversized handkerchief. He pointed to a still-smoldering ruin behind me. "What have we old people done to deserve this?" he sobbed. "Over there stood my house, everything's gone, we couldn't salvage anything."

I asked him if he knew what had happened to the Keminski family. He said the old man had died several months back and the young Keminski was a soldier somewhere. He didn't know where the rest of the family was living. I decided to get in contact with my lawyer, Dr. Schwarz. Perhaps he had some information on their whereabouts. I walked back to the Kantstrasse and found a phone booth where I looked up the doctor's address and number. It was Berlin, NW 7, Friedrichstrasse 103. Since the Leipziger Strasse ran into the Friedrichstrasse, it was relatively easy to find the address. Number 103 was in a tall and still intact building right across from the S-Bahn station. I went to the second floor and was received by a receptionist who referred me to a secretary down the hall. There I was told that Dr. Schwarz did not see clients without an appointment. I had mentioned my name as I was about to explain why I was there, when a distinguished-looking gentleman walked in through a side door. He must have overheard my name because he came up to me and extended his hand. "So you're Herr Friedrich," he said. "What can I do for you?"

"I'd like to know why no one came to my trial to defend me."

"I know," he said apologetically. "That was strictly the court clerk's fault. My firm was never notified. We did, however, receive all the pertinent information as to the outcome. It was a wise decision defending yourself, and you can be pleased with the outcome because I don't think I could have done much better. The verdict was fair, considering the fact that the courts rule much more firmly now than they did before. You must have had a sympathetic judge. By the way, we notified your wife and refunded her the two hundred marks."

"Thank you for your trouble," I said.

"Before you go," he said, "I want to tell you that once you're incarcerated, we can petition for a pardon. You can decide later on if you want to go this route."

I thanked him again and asked if he knew how Alex Keminski was doing. "His case is serious. There isn't much I can tell you, since most of the information is classified. His case will come in front of the Volksgerichtshof next week, and it doesn't look too hopeful. Alex is back in Moabit; Buch was completely emptied. I had to tell him about the destruction of his store. Poor man, he took it hard!"

In leaving, I said good-bye to the secretary, who reciprocated with a loud, joyful "Heil Hitler!" Heil Hitler, I thought. Lady, you're an idiot, and someday you'll eat your words!

Back at the infirmary I thought about what I should do next. I decided that I should try and locate Alex's brother-in-law's Turkish bar in the Kantstrasse, since the lawyer hadn't been able to give me any information.

In the evening the doctor told me my hand would be completely healed within a week to ten days. That would allow me just enough time to look for Alex's sister and perhaps find out something about the Römers by stopping by either Dr. Sommermann's or Dr. Ritz's residences. I checked a telephone directory, but none of the names I was looking for was listed.

Within the next couple of days, I took the subway back to the Kurfürstendamm and got off at the Kantstrasse exit. Surprisingly, I found the Turkish bar in a still-intact building. The building to the left of the bar had been bombed out and the one to the right was only partially standing, its entire front section missing. A handwritten "Closed" sign was taped to the front door of the bar. I walked through a narrow alley that divided the two buildings and peeked through a side door boarded up with wooden planks. Looking inside, I saw that the staircase had collapsed and the building was uninhabitable.

I then recalled Alex telling me that his brother-in-law had once been the manager at one of the cafés at the Haus Vaterland. Early the next morning, I went looking for the building. It was a large structure with many empty rooms. I walked up to the second floor via a wide circular staircase and saw a door with the sign "Türkisches Café." The door was unlocked and I entered into an appropriately decorated but empty little restaurant. I called out, and before long a small fellow came out from behind a heavy curtain.

"We don't open until noon," the man said with a strong accent. Seeing that I was wounded, he asked if I really wanted a cup of Turkish coffee. "Yes, that would be nice, since I'd like to ask you a couple of questions." He came back shortly with a polished brass tray and two tiny cups of thick mocha and looked at me curiously. "You wanted to ask me something?"

"Do you know Herr Clark?" I asked. "He used to work here."

"Oh, yes, Ali, he was manager when I started working here. Nice fellow. He quit after he married a rich Russian lady. He himself was a Turkish resident, although he had an English last name, but I never asked him about that. Unfortunately, I haven't seen him since, but that's how it goes in a big city like this—you meet a person and never see him again."

The friendly man wanted to keep on talking, but I told him I had to go. I thanked him for the coffee, since he had refused to take any money, and left.

Farther down the road, I passed the immense Luftwaffe building and thought about the lieutenant colonel who had worked for both Göring and Fritz's resistance group.

I spent the next two days walking about Berlin. I had a strong feeling that I wouldn't be in this city much longer. I thought that if the relentless bombings and assaults on her didn't stop soon, many of her timeless treasures would be lost forever. But deep down in my heart I felt that Berlin would survive and remain standing with the Spree River and her many lakes and waterways caressing her gently once more.

On March 14, 1943, I was summoned to the chief of surgery's office. The doctor, a pleasant man in his fifties, leaned back in his leather chair as I entered. He motioned me to sit down. In a sympathetic manner he leaned forward and placed his hand on my wounded hand. "I feel almost guilty for not having your hand looked at by Dr. Sauerbruch in person. He would have been able to save at least a couple of your fingers. Unfortunately, in this hospital we don't have any surgeons like him." Then he explained that he couldn't keep me there any longer because the hospital was getting overcrowded with dozens of new arrivals, and besides, it was time for me to serve my sentence. With a slight sigh he handed me my marching orders and a train ticket. "Tomorrow morning you are to report at the Brückenkopf military prison in Torgau. Your train leaves at nine forty-five A.M. from the Anhalter station. Be on time!"

Sleep never came that night. I was up and dressed before sunlight penetrated the large windows. I tried to eat at least some of my breakfast, but I couldn't. Even the ersatz coffee tasted terrible today. I left the hospital earlier than I had planned and boarded the train clutching my bundle of personal belongings in my good hand. The conductor showed me where I was to sit. It was actually a nice compartment for military personnel only. He closed the door behind me and told me I could walk in the corridors as long as I didn't leave the train until Torgau. Otherwise there was no security. This surprised me.

It was not until the train lurched forward on its tracks and Berlin slowly disappeared over the horizon when I started to think about the ordeal behind me and the questionable fate to come. Up to now I had been a prisoner pending trial. Now, however, I was a convicted prisoner. I had no idea what life would be like in a military prison, nor had I ever known anybody who had been incarcerated in one. I had been tried and convicted, but I was not a criminal. I had escaped the death penalty. What kind of society were we living in where two critical statements against the regime and its leaders could send one to prison? I was a brave soldier and a good and loyal citizen as well—so what was I doing on that train? But then, out of the abyss of the darkness, emerged a positive thought. The war was a lost cause—something I had realized already in Russia.

The conductor returned to tell me that the next stop was Torgau. When he noticed the forlorn expression on my face, he added quickly, "You're not the first soldier who's had to get off here, and you won't be the last, believe me."

Once in Torgau I jumped off the train and asked for directions. I had to walk through nearly the entire city before I came to the bridge crossing the swollen Elbe River. Just to the left I saw a semicircular red-brick building encased by a high fortress wall. As I approached the gigantic gate, I heard a distant church bell strike twelve noon.

My stomach started doing flipflops out of sheer nervousness, and I had to take a couple of deep breaths before I could pull the bell cord at a smaller door inside the large gate. I heard the loud echo of the chimes, and just as it faded, a soldier opened the door. It looked to me as if they were expecting me. No words were exchanged as the staring figure turned and directed me to a small shed built up against the fortress wall. The words "Registration Office" were painted on the door. I knocked and entered. As I stood at attention and looked down at a man sitting behind a desk, I thought he hadn't seen me. I waited.

Suddenly he jumped up and made a half turn until he stood just in front of me. "Don't you have any manners?" he barked. I was flabbergasted and didn't quite know how to answer. "Lie down on the floor!" he commanded. I truly thought he was kidding and kept standing there holding my marching papers out to him instead. He grabbed them out of my hand and threw them on the desk. "Didn't you hear me?" he shouted. "Down with your belly on the floor."

I knew now that this man was serious, and I repeated, "Lie down, yes sir." I first kneeled and then, supported by my right elbow, managed to lie flat on the floor. My left hand and arm, which were still in a sling, were under my chest, which was extremely painful.

"You see," came his blistering voice again, "now you have your first refusal to obey a direct order behind you." With his heavy boot on top of my back he started to scream. "Your tired bones will be brought into action soon—I promise you that!"

When I felt him releasing his weight from my back I tried to get up, but once again his boot came down on me and I felt trapped like an insect waiting to be squashed. "I haven't given you permission to get up. This is your second offense today, and you've been here only a few minutes." He finally released me, and pain surged from my hand up through my arm and into my brain. I could have screamed in agony but didn't. As I lay there on the cold cement floor, I followed him out of the corners of my eyes as he disappeared behind his desk. After a few minutes I heard his voice again. He asked me what I had on my body and what the content of the bundle on the chair was. Before I could even get out the first word he screamed again, "Get up on your feet when you're asked a question! Stand at attention, you twerp!"

I really had to struggle to get to my feet, and I know my right hand trembled as I stood at attention. The man behind the desk put his cap on his fat head and once again got up and marched toward me. The man really did not walk—he marched. Next I had to empty all my pockets. I put a handkerchief, an empty money purse, my military watch, and some matches on the desk. My other personal belongings from the bundle on the chair—a pair of socks, an undershirt, and a pair of underpants—I also placed on the desk. The soldier removed a brown paper bag from one of the desk drawers and wrote the numbers 3459/43 and my name in large, legible letters next to it. He put my belongings into it, sealed it, and put an official stamp on the top. Holding the bag up to my face, he shouted, "Engrave these numbers on your stupid brain, because this is you from now on!"

After a few minutes another soldier came for me. He was a silent person who marched me across the courtyard to a brick structure. Upon entering we passed through endless empty corridors and gangways hearing only the tread of our own boots echoing in the distance. There was no one in sight. The silent man came to a sudden stop in front of a cast iron door which he motioned me to enter. When the door was locked behind me, I stood in a dark, unfurnished cell. Scarcely visible in a corner was a gray pail with a wooden lid on it. The foul, musty odor invaded my nostrils. The room was cold and damp, and the closer I got to the pail in the corner the stronger became the smell of human excrement. I thought I could sit on the bucket to rest, but for obvious reasons I quickly felt my way back to the other corner. Spasmodic shivers shook my body as I slid down onto the cold cement floor. I rested my aching head against the cold wall and closed my eyes.

"They can't leave me in here forever. This has to end soon," I thought out loud. Suddenly, amid the pitch darkness of the room, in my imagination, I felt the comforting presence of my wife and daughter. It was then that I knew I had to endure all the hardship and terror and survive. My exhausted brain had become conditioned to this realization and to my hope of someday returning to a society where people would respect each other once again.

CHAPTER 16

A NEW LIFE

I left the Brückenkopf Wehrmacht prison in Torgau on July 7, 1944, having served my sentence. Clutching my small bundle of belongings under my arm, I walked through the same gate I had entered a year and a half before. I took a deep breath. Somehow, the air smelled cleaner outside the compound. I was overcome with mixed emotions. On the one hand I was happy to be a free man, but on the other I was afraid of what lay ahead. I was still a soldier, and my orders called for me to report on that same day to the Freising barracks near Munich.

After I boarded the southbound train I focused on the passengers—a crowd of unsmiling people showing the scars of fear and deprivation on their faces. No one talked to me, and I remained silent as well. Although there was no air raid during the ride, I was appalled at the destruction of the towns and villages we passed through, where many of the ruined houses and buildings were still burning.

I arrived at the Freising barracks before dawn and reported to the reception office, where I was assigned a bed and was given some food. The following morning I reported to the first sergeant, who sent me to an office where I was received by the company commander, a captain. From the moment I saw this man, I knew he was a brutal Nazi in Wehrmacht uniform. After I had given him my personnel information, the first sergeant joined us. "You're from the Torgau-Brückenkopf prison," he began— as if I were not aware of this fact—"and tomorrow morning you will be dispatched to a frontline unit."

I tried to tell him that I had suffered greatly in prison and was hoping to receive a short furlough to restore my mental and physical health. What I didn't tell him was that I had been told by an ex-Wehrmacht lawyer who was an inmate at Torgau that I could demand a furlough even though there was a general suspension of furloughs in effect. As I made my request, the captain's eyes narrowed; he gave me an agitated look and flatly rejected my petition. When I told him that I would appeal his rejection, he reflected for a moment, cleared his throat, and then gave a short laugh. "The appeal has to go through me, and I've already told you that you cannot have a furlough."

"Then I want to appeal to a higher authority," I said.

"The division commander is the only higher authority here," said the captain in a steely voice.

"Very well," I insisted, "I want to make a formal report to the division commander."

By now the captain was flabbergasted and extremely annoyed by my request. I could tell that he wanted to shout at me but he must have realized I had a right to my claim.

Early the following morning I was called to the orderly room. I was informed by the soldier present that I had to appear with the captain in front of the division commander at eleven A.M., dressed in full military gear. He handed me a steel helmet, a gas mask, a waist belt, and a cartridge pouch without ammunition. The soldier whispered to me that they had had to research the regulations the night before, because so far a soldier had never requested a confrontation with the division commander. Shortly after ten A.M., the captain and first sergeant appeared in full uniform, including helmets, sabers, and medals.

When we arrived at the commander's office the captain and first sergeant went in. I was called in shortly thereafter. I stood at attention, as I had learned to do so well in Torgau. The commander looked at me in a puzzled way and asked me what my complaint was. I explained what had led up to my imprisonment and why the High Command of the Wehrmacht (OKW) had sentenced me to prison. Furthermore, I told him that I had petitioned for a furlough to recover my health but that the captain had denied my petition, and that was why I was in front of him appealing the captain's decision.

From his medals I concluded that the gray-haired commander, a distinguished looking man with a weathered face, was a World War I veteran. He looked me straight in the face and to my utter surprise said, "You have a right to a two-week furlough. In addition, I'll also give you four travel days. Go to the office and pick up your papers." I thanked the commander and left his office. Both the captain and first sergeant were subdued as we walked back to our barrack. Surely they had expected a different outcome.

The next morning I received a furlough slip, a train ticket, and some ration coupons.

With a feeling of apprehension, for I felt that I had brought a lot of hardship upon my family, I arrived in my hometown in the middle of the night. These agonizing thoughts soon vanished as I was welcomed home with compassion and love.

I kept an extremely low profile, for I noticed that the Nazis were slowly and surely moving toward a last-minute panic.

The furlough went by fast, and once again I had to report to the barracks in Freising. As I had anticipated, I was among the ones called to be packed off to war. The same captain as before was waiting for me with orders to send me to the front. I immediately complained about the pain in my hand and asked to see the doctor. My request was granted. The captain said he wanted to accompany me. There were several soldiers ahead of me waiting to see the doctor. During a moment when I was not being observed closely by the captain, I asked the soldiers in line if they would let me go to the front. Seeing my desperation, they agreed to let me see the doctor ahead of them.

I explained to the attending physician that there were still many splinters imbedded in my hand and I had to be operated on. He agreed and issued me a transfer to an orthopedic surgeon in Munich. I noticed that the captain, who was by my side during the entire examination, was extremely upset but had no power over the doctor's decision. I went to Munich immediately and the surgeon there wrote orders for me to be sent to a military hospital in Bad Tölz. Dr. Lange, one of Germany's leading specialists, was to construct an artificial hand for me.

Upon my return to Freising from Munich the first sergeant personally selected my work assignments, namely all the dirty work he could think of. I was ordered to clean the toilets, empty the heavy trash containers, mop the barrack floors—which, by the way, was not an easy task to accomplish with only one hand —until I was finally summoned to the hospital in Bad Tölz. Although he performed several operations, Dr. Lange was unable to construct a grasping hand, and after three months of hospitalization he gave me a discharge as not suitable for war.

Again I had to report to a Wehrmacht discharge center, this time in Munich. When I told the commander my history, he asked me why I had not been promoted. When I told him I didn't know, he promoted me to lance corporal then and there and ordered me to go to the office to get my promotion in writing.

Because of my impending discharge from the Wehrmacht I had to report to the discharge processing center in Freising. Three days later, with the proper documents in my hand, I went back to the same barracks that I had become so familiar with. I arrived at noon and was assigned a bed.

I reported to the discharge processing center, which was the last station a soldier had to report to before he was completely discharged from the Wehrmacht. Several high-ranking officers sat at a head table, among them the division commander. He recognized me immediately and asked me if I enjoyed being a soldier, which I affirmed. He told me to see him at his office at four P.M. and dismissed me.

Punctually at four P.M. I presented myself at his office, but a junior officer told me to wait. After a few minutes the commander himself appeared in the doorway and asked me to enter. He motioned me to sit down and leaned forward over his desk with a look of concern on his face. "After all you've gone through, you still want to be a soldier," he started. "Are you aware that any soldier discharged from the Wehrmacht nowadays has to be reported to the Gestapo?" He pointed to a file on his desk with a red card attached to it and warned: "Because you're considered an enemy of the Reich, it will be in your best interest if I furlough you for an indefinite amount of time. You will receive notification from a Wehrmacht discharge processing center near your hometown; this could take weeks. Go and get your papers from the office." I nodded in thanks and left. I now realize, as I reflect back, that the commander clearly knew of the coming collapse.

I left on the following morning with a four-week supply of ration coupons and my service pay.

In the four weeks that followed, I observed how the Nazis' glorious Thousand-Year Reich came to an abrupt end. As the Russians crossed into Germany and marched toward Berlin, and the allies with the Americans in the lead advanced toward Bavaria, the Nazis continued to worship their idol and believed that Hitler would soon make use of his promised secret miracle weapon. But soon, as all their resources were exhausted, their morale hit bottom and their faith began to die. Disillusioned, and in a desperate struggle for survival, the Nazi leaders became hysterical. Kangaroo courts were set up. Any soldier who didn't have the proper identification papers on him was executed, at times in the most gruesome manner. Heads were bashed in or split open with spades and other tools, bodies were hung from lampposts and trees. Many were just shot to death without any kind of appeal.

I had to be extremely careful myself, since I didn't have any discharge papers, only a furlough slip. I tried not to leave my house or be seen in public. Despite my being so careful, the local Nazi party group leader, who was also the village mayor, took notice and reported me to the Wehrmacht office in Coburg. When I went to pick up my service pay I was told that the mayor had questioned my furlough. Fortunately, the officer in charge recognized me—he was my former schoolteacher—and declared that my papers were in order, that I should go home and await a summons from the discharge office in Nürnberg.

On February 13, 1945, I had to report in to the Wehrmacht discharge processing center in Nürnberg, at Gräslein, near the Hauptbahnhof (main train station). In the town of Fürth, one stop before Nürnberg, the train came to an abrupt halt because of an air raid. The passengers disembarked quickly and ran for their lives to a bomb shelter. I was lucky enough to find standing room in a high-rise bunker near the train station. Two hours later, I emerged from the bunker to a shocking sight. It seemed to me as if the entire city was aflame, and the station and most of the surrounding buildings had been destroyed. Since there were no more trains going south, I had no choice but to walk the five kilometers to the Nürnberg Hauptbahnhof. I walked in the middle of the street, through smoke, falling debris, fire, and small explosions, driven by a single thought—to get my furlough extension signed. When I finally arrived at the Nürnberg Hauptbahnhof, the nearby Wehrmacht discharge processing center was nothing more than a smoldering pile of ashes. I saw an officer who stood next to a military vehicle amid the rubble and told him that I had received a summons to appear at the discharge processing center and needed to get a furlough extension signed. He looked at me as if I were insane and said, "Soldier, go home." I told him quickly that I had no intention of going home and risking a kangaroo court. The officer understood this and told me to go to a Wehrmacht post between Nürnberg and Fürth—basically where I had just walked from.

Upon my arrival at the post, the same officer I had met earlier was getting out of his jeep. I approached him and asked him if he could now sign my furlough extension, which he did. Once I had his signature, I requested an official stamp. The officer shook his head and managed a smile. "Man, you're really a persistent person." I followed the officer to his office, where he stamped an official seal on my extension. Satisfied and with the feeling of security of having my legal papers on hand, I took a northbound train back to my hometown. Now I was able to dress in civilian clothes, although technically speaking I was still a soldier.

On this, the thirteenth of February 1945, Germany suffered immensely. The cities of Nürnberg and Dresden were nearly erased from the map. What happened next in Germany was true hypocrisy. The swastika flags, the banners reading "Long Live Our Führer," all quickly disappeared as the first U.S. tanks rolled into the towns. White bed linens or flags of surrender were hung from windows, even though the people knew they were risking the death penalty by displaying them. We watched as the heavy tanks yanked down walls and fences as they rolled by.

When the first U.S. troops came marching through, anxiety and fear rose. Many people, especially women, were afraid to the point that they committed suicide.

People were forced out of their houses to make room for the occupation troops. This would have been the case with our home as well, but my mother-in-law was sick with pneumonia. A U.S. Army doctor came to the house to investigate, and as he spoke fluent German we were able to communicate with him and he allowed us to stay in our home. Most of our neighbors, however, had to leave their houses and stay with friends or relatives.

Remarkably, with the exception of only a few, a large majority of the people had suddenly become anti-Nazi. The occupying forces requested that each adult fill out a questionnaire indicating his or her political orientation. Only the local Nazi group leader, the mayor of my hometown, still paraded around with his Nazi badges and insignia until an American officer tore them off his chest and arrested him.

For a short time thereafter, I was "a very well respected person." When I went to look for work at the Siemens cable factory in Neustadt near Coburg, where I had previously been employed, I was amazed at the courtesy and overwhelming friendliness shown to me by the director. He apologized profusely for the behavior of the two former coworkers who had denounced me. The director personally gave me a tour of the plant and told me I could have any position I wanted. Although I was tempted, deep down in my heart I longed for a position where I could help in the political and economic reconstruction of a Germany in which a Nazi Reich could never rise again. I decided to decline the work offered to me at the factory and went instead to Coburg, where an official American Directive Office had already been established. There I was received by a Maj. Harry Lockland of the U.S. Army who advised me, after listening to my history, that he would like to see me work for the municipality of Coburg, preferably for the criminal division of the police department.

On July 15, 1945, I started my work as a detective for the Coburg police department. From 1946 through 1947 I attended the police academy and graduated with honors. Until 1953 I enjoyed my career in the homicide and vice squad division and solved every case assigned to me for investigation. However, after a physical examination in 1953, and when I had applied for a higher grade, it was decided that all police officials had to have the full use of both their hands. I had no alternative but to accept a supervisory position in the social services department and later in the office of taxation.

During that time I kept a close watch on political developments in Germany. As the allied forces diminished their grip on the country, visible changes took place. The former Nazis who had lurked in the shadows made themselves known again. Most Germans took notice but did not want to admit it, because in their subconscious the legacy of Hitler lived on. I had just cause to be skeptical, for many of the higher positions in public office were filled by East German refugees or former military personnel. This was also the case in Coburg. From the voted-in chief mayor to the small fry bureaucrat, refugees who had fled East Germany or other former German-speaking countries earlier occupied by Hitler and now occupied by the Russians received preference for public office and civil service positions. Of course, none of these people admitted that they had been members of the Nazi party. The deputy police chief in Coburg took the liberty of sending an inquiry to a town in East Germany where the present mayor had come from. He wanted to know if the mayor, an attorney by profession, had been a member of the Nazi party. The recipients of the inquiry sent the letter back to the mayor and subsequently the deputy police chief was fired. His reason for making the inquiry was that the mayor wanted to hire a former Reich Security Office employee as police chief, even though the man had been a known member of the SS and had no experience as a police officer. A similar case of injustice was that the former mayor of my village, who after the Nazis rose to power in 1933 had had people of different political orientations attacked openly in the streets and beaten bloody by his SA mob. He was once more elected as mayor, even though war crime charges had been brought against him by the Americans and he had served a prison sentence. However, I do not wish to dwell on these injustices, which in my mind, are now part of Germany's past.

As time went by, the German people labored hard and struggled immensely to rebuild their country and the *Wirtschaftwunder* of economic growth and ultimate recovery became a reality with the help of their allied friends. Soon Germany was again a well-respected, booming economic and global power. However, since its reunification on October 3, 1989, acute problems have arisen that have to be dealt with. Storm clouds have once again gathered over Germany with its escalating unemployment, ruthless attacks on foreign workers, and a new wave of unrest and violence against innocent people. Watching the mounting feelings of insecurity, I am reminded of the destructive forces that emerged and shaped political life around 1933, when the Third Reich was born. I only hope fate will protect Germany and give strength and endurance to its democracy so that a totalitarian regime such as that of the Nazis can never appear again.

Over the years, I often thought of the other possible survivors of cell 7: Willi, the deserter; Alex, the dilettante; and Richard, the "good German."

I never learned their fates. I only hope that if they did manage to survive their ordeals as Hitler's prisoners, they were, like me, able to get on with their lives.

After I retired from public office, my wife and I often visited our daughter, who had emigrated to the United States to live with my uncle. During these many visits, I became impressed with the American way of life, the spirit and friendliness of its people, and most of all the freedom and pursuit of happiness granted to everyone, of any age.

In August 1974, my wife and I decided to leave Germany and move in with our daughter, who in the meantime had married and established a family of her own. We now live in peace and harmony with our extended family on the shores of the Occoquan River in Virginia, a state of diverse natural beauty.

Although I always will have a special love for my homeland, with its majestic mountains, its lush green meadows, and the serenity of its cultivated forests and parks, the scars of war remain deeply imbedded in my soul. The carnage on the battlefields, the mindless genocide, and the memories of my unfortunate cell mates at Buch have left an indelible impression on my life, memories I can never erase.

ABOUT THE AUTHORS

ERICH FRIEDRICH was born in 1911 in Köppelsdorf, a small town in Thuringia, Germany. After completing school, he worked at two glassworks before starting his own business. Driven out of business by the Nazis, he later worked in an armanents factory. He was drafted into the army and served as a machine gunner on the Russian front, receiving the Iron Cross second class for valor. While recuperating in a hospital after his left hand was mangled by schrapnel during an atrtillery bombardment, he told the truth about conditions at the front and spoke his views of the Nazi leadership. He was arrested for subversion, tried and convicted of the charges, and served eighteen months in a military prison. During the postwar Allied occupation, Mr. Friedrich became a police detective, serving for almost a decade on the police force of Coburg as a member of the criminal investigation division, including homicide and vice squad. Later he joined the municipal administration of Coburg, serving in supervisory positions in both the social services department and the office of taxation. Now retired, he lives in Woodbridge, Virginia, with his wife, Hildegard, and travels regularly to Germany.

RENATE VANEGAS, Erich Friedrich's daughter, was born in Mönchroden, near Coburg, Germany. She came to the United States in 1959 after receiving her liberal arts education in Germany. Mrs. Vanegas devoted years to translating her father's copious prison notes and extensive manuscript of *Hitler's Prisoners* from German to English. She lives in Woodbridge, Virginia, and works for American Management Systems, Inc., an international computer firm. Married to a civil engineer, she is the mother of three children.